Careers and Basics of Business, Marketing, and Finance

McGraw Hill

1 2 3 4 5 6 7 8 9 LWI 27 26 25 24 23

ISBN 978-1-26-660595-6
MHID 1-26-660595-9

Cover Image: metamorworks/Shutterstock

Interior Image (abstract background):
All credits appearing on page or at the end of the book are considered to be an
extension of the copyright page.

The Internet addresses listed in the text were accurate at the time of publication.
The inclusion of a website does not indicate an endorsement by the authors
or McGraw-Hill Education, and McGraw-Hill Education does not guarantee the
accuracy of the information presented at these sites.

Meet Our Lead Content Architect

Courtesy of Kandis Spurling

Tim Broxholm (MA, Seattle Pacific University)

For many learners, their business education journey begins with Introduction to Business. Tim has had the pleasure of educating numerous unique students in this course. His innovative teaching methods, applications of learning science, and educational technology have taken this foundational course to the next level. He arms students with the skills needed to perform like pros in the world of work, excel in future college courses, build wealth, and become savvy consumers.

Tim has been teaching marketing, management, and entrepreneurship courses at Green River College in Auburn, Washington, since 2010. He was tenured in 2015 and is best known for co-creating and then leading the country's first Bachelor of Applied Science (BAS) in Marketing and Entrepreneurship. Tim also developed an Applied Management BAS program. Affordable schools.net has recognized the Marketing & Entrepreneurship program as the #1 most affordable entrepreneurship program in the country and the #7 most affordable entrepreneurship program by UniversityHQ. Tim is a recipient of Green River College's Distinguished Faculty Award.

In addition to teaching and authoring, Tim works in the technology industry as a Senior Manager at Microsoft, which provides him the ability to bridge the divide between today's higher education curriculum and the rapidly changing needs of today's employers. While Tim serves in many roles, his most important role is as husband to his wife, Danielle, and dad to his sons, Raymond and Joey.

Acknowledgments

Careers and Basics of Business, Marketing, and Finance would not have been possible without the generosity, innovation, and expert contributions of the following:

Content Contributors

Lisa Cherivtch, *Oakton Community College*

Helen Davis, *Jefferson Community and Technical College*

Scott Elston, *Iowa State University*

Chris Finnin, *Drexel University*

Charla Fraley, *Columbus State Community College—Columbus*

Peter Natale, *ECPI University Roanoke*

Robin James, *William Rainey Harper College*

Krissy Jones, *City University of Seattle*

Tim Rogers, *Ozarks Technical Community College*

Alice Stewart, *North Carolina A and T University*

Content Reviewers

Rebecca Adams, *Kansas State University*

Deolis Allen Jr., *Wayne County Community College*

Eric Alston, *University of Colorado—Boulder*

Lydia Anderson, *Fresno City College*

Mark Arnold, *Saint Louis University*

Wayne Ballentine, *Prairie View A and M University*

Susanne Bajt, *Harper College*

Kimberly Baker, *Bryant & Stratton College*

Laura Bantz, *McHenry County College*

Brian Bartel, *Mid-State Technical College*

Denise Barton, *Wake Technical Community College*

Michael Bento, *Owens Community College*

Gene Blackmun, *Rio Hondo College*

Curtis Blakely, *Ivy Tech Community College—Richmond*

Kathleen Borbee, *Monroe Community College*

Nicholas Bosco, *Suffolk County Community College*

David Button, *State University of New York—Canton*

Derrick Cameron, *Vance Granville Community College*

Margie Campbell Charlebois, *North Hennepin Community College*

Rafael Cardona, *Glendale College*

Janel Carrigan, *Fresno City College*

Patricia Carver, *Bellarmine University*

Carlene Cassidy, *Anne Arundel Community College—Arnold*

Lisa Cherivtch, *Oakton Community College*

Christopher Chin, *Glendale Community College*

Katherine Clyde, *Pitt Community College*

Gary M. Corona, *Florida State College at Jacksonville*

Anastasia Cortes, *Virginia Tech*

Sandy Dantone, *A-B Tech Community College*

Helen Davis, *Jefferson Community and Technical College*

Mark DeCain, *Wake Technical Community College*

Gustavo Demoner, *West Los Angeles College*

Carrie Devone, *Mott Community College*

Tina Donnelly, *Horry Georgetown Technical College*

Glenn Doolittle, Jr., *Santa Ana College*

Steve Dunphy, *Indiana University—Northwest*

Christopher Enge, *Mott Community College*

Mary Ewanechko, *Monroe Community College*

Christina Force, *Bloomsburg University of Pennsylvania*

Jill Friestad-Tate, *Des Moines Area Community College—West*

Tina Gaffey, *Horry Georgetown Technical College*

Prachi Gala, *Elon University*

Barbara Garrell, *Delaware County Community College*

Kimberly Gleason, *University of Houston—Downtown*

Joey Goodman, *Davidson County Community College*

Richard Gordon, *Illinois State University*

Francine Guice, *Oakland University*

Andrew W. Gump, *Liberty University*

Brian Gurney, *Montana State University—Billings*

Marie Halvorsen-Ganepola, *University of Arkansas*

Michele Hampton, *Cuyahoga Community College*

Stanton Heister, *Portland State University*

Austin Hill, *Harford Community College*

Linda Hoffman, *Ivy Tech Community College*

Phil Holleran, *Mitchell Community College*

Jianli Hu, *Cerritos College*

Julie Huang, *Rio Hondo College*

Miriam Huddleston, *Harford Community College*

Allison Hudson, *Miami Dade College*

Veronika Humphries, *The University of Louisiana Monroe*

Robin James, *William Rainey Harper College*

Russell Johnson, *Utah Valley University*

Gina Kabak, *Union County College*

Ahmad Karey, *Salt Lake Community College*

Eileen Kearney, *Montgomery County Community College*

Lindsay King, *James Madison University*

Greta Kishbaugh, *St. Petersburg College*

Elko Klijn, *Old Dominion University*

Mary Beth Klinger, *College of Southern Maryland*

Stephen Konrad, *Mount Hood Community College*

Jonathan Krabill, *Columbus State Community College—Columbus*

John Kurnik, *St. Petersburg College*

Eduardo Landeros, *San Diego Mesa College*

Marie Lapidus, *Harper College*

Kimberly B. Leousis, *University of Mobile*

Tammira Lucas, *Harford Community College*

Greg Luce, *Bucks County Community College*

Trina Lynch-Jackson, *Ivy Tech Community College—Lake County Campus*

Monty Lynn, *Abilene Christian University*

Anne Makanui, *North Carolina State University*

Jennifer Malfitano, *Delaware County Community College*

Marcia Marriott, *Monroe Community College*

Theresa Mastrianni, *Kingsborough Community College*

Chris McChesney, *Indian River State College*

Derine McCrory, *Mott Community College*

Donna McCubbin, *Clemson University*

Carlespie Mary Alice McKinney, *Oakland Community College*

Chris McNamara, *Finger Lakes Community College*

Ken Mullane, *Salem State University*

Jennifer Muryn, *Robert Morris University*

Shawn Myers, *Lincoln University*

Kristi Newton, *Chemeketa Community College*

Mihai Nica, *University of Central Oklahoma*

Lisa Novak, *Mott Community College*

Don Oest, *University of Colorado—Boulder*

Lois Olson, *San Diego State University—San Diego*

Hussein Othman, *Oakland Community College*

Pallab Paul, *University of Denver*

Jeffrey Penley, *Catawba Valley Community College*

Marc Postiglione, *Union County College*

Andrew Pueschel, *Ohio University—Athens*

Anthony Racka, *Oakland Community College—Auburn Hills*

Bharatendra Rai, *University of Massachusetts—Dartmouth*

Greg Rapp, *Portland Community College—Sylvania*

Chris Retzbach, *Gloucester County Institute of Technology*

Daniel Rhem, *Pitt Community College*

Raina Rutti, *Dalton State College*

Amber Ruszkowski, *Ivy Tech Community College*

Whitney Sanders, *Quinnipiac University*

Richard Sarkisian, *Camden County College*

Susan Schanne, *Eastern Michigan University*

Douglas Scott, *State College of Florida*

Raj Selladurai, *Indiana University—Northwest*

Sarah Shepler, *Ivy Tech Community College—Terre Haute*

Elizabeth Sikkenga, *Eastern Michigan University*

Amy Simon, *Jacksonville State University*

Jen Smith, *University of Idaho*

Harris Sondak, *University of Utah*

Jacob Stanford, *Chattanooga State Community College*

Alice Stewart, *North Carolina A and T University*

Theresa Strong, *Horry-Georgetown Technical College*

Mary Stucko, *Lansing Community College*

Chao Sun, *Eastern Michigan University*

Yvette Swint-Blakely, *Lansing Community College*

Jared Taunton, *Pitt Community College*

David L. Taylor, *Indiana University*

Ronda Taylor, *Ivy Tech Community College*

Jarvis Thomas, *Lone Star College*

Ron Trucks, *Jefferson College*

Gary Tucker, *Lone Star College—University Park*

Elizabeth Turnbull, *University of Alabama at Birmingham*

Mallory Tuttle, *Old Dominion University*

Alex Wadford, *Pitt Community College*

John Ward, *Rochester Institute of Technology*

Timothy Weaver, *Moorpark College*

Ann Weiss, *Ivy Tech Community College*

James Welch, *University of Tampa*

Ruth White, *Bowling Green State University*

Miriam Wiglesworth, *Harford Community College*

Irene Wilder, *Jefferson Community College*

Amy Williams, *Valdosta State University*

Deric Williams, *Wayne State University*

Luke Williams, *Central Washington University*

Mark Williams, *Community College of Baltimore County*

Shallin Williams, *Tri-County Technical College*

Rick Wills, *Illinois State University*

Elizabeth Wimer, *Syracuse University*

Ray Wimer, *Syracuse University*

Bruce Yuille, *Mid Michigan College*

Marisa Zakaria, *Glendale Community College*

Nancy Zimmerman, *Community College of Baltimore County—Cantonsville*

Symposia and Focus Group Participants

Elsa Anaya, *Palo Alto College*

Norma Anderson, *Ivy Tech Community College*

Rocky Belcher, *Sinclair Community College*

Connie Belden, *Butler Community College*

Michael Bento, *Owens Community College*

William Bettencourt, *Edmonds Community College—Washington*

Koren Borges, *University of North Florida*

Maurice Brown, *Harford Community College*

Carlene Cassidy, *Anne Arundel Community College*

Basil Chelemes, *Salt Lake Community College*

Lisa Cherivtch, *Oakton Community College*

Rachna Condos, *American River College*

Debra Crumpton, *Sacramento City College*

Tyler Custis, *University of South Dakota*

Gustavo Demoner, *West Los Angeles College*

John DeSpagna, *Nassau Community College*

Tina Donnelly, *Horry Georgetown Technical College*

Erik Ford, *University of Oregon*

Tracy Fulce, *Oakton Community College*

Kathleen Gallagher, *Johnson County Community College*

Wayne Gawlik, *Joliet Junior College*

Kimberly Gleason, *University of Houston—Downtown*

Shari Goldstein, *San Jacinto College*

Mark Grooms, *Orange Coast College*

Michele Hampton, *Cuyahoga Community College*

Phil Holleran, *Mitchell Community College*

Julie Huang, *Rio Hondo College*

Miriam Huddleston, *Harford Community College*

Samira Hussein, *Johnson County Community College*

Ralph Jagodka, *Mt. San Antonio College*

Robin James, *William Rainey Harper College*

Jonathan Krabill, *Columbus State Community College—Columbus*

Janet Kriege-Baker, *Ivy Tech Community College*

Steven Levine, *Nassau Community College*

Catalin Macarie, *University of Cincinnati*

Theresa Mastrianni, *Kingsborough Community College*

Paulette McCarty, *Northeastern University*

Kimberly Mencken, *Baylor University*

Steven Mohler, *Ivy Tech Community College*

Peter Natale, *ECPI University Roanoke*

Mihai Nica, *University of Central Oklahoma*

John Nobles, *Ohio University*

Margaret O'Connor, *Bloomsburg University of Pennsylvania*

Kathy Osburn, *Antelope Valley College*

Andrew Pueschel, *Ohio University*

Ujvala Rajadhyaksha, *Governors State University*

Steve Riczo, *Kent State University—Kent*

Donald Roomes, *Florida International University—Miami*

Carol Rowey, *Community College Rhode Island—Lincoln*

John Russo, *Irvine Valley College*

Raina Rutti, *Dalton State College*

Mark Ryan, *Hawkeye Community College*

Amy Santos, *State College of Florida—Manatee*

Steven Sedky, *Santa Monica Community College*

Phyllis Shafer, *Brookdale Community College*

Carl Smalls, *Guilford Technical Community College*

Nayrie Smith, *Miami Dade College*

Ray Snyder, *Trident Technical College*

Jeff Spector, *Middlesex County College*

Alice Stewart, *North Carolina A and T University*

Theresa Strong, *Horry Georgetown Technical College*

Ronda Taylor, *Ivy Tech Community College*

George Valcho, *Bossier Parish Community College*

Jacob Voegel, *Coastal Carolina University*

Ruth White, *Bowling Green State University*

Rick Wills, *Illinois State University*

Doug Wilson, *University of Oregon*

Mark Zorn, *Butler County Community College*

Board of Advisors

A special thank you goes out to our Board of Advisors:

Koren Borges, *University of North Florida*

Elisabeth Cason, *Bossier Parish Community College*

Gustavo Demoner, *West Los Angeles College*

Katie Gallagher, *Johnson County Community College*

Miriam Huddleston, *Harford Community College*

Greg Luce, *Bucks County Community College*

Kimberly Mencken, *Baylor University*

Phyllis Shafer, *Brookdale Community College*

Table of contents

Chapter 6: Organizational Behavior

Chapter 7: Introduction to Marketing

Chapter 8: Accounting and Financial Statements

1 Fundamentals of the Business World

What To Expect

By the end of the chapter, you will be able to:

- Compare and contrast for-profit and nonprofit organizations.
- Differentiate among revenue, profit, and loss.
- Classify business offerings as goods or services.
- Summarize how the American economy has evolved over time.

Chapter Topics

- **1-1** Business and Profits
- **1-2** The Role Business Plays in Society
- **1-3** Entrepreneurial Risk and Factors of Production
- **1-4** The Forces of the Business Environment
- **1-5** Stakeholders in Business

Copyright ©McGraw Hill / Paul Burns/Image Source.

"What Basic Information Do I Need to Launch a Successful Business?"

Pets are big business in the United States. The Humane Society of the United States estimates that 65% of U.S. households own a pet.

That's about 80 million U.S. households owning more than 163 million dogs and cats. The average amount spent on vet care each year, per pet, is more than $1,250.1 Total annual spending on pets reaches nearly $70 billion per year!

Ana is an entrepreneur who sees the opportunity to thrive in the pet market. She is just about to launch her first business—a pet-supply store named PETZ.

Ana is nervous because she's heard that many new businesses fail, and she doesn't want to become another statistic.

Ana's friend Calvin has built a successful catering business, and like any good entrepreneur, Ana is seeking guidance from an expert.

PETZ's grand opening is next month. I'm excited and also terrified.

What are you going to sell?

Basic supplies for cats and dogs. Food, toys, collars, leashes. Plus other merchandise for pet lovers, like stuffed animals, magnets, and bumper stickers

This is a great concept. We want to make sure you are also differentiating yourself from your competitors

Definitely. PETZ is going to be different from the big-box stores. It'll be a place where people can bring their pets and get personalized advice from experts.

Another opportunity you could consider is providing services, too, like dog grooming, training, and boarding. I think the profit margins on those services are quite high.

Great idea! I'm planning to start small and then expand a little at a time, because money's so tight right now. Besides, I don't know any dog groomers or trainers.

That's okay, you've hustled and made it this far. In terms of connecting with providers, one suggestion would be to leverage LinkedIn as well as just simply search for providers online and reach out to them to talk about the opportunity. Building relationships is a cornerstone of business.

Lesson 1-1
Business and Profits

Many people start their own business because they want to be their own boss and earn a good living. They equate their love of something (for example, animals, fashion, music, books) with their ability to base a business on it.

Unfortunately, many people start their own business without understanding the business environment. Lacking funds, experience, and a basic knowledge of business practices, they cannot make enough money to stay in business. In fact, only about 20% of new businesses survive beyond their first year.

Before Ana starts her business, she should understand the fundamentals of business. What questions should she ask as she gets her business off the ground?

In this lesson, we will gain a better understanding of the different types of businesses and their goals. By the end of the lesson you'll be able to understand the role of profit and explain why Calvin advised Ana to provide services for pet owners.

What Is a Business Organization?

It is helpful to distinguish between an *organization* and a *business*.

An **organization** is a group of people who work together to accomplish a specific purpose. There are two types of organizations—*for-profit* and *nonprofit*.

- A **for-profit organization** is formed to make money, or profits, by selling goods or services.

- The purpose of a **nonprofit organization** is to earn enough profit to cover its expenses and further its goals.

A **business** is any activity that seeks to make a profit by satisfying needs through selling goods or services and generating revenue.

For-Profit Organizations	Nonprofit Organizations
• PetSmart	• Red Cross
• Camping World	• NFL (National Football League)
• Under Armour	• Humane Society
• Uber	• Some hospitals
• Facebook	• Some colleges and universities
	• United Autoworkers

Some nonprofits operate in the *public sector*, which are controlled by the government. Others are in the *private sector*, which are not controlled by the government.

Copyright © McGraw Hill   Daisy-Daisy/Alamy Stock Photo

The biggest difference between for-profit businesses and nonprofit organizations is the measure of accomplishment.

- In for-profit organizations, the measure generally is profit (or loss).
- In nonprofit organizations, money and expenses are important, but success is measured by how effectively services are delivered or by other criteria.

Decisions

Based on the conversation between Ana and Calvin, which type of organization is PETZ, Nonprofit or for-profit?

Correct Answers: For-profit

What Is the Lifeblood of Business? Profit!

A business seeks to make a profit by selling goods or services to generate revenue. There are three components of making a profit.

1. **Selling** is the exchange of goods or services for an agreed sum of money.

2. By selling, a company generates **revenue,** which is the total amount of money that the selling of goods or services produces during a defined period of time: daily, weekly, monthly, quarterly, yearly.

3. It takes money to make money. **Expenses** are the costs incurred in running the business, such as salaries and rents.

Subtract expenses from revenue to generate profit.

Revenue − Expenses = Profit

Profit is the amount of money a business makes after paying for all of its costs. The opposite of profit is a **loss,** which occurs when business expenses exceed revenues.

Decisions

Use Ana's revenue and expense figures for PETZ during her first two years of operation to answer the following questions.

Year	Revenue	Expenses
1	$150,000	$185,000
2	$180,000	$120,000

1. In Year 1, PETZ _____.

    A. earned a profit

    B. incurred a loss

2. From Year 1 to Year 2, what happened to PETZ's expenses?

    A. Its expenses decreased.

    B. Its expenses increased.

3. What was PETZ's profit in Year 2?

    A. $60,000

    B. $120,000

    C. $30,000

    D. $180,000

Correct Answers: 1. B; 2. A; 3. A

What Do Businesses Sell?

Businesses sell goods, services, or both.

- **Goods** are tangible products—things you can touch—such as food, clothing, appliances, gasoline, and books.
- **Services** are intangible products—things you can't touch—such as education, recreation, or health care. Think of a service as a task that is performed for you, such as house cleaning or tax preparation.

The U.S. economy has evolved over the centuries. For more information on the evolution of the U.S. economy from agricultural to industrial to knowledge, technology, and service, see below.

From an economic standpoint, most American jobs today involve the provision of services. For example, editors provide services by editing books, magazines, and websites; stockbrokers provide services by helping investors buy and sell stocks. But the dominance of service-based jobs is relatively recent.

The Evolution of the U.S. Economy

18th Century: The Agricultural Economy

Early in the history of the United States, the great majority of the workforce was employed in agriculture, producing and selling goods made on farms and ranches, such as food, cotton, and leather. Today, technology has made farming and ranching so efficient that only about 2% of the U.S. population is now employed in agriculture.

Late 19th to Early 20th Century: The Industrial Economy

During the late 19th and early 20th centuries, the United States evolved from an agricultural nation into an industrial one, selling manufactured goods: steel, tools, and machines—everything from ships to locomotives to automobiles to toasters. Indeed, America's industrial development became the envy of the world and made a huge difference in turning the tide toward victory during World War II.

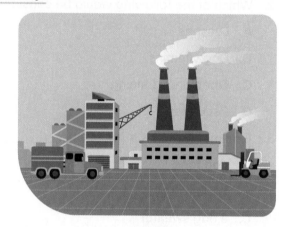

Late 20th Century: The Service Economy

By the late 20th century, the United States had evolved into the service economy it is today. Indeed, during the last 50 years, jobs involving manufacturing—the production of goods—have declined, mainly because of global outsourcing or offshoring, the use of suppliers outside the United States (such as suppliers in China and India) to provide labor, goods, or services. Many of the goods formerly produced in the United States are now produced overseas. In the United States in the last 25 years, most new jobs can be attributed to the growth in services: entertainment, health, legal, financial, educational, personal care, repair, janitorial, and other services.

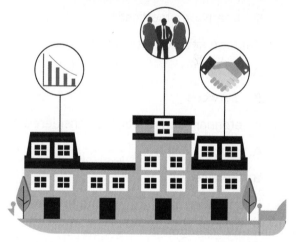

Decisions

After Ana's conversation with Calvin, she is taking a look at her business strategy to analyze what she will be offering her customers. Help Ana classify the items as goods or services.

1. Which of the following would be considered goods? (Check all that apply.)

    A. Pet crates

    B. Cat sitting

    C. Dog walking

    D. Cat food

2. Which of the following would be considered services?

    A. Leashes

    B. Dog vitamins

    C. Obedience training

    D. Pet crates

3. Flea medication is a good, while _____ is a service.

    A. dog food

    B. dog grooming

    C. a dog sweater

    D. heartworm medication

4. Cat food and dog vitamins are _____.

    A. Goods

    B. Services

5. A veterinary consultation is considered a _____.

    A. Good

    B. Service

6. Dog walking is a _____, and the leashes used to walk them are _____.

    A. service; goods

    B. good; services

Correct Answers: 1. A & D; 2. C & B; 3. B; 4. A; 5. B; 6. A

The Role Business Plays in Society

By the end of this lesson, you will be able to:

- Provide examples of the ways business can impact quality of life.
- Provide examples of the four ways business can advance the interests of society.

Where Does PETZ Fit in the Bigger Picture?

"How Does My Business Benefit Society?"

In opening PETZ, a pet-supply and service store, Ana is guided by the profit principle: She wants PETZ to bring in more revenue than it pays in expenses.

With all of her energy focused on getting the store opened, Ana hasn't thought about the exciting role her business can play in her community.

A week after the PETZ grand opening, Ana's friend Calvin (a successful catering entrepreneur) stops by to pick up some catnip for his cat, Whiskers.

Hey Ana, how's business?

People have been really supportive! PETZ has been open for only one week, and I've already had repeat customers.

What do they like most about the store?

They like having a local place where they can talk about their pets and get advice. Also, I have a refrigerated section of fresh pet foods. A lot of customers want only fresh, organic food for their cats and dogs, so they can't buy more than three or four days' worth of pet food at a time. So, they say they'll be stopping in a couple of times a week.

What a great opportunity for you. Are you taking "reservations" for the foods? You'll build customer loyalty if they know you're saving inventory for them.

I'm already covered on that! I've even been working out the details of delivering the fresh foods to people's houses.

Isn't being an entrepreneur great? Not only are you earning a profit for yourself, you're also providing a benefit to your community and to local pet owners.

Ana's main goal in starting her business was to earn a profit. Though she did not realize it at first, Ana's business also improves other people's lives, too. How exactly does Ana's business benefit society?

In this lesson, we will learn about the larger social context in which business operates. We will explore how businesses help to improve people's overall quality of life and advance society's interests. We will gain insight into how for-profit businesses have the opportunity to benefit many people, not just their owners.

How Does Business Improve a Society's Standard of Livig?

Business can raise people's standard of living, enabling them to live longer and healthier lives. It can also contribute to human knowledge.

Quality of life refers to a society's general well-being as measured by standard of living, health care, educational opportunities, freedom, happiness, and environmental health. A synonym for quality of life is *human development*.

A large part of an enhanced quality of life results from an improved **standard of living**, which is defined by how many goods and services people can buy with the money they have.

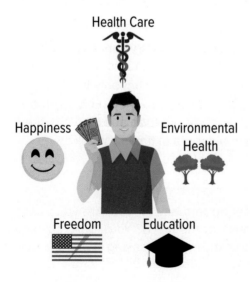

Health Care

Happiness

Environmental Health

Freedom   Education

How Do Businesses Support Community Interests?

In addition to increasing quality of life, business can advance the interests of society in four key ways.

Producing Goods and Services

Food and medicine, clothing and shelter, heat and light, and many other necessities of life are produced by businesses.

Providing Paychecks and Benefits for Employees

Typically, dozens or hundreds of employees depend on an individual business owner for paychecks and benefits, such as health insurance and a retirement plan.

Paying Taxes to Support Government Spending

Most businesses pay taxes. Moreover, employees pay payroll taxes. The government uses these taxes to fund public health programs, Social Security, education, defense, and other essential services.

Donating Funds, Goods, and Services for Community Causes

In many communities, businesses are strong supporters of charitable causes. For example, they donate supplies to help earthquake disaster victims, contribute money to the United Way, and sponsor Little League baseball teams.

Decisions

Ana is reflecting on how her business helps society. Choose the most applicable label for each of Ana's thought and actions.

1. PETZ provides pet goods, services, and supplies under one roof, making it convenient for pet owners to find everything they need to care for their animal.

   A. Providing paychecks and benefits for employees

   B. Donating funds, goods, and services for community causes

   C. Paying taxes to support government spending

   D. Producing a good or service

2 While Ana has only a few employees right now, she aspires to grow her business. If she continues opening new stores in different locations, she could end up with hundreds of employees.

   A. Providing paychecks and benefits for employees

   B. Producing a good or service

   C. Donating funds, goods, or services for community causes

   D. Paying taxes to support government spending

3. Ana withholds taxes from her employees' paychecks and pays all the required local, state, and federal taxes.

   A. Paying taxes to support government spending

   B. Donating funds, goods, or services for community causes

   C. Providing paychecks and benefits for employees

   D. Producing a good or service

4. Ana provides donations to the local animal shelter and hosts pet adoptions on a monthly basis.

   A. Producing a good or service

   B. Paying taxes to support government spending

   C. Donating funds, goods, or services for community causes

   D. Providing paychecks and benefits for employees

Correct Answers: 1. D; 2. A; 3. A; 4. C

Lesson 1-3
Entrepreneurial Risk and Factors of Production

By the end of this lesson, you will be able to:

- Explain why entrepreneurs are important to an economy.
- Apply the factors of production to a business setting.

Is Ana an Entrepreneur?

"What Are the Risks and Benefits of Entrepreneurship?"

Ana's pet-goods store, PETZ, is up and running. She is feeling and experiencing the joy and challenge of owning a business.

Ana invites her trusted friend and advisor, Calvin, to lunch to discuss the challenges of entrepreneurship.

How is the business going?

Its going well, for now I'm able to generate only a small salary for myself. But after I make the payroll, there's nothing left over.

Hang in there, it takes time to get a return on the investment.

It's stressful. Every time a customer walks into the store, I hope that she'll spend hundreds of dollars. When she buys a cat toy for three bucks, I feel like I'm doing something wrong.

That's the key challenge of entrepreneurship, Ana. You have the potential to make a really large profit, but in the meantime you carry all the risk.

It is definitely stressful. I used every penny of my savings to open the store, and I borrowed money from my parents and from the bank. Even if the store fails, I still have to pay them back.

Copyright © McGraw Hill

Chapter 1 · Fundamentals of the Business World   **13**

Because Ana takes all the risks of opening her own business, she is truly an entrepreneur.

In this lesson, we will explain the key element that defines entrepreneurship. Because most entrepreneurs seek profits, we also discuss the building blocks of wealth, which will help us see what Ana needs to do to make make PETZ into a profitable, ongoing business.

What Is an Entrepreneur? How Does an Entrepreneur Differ from an Employee?

Entrepreneurs play a vital role in our economy. Understanding what makes them special and how they impact others is key to understanding what role you could play. How would you respond to the following questions:

What Risks Do Entrepreneurs Take?

In the business realm, **risk** is defined as the possibility that the owner or owners of a business may invest time and money in the enterprise and fail. Entrepreneurs take a larger risk in starting a business compared to employees who work for that business. Although the employee is risking his/her commitment of time and effort in following a particular career path, an entrepreneur can face the loss of time, effort, reputation, and money.

Taking risks is what entrepreneurs do. An **entrepreneur** is a person who sees a new opportunity for a product or service and risks time and money to start a business with the goal of making a profit.

Why are Entrepreneurs Essential to an Economy?

Entrepreneurs are essential to an economy because they provide the catalyst that drives innovation. Most entrepreneurs start small businesses designed to capture, meet, or improve a segment of a market that is underserved. It is this essential action that consumers want in order to make their lives more efficient and/or enjoyable, and it is what an economy needs to grow.

Decisions

1. During one week, the following people come into PETZ and talk with Ana. Which one of them is an entrepreneur?

    A. A sales representative for the country's largest supplier of dry dog food

    B. A recent college graduate who works for an SEO (search engine optimization) company and offers the company's services to Ana

    C. A customer who works as a hair stylist at a local salon

    D. The proprietor of a company who created dog toys that are indestructible

Correct Answer: 1. D

What Are the Factors of Production?

Whether a business is an individual pursuit by one person or an organization with thousands of employees, it relies on the *factors of production*. Here are some factors of production:

Entrepreneurship

An entrepreneur is a person who sees a new opportunity for a product or service and who risks his or her time and money to start a business with the goal of making a profit.

Natural Resources

Natural resources consist of production inputs that are useful just as they appear in nature. Most natural resources can't be created; they must be mined, harvested, harnessed, or purified. They include land, forests, water, wind, sunlight, and mineral deposits.

Capital

Capital includes the buildings, machines, tools, and technology used to produce goods and services. Capital does not include money, although money is used to acquire buildings and other capital.

Human Resources

Human resources consist of labor, the physical and intellectual contributions of a company's employees.

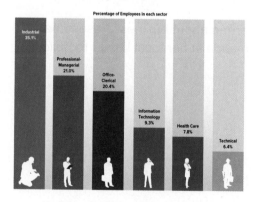

Percentage of Employees in each sector

Industrial 35.1%
Professional-Managerial 21.0%
Office-Clerical 20.4%
Information Technology 9.3%
Health Care 7.8%
Technical 6.4%

Knowledge

Knowledge is composed of the facts, information, and skills acquired by a person through training or education. It has been revolutionized by computers, telecommunications, and databases, which allow entrepreneurs to quickly determine and meet customers' wants and needs.

Decisions

Select the factor of production that best applies to PETZ.

1. Ana's physical store is located on land the city has zoned for commercial use.

   A. Capital

   B. Natural resources

   C. Knowledge

   D. Human resources

   E. Entrepreneurship

2. When Ana launched PETZ, she invested in a point of purchase system to track inventory, run financial reports, and take payments from her customers.

   A. Human resources

   B. Capital

   C. Entrepreneurship

   D. Natural resources

   E. Knowledge

3. Ana hired sales associates who have a passion for pets and a desire to grow their knowledge. Ana knows her staff is more than labor as these employees also contribute ideas on how to grow the business.

   A. Knowledge

   B. Human resources

   C. Natural resources

   D. Entrepreneurship

   E. Capital

4. Ana was able to launch PETZ because she learned about business, researched the industry, and utilized the plethora of information at her local library to build her business plan.

   A. Human resources

   B. Entrepreneurship

   C. Natural resources

   D. Knowledge

   E. Capital

Correct Answers: 1. B; 2. B; 3. B; 4. D

The Forces of the Business Environment

By the end of this lesson, you will be able to:

- Summarize the importance of the macroenvironment.
- Classify examples of the impacts of economic, political/legal/regulatory, technological, competitive, global, and social forces on businesses.

Survive and Thrive in the Business Environment

"What Social and Economic Forces Affect Ana's Business (PETZ)?"

Business does not operate in a bubble. Rather, it is part of an ecosystem that is comprised of micro and macro elements that impact the business.

Ana meets with her friend Calvin to discuss what's going on in the business environment

Ana how have you been doing! Every time I go by PETZ it is filled with customers.

Things are going well in the store. I am starting to realize there are some other elements outside of our four walls that impact the business.

You've got it, this is what we call the business environment and it changes and evolves, and if you don't stay apprised you may find yourself going out of business.

Yes, for example we are taking advantage of some changes in demographics by spending more time promoting on social media. We can definitely see the bond between pets and their humans are strong as ever.

That's awesome! You'll also want to keep an eye out on some potential legislation that could impact small business. Also, don't lose sight of what your competitors are doing.

In this lesson, we will examine the social and economic environments in which a business operates. Businesses are affected by many factors that can spur or limit their success. Understanding these factors is essential for both short-term and long-term business planning.

By recognizing these forces and understanding how they affect her, Ana can become a more proactive entrepreneur—one who balances a focus on the store's day-to-day operations with an understanding of the trends that may require a change in her business strategies.

What Forces Affect the Business Environment?

Business and entrepreneurship don't exist in a vacuum. All companies operate within the **business environment**, the arena of forces that encourage or discourage the development of business. These forces can be divided into six categories:

Learn more about the Business Environment.

Economic Forces: The Tension Between Freedom and Restraint

Business owners face a continual tension between the freedoms to operate a business and the regulations provided by governments. Several common areas include:

- **Taxation:** Some countries have higher tax rates on businesses, which can restrict how much companies can invest in initiatives and how much profit is retained in the business.
- **Contract enforcement:** In countries that do not strongly enforce contract laws, businesspeople are reluctant to enter into business relationships.
- **Corruption:** Countries that don't punish corruption and bribery create an atmosphere of uncertainty that can hurt honest businesspeople.

Technological Forces: The Effect on Productivity and Security

Technology includes not only digital technology (computers, telecommunications, and giant data storage) but also all machines required to help a company get things done, including delivery vans, vending machines, and surveillance cameras.

Technology has given rise to **e-commerce**, or **electronic commerce**, the buying and selling of products or services over computer networks. E-commerce is reshaping entire industries and revamping the very notion of what a company is.

Information technology has also facilitated **e-business**, using the Internet to facilitate every aspect of running a business. Some impacts include:

- **Productivity:** The purpose of all technology is to improve **productivity**, defined as the amount of output given the amount of input—such as the number of doughnuts produced by one worker in an hour.

- **Security:** Technological systems can enhance productivity, but they can also compromise security—for example, by allowing hackers to steal credit card information.

Competitive Forces: The Influence on Customers, Employees, and Investor Satisfaction

Competitors are people or organizations that are rivals for a company's customers or resources. The rivalry that exists between businesses in certain industries can be extremely difficult for a business to operate within, causing some businesses to fail. Because all businesses must deal with competition, businesses strive to create a **competitive advantage** to allow the organization to create products, systems, or cultures that are not easily replicable.

Customers: A company such as a public utility that is the only one in its industry has no particular incentive to improve service with its customers because it knows they have nowhere else to go.

Employees: A technology company trying to recruit and keep top talent will go to greater lengths if it knows there are other companies fiercely competing for that talent.

Investors: A bank that is the only one in a state or country may pay its investors whatever it wants.

Social Forces: The Impact of Demographics

Changes in a country's demographics, the population's measurable characteristics such as gender, age, race, and family composition, can change a business's number of customers. Customers' changing needs and tastes can also affect the business.

Global Forces: The Effect on Trade and Stability

Businesses today operate in a global economy, one in which customers can be located a mile away or halfway around the globe. **Globalization** refers to the movement of the world economy toward becoming a more interdependent system.

Global forces include all of the following:

- Trade pacts and economic unions: Formal trade agreements can facilitate the exchange of goods and services between nations, which in turn can affect a nation's manufacturing capacity, employment level, and travel policies.

- Military alliances
- Currency exchanges
- Immigration policies
- Environmental regulations

All of these forces can affect national stability. Wars, terrorism, recessions, currency panics, epidemics, refugee flows, and ecological changes can undermine national stability—thereby increasing risk to business owners.

Political/Regulatory/Legal: The Rules Business Must Abide By

Both nationally and internationally, regulations, laws, and politics set the rules businesses must abide by to stay in business and out of trouble.

For example, new laws and regulations were implemented after the recession to protect consumers from predatory lending practices.

Decisions

Review each statement, choose which aspect of the business environment is being described.

1. There is local legislation being considered that would increase a local sales tax. Ana is concerned this could impact sales.

   A. Technological

   B. Competitive

   C. Global

   D. Social

   E. Economic

   F. Legal/Regulatory/Political

2. Ana recently implemented an automated, Internet-based system ensuring she never runs out of inventory of her most popular brand of dog food.

   A. Economic

   B. Competitive

   C. Legal/Regulatory/Political

   D. Global

   E. Social

   F. Technological

3. A new, larger pet store has opened around the corner from PETZ.

   A. Technological

   B. Economic

   C. Social

   D. Legal/Regulatory/Political

   E. Global

   F. Competitive

4. Ana is able to increase her profit margins by purchasing dog collars and other pet supplies from manufacturers in China and the Philippines.

   A. Social

   B. Technological

   C. Economic

   D. Legal/Regulatory/Political

   E. Global

   F. Competitive

5. Ana recently read a study that said millennials have increased their spending on pets by 15% and are more likely to splurge on their pets than consumers 5 years ago.

   A. Global

   B. Economic

   C. Technological

   D. Competitive

   E. Legal/Regulatory/Political

   F. Social

6. The city government where Ana lives is considering implementing a new law that would restrict the number of pets to one per household.

   A. Competitive

   B. Global

   C. Technological

   D. Legal/Regulatory/Political

   E. Economic

   F. Competitive

   G. Social

Lesson 1-5
Stakeholders in Business

By the end of this lesson, you will be able to:

- Recall the types of stakeholders that businesses must recognize and satisfy.

PETZ: Changes and Surprises

"Who Are the Stakeholders in My Business? What Trends in the Business Environment Must I Be Aware of?"

Ana, the owner of PETZ pet-supply store, meets her friend and successful entrepreneur Calvin for dinner and to share ideas to continue growing the business.

Ana, I am excited to brainstorm ideas on how to grow your business.

Thanks Cal, you know from the beginning I wanted PETZ to be a place where animal lovers could gather and find everything they need. I love animals, and I wanted my customers to know that their pets' health and happiness is PETZ's key goal. Customers have responded really well to that.

I think the results are demonstrating this is a great business approach.

I also think I did a good job in hiring people who want the business to succeed as much as I do. They are passionate about animals, care about customers, and are excited to grow with the company.

What were the biggest challenges for you?

Copyright © McGraw Hill

I can't believe how quickly things change. I was shocked when a competitor opened around the corner. At first I was paralyzed by it. Then I realized I needed to start working much harder to gain and keep customers.

How's that going?

Really well, we've greatly increased our presence on social media, we started an e-mail list, and we're about to launch a pet-sitting service and an app that will let customers place standing orders for pet products.

It sounds like you're doing everything you can to please your various stakeholders.

Ana has learned that business is about hustle, grit, and resilience. One of Ana's key metrics of success is her ability to take care of her stakeholders.

In this lesson, we will examine these different groups of stakeholders. Running a business often feels like a balancing act of trying to keep different groups of stakeholders happy; understanding each group's desires and interests is essential.

Management and Stakeholders

Business people practice the art of management, planning, leading, organizing, and controlling the activities of an enterprise according to certain policies to achieve certain objectives.

Copyright © McGraw Hill   Ground Picture/Shutterstock

Managers and entrepreneurs operate in an organizational environment composed of various stakeholders, those who have any sort of stake or interest in the business.

Key Stakeholders in a Business

Let's learn about some key stakeholders in business.

Customers: The Focus of Business

Customers are the people or companies that pay to use an organization's goods or services. For-profit companies and nonprofit organizations both focus on customers. For example, the customers of a nonprofit university are its students.

Employees: The Need for Performance

Employees are typically a key stakeholder in a business as they provide the labor, create the culture, and provide the service that ultimately makes a business succeed or fail. Have you ever worked for a "toxic organization"? This is the name that Stanford University business professor Jeffrey Pfeffer gives to firms with high turnover and low productivity, companies that drive employees away. "Companies that manage people right will outperform those that don't by 30% to 40%," he says.

Suppliers: Providing Parts and Products

A *supplier*, or *vendor*, is a person or an organization that supplies raw materials, services, equipment, labor, energy, and other products to other organizations.

Distributors: Directing Products to Customers

A *distributor* is a person or an organization, such as a dealer or retailer, that helps sell goods and services to customers. Distributors can be quite important in terms of ensuring that customers have a place to purchase a product. For example, many small publishers have distributors to sell their books to libraries and bookstores.

Lenders: Carrying the Company When Money Is Short

Businesses often rely on lenders such as banks to give them loans to start a business, to keep the business afloat when revenues are low, or to expand their operations. Some entrepreneurs finance their new enterprises by using their personal credit cards for cash advances or expenses.

Nearby Communities: The Local Environment

Nearby communities are important stakeholders because schools and municipal governments rely on businesses for a portion of their tax base. In addition, families and merchants depend on the employee payroll for their livelihoods, and nonprofit organizations such as sports leagues may depend on them for donations.

Government Regulators: Local, State, Federal, and World

Government regulators are government agencies that establish rules and regulations under which organizations must operate; in turn, regulators are often affected by organizations. Regulatory bodies may range from local planning departments to state commissions to federal agencies and international agencies (such as the World Trade Organization, which oversees international trade).

Interest Groups: People with Specific Issues

The Sierra Club, the United Auto Workers, and the Chamber of Commerce are examples of *interest groups* or *special-interest groups*—groups whose members try to influence businesses and governments on specific issues. Interest groups may try to exert political influence, as in contributing funds to lawmakers' election campaigns or in launching letter-writing efforts to businesses and politicians.

Media: From Print to Internet

No businessperson can afford to ignore the power of news and entertainment media, which include not only newspapers, magazines, radio, and TV but also Internet social media, such as Snapchat, Twitter, Instagram, Facebook, and YouTube. Because the media can rapidly and widely disseminate both bad news and good news, most mid-sized and larger businesses have a public-relations person or media department to communicate effectively with the press. In addition, top-level executives often receive special instruction on how to best deal with the media.

Decisions

As Ana strategizes on how she is going to grow the business, she jots down the list of her stakeholders. Ana is committed to meeting the needs of her customers, but knows that she has to be committed to *all* stakeholders to succeed.

1. Ana is the sole investor in her company. She is the _____.

   A. distributor

   B. lender

   C. employee

   D. owner

2. The people who need PETZ's goods and services are the _____.

   A. suppliers

   B. interest groups

   C. employees

   D. customers

3. PETZ purchases its products from _____.

   A. interest groups

   B. distributors

   C. nearby communities

   D. owners

4. The group responsible for PETZ's location in the downtown area is the _____.

   A. interest groups

   B. government regulators

   C. media

   D. employees

Correct Answers: 1. D; 2. D; 3. B; 4. B

Fundamentals of the Business World: Test

1. Barb, the owner of a lawn mowing business, gave half of her monthly revenue to a local homeless shelter. From this information, you can conclude that Barb's company is a

   A. for-profit organization.

   B. nonprofit organization.

   C. charitable business.

   D. public company.

   E. not-for-profit business.

2. A(n) _____ is any activity that seeks to make a profit by satisfying needs through selling goods or services and generating revenue.

   A. entity

   B. business

   C. organization

   D. association

   E. sector

3. A small business owner sold $2500 worth of product in one month. The owner had to pay rent of $500 and materials costs of $1250. What was the profit for the month?

   A. $750

   B. $500

   C. $1000

   D. $2500

   E. $2000

4. Since Maia moved to Nebraska, she is finding that she can buy more with her money than she could in Hawaii. Maia is experiencing an improvement in her

   A. earning potential.

   B. return on investment.

   C. standard of living.

   D. human potential.

   E. psychological benefits.

5. Patrice knows that investing her own money in a start-up business may be a mistake, but she believes she can make it work. Patrice is willing to

   A. take a risk.

   B. follow others' advice.

   C. live on a small salary.

   D. forgo rewards.

   E. buck the trend.

6. Capital does *not* include

   A. money.

   B. buildings.

   C. tools.

   D. technology.

   E. machines.

7. Plus Size has been selling larger size clothing in the same location for 10 years. Big Girls just opened across town and is threatening Plus Size's business. Big Girls is a(n) _____ of Plus Size.

   A. customer

   B. investor

   C. employee

   D. partner

   E. competitor

8. The United States has imposed trade sanctions on North Korea. This is primarily a _____ force in the business environment.

   A. legal/regulatory/political

   B. social

   C. global

   D. competitive

   E. technological

9. When Russia invaded Crimea, the United States imposed sanctions on Russia. What category of forces is impacting the business environment with these sanctions?

   A. legal/regulatory/political

   B. social

   C. global

   D. competitive

   E. technological

10. Holidays Galore is a seasonal business, so in the off season when it is buying inventory, it is often short of cash. The business usually borrows money from the bank to tide it over until the busy season begins. The bank is Holidays Galore's

    A. shareholder.

    B. supplier.

    C. distributor.

    D. interest group.

    E. lender.

11. AARP is an example of a(n) _____ whose members try to influence businesses and governments on specific issues.

    A. for-profit organization

    B. government regulator

    C. shareholder

    D. media outlet

    E. interest group

12. Smart Telephony has $500,000 in revenue and $600,000 in expenses this year. Which situation best describes the company's financial situation for the year?

    A. nonprofit

    B. loss

    C. profit

    D. risk-adverse

    E. competitive disadvantage

13. Shamira runs a small catering business in her hometown. Every three months, Shamira and her staff take hot meals to a homeless shelter across town. In this example, how is Shamira most helping society with her business?

    A. by producing services

    B. by paying taxes

    C. by providing benefits to her staff

    D. by sharing her profits

    E. by donating goods

14. Ingmar receives a substantial pay increase from his employer. He can now afford the new car he has been dreaming about for years. Ingmar can *best* be described as having

    A. better environmental health.

    B. an improved standard of living.

    C. more consumer freedom.

    D. a lower tax bracket.

    E. more community support.

A large part of an enhanced quality of life results from an improved standard of living, which is defined by how many goods and services people can buy with the money they have.

15. Seabass, Incorporated recently implemented an online training program to facilitate continuing education for its employees. Senior leadership believes the new training will increase efficiency and quality. This implantation will *most likely* impact which of the following factors of production?

    A. natural resources

    B. standard of living

    C. competitive advantage

    D. knowledge

    E. capital

Knowledge is composed of the facts, information, and skills acquired by a person through training or education. It has been revolutionized by computers, telecommunications, and databases, which allow entrepreneurs to quickly determine and meet customers' wants and needs.

16. Ozara is the plant manager for Estate Manufacturing. He is leading the efforts to double plant capacity with a new building. Which of the five factors of production is Ozara most impacting?

    A. human resources

    B. equity

    C. capital

    D. natural resources

    E. knowledge

17. Endellion owns a small delivery company. He decides to hire an office assistant and buys her a laptop to handle some of the administrative responsibilities for the company. This laptop is best described as which factor of production?

    A. equity

    B. capital

    C. knowledge

    D. human resources

    E. tangible product

18. As more and more individuals in Generation Z move out into the world, the housing market has shifted to meet their changing needs. This change is best represented by the _____ forces in the business environment.

    A. social

    B. competitive

    C. technological

    D. economic

    E. capital

19. Armida is a lawyer with the American Civil Liberties Union (ACLU). She is regularly in court working to ensure fair treatment of all individuals in the business world. The ACLU can *best* be described as a(n)

    A. government regulator.

    B. employee shareholder.

    C. contract enforcement group.

    D. special-interest group.

    E. demographic compliance group.

20. Which example best demonstrates how a large company could impact the town in which it operates?

    A. The town is more likely to be approved for a bank loan to build a new pool.

    B. Town schools are more likely to receive tax credits.

    C. Distributors are more likely to open businesses in the town.

    D. Customers are more likely to relocate to the town.

    E. Suppliers are more likely to offer discounts on bulk shipping to the town.

2 Ethical and Social Responsibility in Business

What To Expect

By the end of the chapter, you will be able to:

- Classify a company's action as legal/illegal and ethical/unethical.

- Determine whether a business action is ethical or unethical, given the host country's cultural values and norms.

Chapter Topics

- **2-1** Understanding Ethics
- **2-2** Building an Ethical Culture
- **2-3** Corporate Social Responsibility and the Social Audit
- **2-4** The Payoffs from Doing Good: The Benefits to Stakeholders

Copyright McGraw Hill Space_Cat/Shutterstock

"Conflict with My Job Duties or Desire to Profit?"

The American Journal is a highly successful online news and opinion website that covers many aspects of U.S. society, including business, politics, entertainment, sports, lifestyle, health, and pop culture. The journal both reproduces articles originally published by other sources and commissions its own news stories.

Thomas, who double-majored in communication and journalism, started as a reporter for the business section; he has since risen to become the site's editor-in-chief. Today, he is talking with Marissa, a junior reporter, about a story that she wants to publish on *The American Journal*'s homepage.

Thomas is faced with a decision that many businesspeople encounter: the choice between increasing revenue and profits or passing up an opportunity because it conflicts with personal or company values (or because it is against the law). What information can Thomas use to make a final decision about the story that Marissa wants to write?

In this lesson, we will introduce the concepts of ethics, values, and laws, which are used for making business decisions. We will distinguish between what is legal and what is ethical, and we will offer suggestions for conducting business with an emphasis on core values that benefit society.

You're not going to believe this, Thomas. You know who Dirk Matthews is?

Of course—he owns the company Picassio. It allows anyone to turn their photos into Picassio-style photos. It's one of the most downloaded apps in the app store.

There is talk that the technology behind the app is not actually his and that he stole it from another developer. This story would be perfect for the lead on the homepage.

Do you have reliable sources to back up the story?

Just a couple of people who overheard him talking at a social event about how the company started, but why would they make up something like that? I don't think they have anything against him personally.

Do we know for sure? Are there records? Have we reached out to him for comment?

My sources said he was definitely talking about someone who was involved at the beginning but "didn't hang in there," and that he is "lucky" as he would have had to split the shares otherwise.

This seems like gossip to me, not real news.

Come on, Tom, you know our readers click on these stories.

But we're talking about a man's reputation here as well as the integrity of our company.

But this story will get our homepage 100,000 hits or more! And the greater our numbers, the more we can charge for ads.

Right, but if we get our facts wrong, we can get sued for libel and slander.

Lesson 2-1
Understanding Ethics

What are *ethics*, *values*, *laws*, and *cultural norms*? Let's take a closer look at these important terms, which form the basis for business decision making.

Ethics, Values, Laws, and Cultural Norms

Ethics

Ethics are principles of right and wrong that influence behavior. They help instruct how people deal with and treat one another. Some ethical standards are nearly universal, such as the belief that killing is never justified, except for the most justifiable of reasons (such as self-defense). Other ethical standards are culturally based, varying according to what a particular culture considers right or wrong.

Values

Values are the relatively permanent and deeply held underlying beliefs and attitudes that help determine people's behavior. Values are the underpinnings for ethical systems (as in the Hippocratic Oath physicians take to "first do no harm" to a patient) and legal systems (as in lawyers' pledges to uphold the law). CEOs and financial advisors may also have fiduciary responsibilities (to act in the best interest of their investors and clients).

Laws

Laws are rules of conduct or action formally recognized as binding or enforced by a controlling authority, such as police officers and the court system. In our society, laws are based on ethical considerations and values. However, what is ethical may not always be legal, and vice versa.

Cultural Norms

Cultural norms are the ethics, values, attitudes, and behaviors that are deemed to be normal or typical in a given culture. For example, in the United States, a cultural norm is that we shake hands when formally meeting someone.

Is It Legal? Is It Ethical?

When people are faced with decisions, how can they determine the most ethical action? Four questions help make this determination:

1. Is the action legal?

2. Is the action ethical?

Copyright © McGraw Hill

3. Would I want to be treated like this?

4. Will the outcome of my decision make me feel guilty?

In addition, as we noted above, what is ethical may not always be legal, and vice versa. Read the examples in each of the boxes below to understand more about the distinction between what is legal and what is ethical. Note that these examples refer to business practices in the United States. Other countries may differ in terms of what they consider legal or ethical.

Distinctions Between Legality and Ethics

Legal but Unethical

- Making low-quality products that break easily
- Canceling a company retirement plan
- Avoiding taxes on U.S. revenues by using offshore banks
- Charging a very high price for brand-name drugs when inexpensive generic versions are available

Legal and Ethical

- Boycotts of businesses
- Consumer-friendly policies
- Employee fringe benefits
- Diversity policies (including affirmative action)

Illegal and Unethical

- Embezzlement
- Consumer fraud
- Sexual harassment
- Cash payments to avoid taxes
- Bribes

Illegal but Ethical

- Paying more despite union contract limits
- Selling raw milk for human consumption across state lines
- Taking usable items from corporate dumpsters and donating them

Decisions

Thomas is pondering whether to run with the story proposed by Marissa. How would you respond to the following questions?

If *The American Journal* publishes false information, the injured party may sue. Therefore, *The American Journal* (and all other U.S. businesses) must work within the framework of U.S. _____.

> **A.** law
>
> **B.** corporate social responsibility
>
> **C.** values
>
> **D.** ethics

Thomas has a deeply held _____ that journalists are required to publish the truth and to verify all the information in their stories.

> **A.** law
>
> **B.** corporate social responsibility
>
> **C.** value
>
> **D.** ethic

Thomas's _____ tell him it is not morally acceptable to ruin a man's career based on gossip.

> **A.** set of laws
>
> **B.** corporate social responsibilities
>
> **C.** goals
>
> **D.** ethics

Correct Answers: A; C; D

Lesson 2-2
Building an Ethical Culture

By the end of this lesson, you will be able to:

- Explain how leadership helps foster high ethical standards.
- Explain how a code of ethics helps to create an ethical environment.
- Summarize the ways that organizations foster high ethical standards.
- Apply the Sarbanes–Oxley Act to a business case.

Creating an Ethical Culture at *The American Journal*

"How do I create an ethical work environment and set a good example for my employees?"

Thomas feels disconcerted that Marissa would propose a major story based on hearsay. He decides to discuss the situation with Viola, *The American Journal*'s publisher and "head honcho."

As top managers of a popular news and opinion website, Viola and Thomas are aware of the importance of setting the right example for their staff. They understand the ethics of journalism, but some of the less experienced staff at *The American Journal* have not yet developed the same understanding.

Viola, yesterday Marissa came to me with a possible story for the homepage. A couple of sources told her that Dirk Matthews, founder of Picassio, used another person's intellectual property to create his successful app.

The problem is that the story is based completely on gossip. Marissa can't find proof to back up the story. A story like this could wreck his reputation.

What did you tell her?

I said we can't run the story until we have the facts. Now she's upset because she thinks the story would be great exposure for her career. She thinks another news outlet will get a hold of the story and run it, and she'll miss a career-making opportunity.

What worries me is that Marissa thought I'd support publishing the story. Any journalist should know that would violate journalistic ethics.

(sighs) I feel for her, Tom. We've all been in her situation at some point in our career. . . . I'm glad you came to see me; it's important that our staff sees ethical journalism as a topic important to us all—not just something that you are stuck on.

The American Journal has been growing so fast . . . I think it's time to write a specific ethics policy and require the entire staff to undergo ethics training.

In this lesson, we will follow Thomas and Viola as they work to create a highly ethical climate at *The American Journal*. Making ethical decisions requires strong critical thinking about actions and their consequences, as well as the legal ramifications of those decisions. We will discuss the roles of an organization's owners, managers, and employees in setting and maintaining ethical standards. We'll also discuss some important legislation that affects business decisions.

Doing the Right Thing: How Organizations Can Promote Ethical Behavior

To foster high ethical standards, a company must have top managers who support a strong ethical climate, hire ethical employees, and institute a code of ethics as well as implement training programs in ethics.

As you explore the four ways of fostering an ethical culture listed here, think about the situation in which Viola and Thomas find themselves. Can they implement any of these best practices to promote a culture of ethical journalism at *The American Journal*?

Fostering High Ethical Standards

"We're Not Just Giving Lip Service"

Many, perhaps even most, lower-level employees will act ethically and honorably. But if top executives wink at ethical problems, ignore or reward ethical lapses, use legal loopholes to dodge ethical obligations, or use public relations to "spin" their unethical behavior into something more appetizing, they are clearly failing to lead by example.

Such behavior from top management will foster a loose ethical climate. Why should a clerk not steal from the office supply cabinet when the people at the top are using the company jet for personal vacation travel?

"We Want Honest Employees"

Few companies deliberately try to hire dishonest, irresponsible employees, but employers need to emphasize the company's ethical culture in its recruitment, interviewing, and hiring practices to recruit employees that fit the culture they want.

With the help of the human resources department, managers can design a talent management system that screens for strong personal values and a commitment to ethical behavior.

For example, the interviewing process may require applicants to share past experiences that demonstrate the behaviors, values, and ethics required by the organizational culture.

"We Need to Share Our Expectations"

A *code of ethics* is a set of ethical standards to help guide an organization's actions. Most ethical codes state top management's expectations for employees, offering guidance on how to treat customers, suppliers, and competitors. They also list and explain prohibited and ethically questionable behaviors, such as nepotism (hiring family members), bribery, accepting gifts from suppliers or vendors, and "cooking the books" to make the company's finances look stronger than they really are.

To reinforce their ethics, many companies provide ethics training, often presenting employees with possible ethical dilemmas they may eventually encounter.

"We Should Discipline Appropriately"

Companies must also work to ensure that their management and systems reward ethical behavior and punish unethical behavior.

What Are the Two Types of Ethical Codes?

Ethics codes may be either compliance-based or integrity-based:

- A **compliance-based ethics code** attempts to prevent criminal misconduct by increasing control and by punishing violators. For instance, many companies ask employees to sign nondisclosure agreements (NDAs) in which the signers acknowledge that they can be fired and even sued if they leak confidential information.

- An **integrity-based ethics code** seeks to foster responsible employee conduct by creating an environment that supports ethically desirable behavior. This approach stresses a culture of fair play, honesty, and diversity. It also emphasizes shared accountability among employees.

Individuals in organizations often view compliance-based codes as laws that should not be violated and integrity-based codes as ethics and values that should be promoted. When used together, these codes help promote a healthy environment where employees know which behaviors are discouraged and which behaviors are encouraged.

What Do Ethical Companies Do?

As you are beginning to understand, ethics starts with each of us. It is the individual actions of each person that collectively steer the entire organization.

Although individuals in the organization are responsible for their own behavior, managing the behaviors of numerous employees can become a daunting task, which is why large companies frequently have an ethics office, headed by an ethics officer. The job of the **ethics officer** is to integrate the organization's ethics and values initiatives, compliance activities, and business practices into the company's decision-making processes.

Human resources personnel are also involved in ensuring a company creates a code of ethics, institutes ethical training programs, and fosters an ethical screening and hiring process.

All of these actions lead to an organizational culture that values ethical behavior and decision making.

Thomas and Viola are discussing the need for an ethics code.

Viola, I think we need to re-think how we are operating. The situation with Marissa is a good reminder that we need to make sure our staff understand our code of ethics and that we clearly outline expectations and guidance for how we act and operate.

You are right Tom. I think we need to get even more clear in our policies. We also need to model this starting with you and me.

I agree. I think it starts with updating our policies to remind everyone that if we don't do things correctly, we could get sued.

Yes, this needs to be highlighted and trained via our compliance-based code of ethics. In fact, I think we should get a group of employees together to discuss our culture and develop an ethical code in which we focus on fair play, honesty, and diversity.

That's an excellent idea. This will emphasize shared accountability among employees. I also think we should look at hiring an ethics officer to help us integrate the organization's ethics and values initiatives, compliance activities, and business practices into the company's decision-making processes.

Decisions

At *The American Journal*, who is responsible for implementing and holding to the organization's code of ethics?

A. Viola, the CEO and publisher

B. Thomas, the editor-in-chief

C. Marissa, a reporter

D. All of the above

Correct Answer: D

Whistleblowers and the Sarbanes–Oxley Act

Sometimes a company develops an ethical climate the hard way—by having its illegal and/or unethical behaviors exposed by a **whistleblower**, an employee who reports organizational misconduct to the government or the public. Such misconduct may include corruption, fraud, overcharging, or health and safety problems.

Imagine you uncovered your supervisor's wrongdoings and then confronted your supervisor or reported this information to someone outside the organization. There is a good chance your supervisor and/or organization will not be pleased. Today, you would not face repercussions for such an action. However, in the past, this was not the case—as recently as 2001, many whistleblowers were fired for reporting the wrongdoings of their employers.

What changed? In 2002, President George W. Bush signed into law the *Sarbanes–Oxley Act*, which gave whistleblowers protection from retaliation. The Sarbanes–Oxley Act of 2002, often known simply as SOX or SarbOx, established protections for whistleblowers, record-keeping requirements for public companies, and penalties for noncompliance. The figure below outlines 10 key provisions of the law.

Principal Provisions of Sarbanes–Oxley

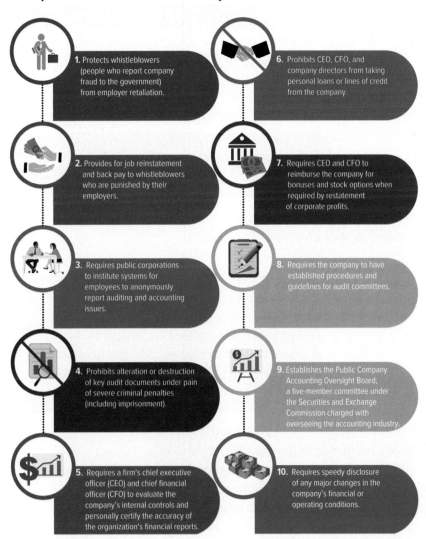

1. Protects whistleblowers (people who report company fraud to the government) from employer retaliation.

2. Provides for job reinstatement and back pay to whistleblowers who are punished by their employers.

3. Requires public corporations to institute systems for employees to anonymously report auditing and accounting issues.

4. Prohibits alteration or destruction of key audit documents under pain of severe criminal penalties (including imprisonment).

5. Requires a firm's chief executive officer (CEO) and chief financial officer (CFO) to evaluate the company's internal controls and personally certify the accuracy of the organization's financial reports.

6. Prohibits CEO, CFO, and company directors from taking personal loans or lines of credit from the company.

7. Requires CEO and CFO to reimburse the company for bonuses and stock options when required by restatement of corporate profits.

8. Requires the company to have established procedures and guidelines for audit committees.

9. Establishes the Public Company Accounting Oversight Board, a five-member committee under the Securities and Exchange Commission charged with overseeing the accounting industry.

10. Requires speedy disclosure of any major changes in the company's financial or operating conditions.

Corporate Social Responsibility and the Social Audit

By the end of this lesson, you will be able to:

- Discuss Carroll's Corporate Social Responsibility Pyramid and describe how organizations use it.
- Discuss the viewpoints surrounding corporate social responsibility and profitability.
- Discuss how companies are monitored to ensure they are meeting their social responsibilities.

"Which is more important: earning a higher profit or being socially responsible?"

Thomas and Viola are discussing the relationship between profits and social responsibility, trying to find ways for the company to accomplish both goals simultaneously.

I think the first draft of *The American Journal*'s code of ethics is looking good.

The team did great; I ran it past a few of my staffers, and they said they felt inspired by it.

It's long overdue, that's for sure.

Marissa brought up an important question that we're going to have to deal with. She was disappointed that we wouldn't run her story. Sure enough, *Gotcha!* (a gossip website) ran the story a day later, and it got hundreds of thousands of hits.

(sighs) That's hundreds of thousands of hits we could have had. At the same time, these are still accusations, and we are committed to holding ourselves to a higher standard.

Copyright © McGraw Hill

I agree—it's just tough when the other guy is getting the clicks and ad revenue that comes with those numbers. But we did the right thing.

We have to figure out how to deal with this. New competitors are launching every day, and we have to stay profitable and do what's right. If we don't, *The American Journal* will be financially impacted, which could impact our business and potentially our workforce.

There has to be a middle ground—a way for us to operate profitably and in a socially responsible manner.

You're right. It's our job to find that middle ground and set the right example.

Thomas and Viola are encountering a dilemma that top managers often face: how to balance social responsibility with a commitment to maximizing profit. Businesses of all sizes, including small companies run by ambitious entrepreneurs, face the same dilemma.

In this lesson, we will help Thomas and Viola examine *The American Journal*'s approach to social responsibility. Corporate social responsibility means taking actions that will benefit the larger society and not just the business and its employees. We will review both sides of the profit/social responsibility debate. We'll also discuss several key initiatives that companies undertake to demonstrate their commitment to social responsibility.

Should Corporate Social Responsibility Be Secondary to Profit?

Carroll's Global Corporate Social Responsibility Pyramid

A business is any activity that seeks to provide goods and services to others while operating at a profit, but some individuals believe the role of a business goes beyond just making a profit by fulfilling philanthropic responsibilities. The

University of Georgia business-ethics scholar Archie B. Carroll provides a guide for thinking about the day-to-day practical and moral matters that businesses encounter. **Carroll's Global Corporate Social Responsibility Pyramid** suggests that an organization's obligations in the global economy are comprised of **economic**, **legal**, **ethical**, and **philanthropic** responsibilities that are present in a firm's **host country**.

Corporate Social Responsibility: Pros and Cons

If individual ethical responsibility is about being a good individual citizen, **corporate social responsibility (CSR)** is about being a good organizational citizen. CSR is a concern for taking actions that will benefit the interests of society as well as the organization. CSR may range from sponsorship of Little League teams to sending supplies to hurricane victims. At the end of the day, it is about contributing to society in positive ways that make a difference to the community. And as many companies have found, CSR and ethics go hand in hand: acting ethically and with a sense of social responsibility are often one and the same.

Some companies feel the goal for maximum profit pulling them in one direction while the desire to be socially responsible pulling them in a different direction, because money from the organization is used to fund these social causes instead of being returned to the business or the owners of the business. The figure below outlines the rationale of these opposing viewpoints. Blending these two viewpoints together into one creates a "concurrent pursuit of value—both social and financial."

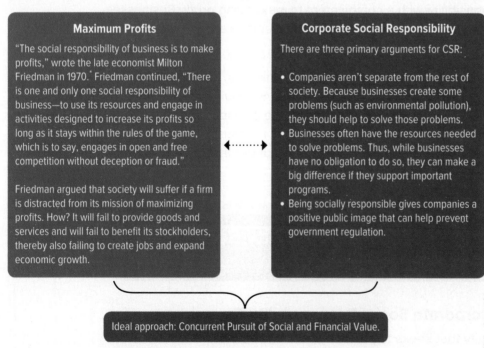

Maximum Profits

"The social responsibility of business is to make profits," wrote the late economist Milton Friedman in 1970.* Friedman continued, "There is one and only one social responsibility of business—to use its resources and engage in activities designed to increase its profits so long as it stays within the rules of the game, which is to say, engages in open and free competition without deception or fraud."

Friedman argued that society will suffer if a firm is distracted from its mission of maximizing profits. How? It will fail to provide goods and services and will fail to benefit its stockholders, thereby also failing to create jobs and expand economic growth.

Corporate Social Responsibility

There are three primary arguments for CSR:

- Companies aren't separate from the rest of society. Because businesses create some problems (such as environmental pollution), they should help to solve those problems.
- Businesses often have the resources needed to solve problems. Thus, while businesses have no obligation to do so, they can make a big difference if they support important programs.
- Being socially responsible gives companies a positive public image that can help prevent government regulation.

Ideal approach: Concurrent Pursuit of Social and Financial Value.

* Source: M. Friedman, "The Social Responsibility of Business Is to Increase Its Profits," *New York Times Magazine*, September 13, 1970, pp. 17–20.

What Is the Goal of a Business?

Thomas and Viola recognize *The American Journal*'s potential to be a business that makes a profit and impacts society. By running stories about important local, national, and world events, *The American Journal* can increase sales while enhancing public awareness about issues that society needs to address.

The American Journal can engage in social responsibility by taking actions such as supporting a scholarship for future journalists, donating a percentage of profits to local charities, and providing paid time for employees to serve the community.

Decisions

Which of the following demonstrates a commitment to corporate social responsibility at *The American Journal*?

1. Create a corporate matching program where the company will match an employee's donation to a charity.

2. Allow employees flex scheduling so they can reduce driving to reduce carbon emission.

3. Create a free literacy course to help readers better analyze the news.

4. All of these are forms of corporate social responsibility.

Correct Answer: 4

The Social Audit: Evaluating Corporate Social Responsibility

How can a company evaluate its social performance? A *social audit* is a systematic assessment of a company's performance in implementing socially responsible programs, often based on predefined goals.

Social audits often focus on six key areas, as explained below.

Social Audits

Corporate Policy: Positions on Political and Social Issues

Corporate policy describes a company's stated positions on political and social issues. Many companies take positions on environmental matters. For example, Patagonia (a manufacturer of high-quality outdoor clothing and equipment) gives 1% of its profits to environmental preservation groups in addition to supporting dozens of other environmental programs.

Community Activities: Sponsorship, Fundraising, Donations, and Other Support

Many companies contribute to charities, sponsor sports teams, buy ads in school newspapers, donate to museums, permit employees to volunteer at charities, and support similar community activities.

Cause-Related Marketing: Supporting Worthy Causes

Cause-related marketing, or simply **cause marketing**, is a commercial activity in which a business forms a partnership with a charity or nonprofit to support a worthy cause, product, or service.

A good example of cause marketing is Box Tops for Education. General Mills began the program in 1996 with special box tops on certain cereals, including Total and Cheerios. Parents clip the box tops and send them to their local schools, which then trade the box tops for cash. The program has been so successful that it now includes many other brands, including Pillsbury, Ziploc, Kleenex, and Green Giant. By participating in the Box Tops program, American schools have earned more than $800 million to date.

Social Entrepreneurship: Leveraging Business for Social Change

Social entrepreneurship is defined as an innovative, social value–creating activity that can occur within or across the for-profit and nonprofit sectors.

The focus is generally on creating value while doing good in the world.

Social entrepreneurship is also characterized by *innovation*, through finding an opportunity to create something new, rather than simply repeating existing business models or practices.

Sustainability: Green Is Good

Sustainability is economic development that meets the needs of the present without compromising the ability of future generations to meet their own needs. Companies large and small have launched green marketing campaigns promoting environmentally friendly causes, products, or stores.

Philanthropy: Not Dying Rich

"He who dies rich dies thus disgraced." So said 1880s steel manufacturer Andrew Carnegie, after he turned from making money to *philanthropy*, making charitable donations to benefit humankind. Carnegie became well known as a supporter of free public libraries, among other good works.

Among the most famous and generous philanthropists in the United States today are Bill Gates (founder of Microsoft), Warren Buffett, and Mark Zuckerberg (founder of Facebook) and his wife, Priscilla Chan, who have pledged to give away 99% of their net worth (estimated at more than $45 billion) in the course of their lifetimes.

Decisions

1. *The American Journal* is a media company that relies on a literate, educated public as the foundation of its success. Suppose *The American Journal* conducts a social audit and, as a result, decides to engage in more cause-related marketing. Which of the following causes is most related to *The American Journal*'s mission as an organization?

   A. Organic farming

   B. Animal rights

   C. Literacy training

   D. Consumer advocacy

2. *The American Journal* is based in Miami, Florida. As a result of its social audit, it decides to increase its philanthropic efforts. Which of the following would be most relevant to those who live in the Miami region?

   A. Charities that help the local victims of hurricanes and other natural disasters

   B. Environmental organizations attempting to preserve the Great Lakes

   C. United Nations food relief for starving children in Africa

   D. Job-retraining programs for West Virginia coal miners who have lost their jobs

Correct Answers: 1. C; 2. A

Lesson 2-4

The Payoffs from Doing Good: The Benefits to Stakeholders

By the end of this lesson, you will be able to:

- Contrast the ways in which illegal and/or unethical behaviors can harm a business with the ways that ethical and legal behavior can positively impact a business.

Doing Good: Good for Business at *The American Journal*

"How do my customers, employees, and community benefit from my company's ethical business practices and commitment to corporate social responsibility?"

Because *The American Journal*'s employees are scattered all over the country, Thomas schedules a WebEx meeting to roll out the code. An important part of the meeting is a Q&A (question and answer) session with *The American Journal*'s staff. Thomas completes his presentation and asks for questions.

The American Journal plans to have the code of ethics as a major link on our homepage, so it's there whenever we need it. I think that putting it on our homepage also makes a very positive statement to our readers.

This is great, Thomas. I like that the code of ethics isn't vague and general. It provides the specific guidance we need in tricky situations.

Two weeks from now, everyone will get a link to an online training module that walks you through the code, step by step. It provides several scenarios and asks some tough questions. It should take you about two hours to complete.

Copyright © McGraw Hill

Oh, come on, Tom. Ethics are common sense, and time is precious. Do I really have to spend two hours with a hokey simulation when I can be out in the field looking for good stories?

We respect your time, Rory, but ethics training is essential. I guarantee that it's time well spent.

Are you doing this because of some new law requiring you to train us on ethics?

Absolutely not. Having a written code of ethics, and making sure everyone understands it, are essential to our values as a publishing organization. So, look at the training module as a learning opportunity.

And remember that Thomas and I are always available if you need to discuss a situation that may compromise either your ethics or *The American Journal*'s.

When introducing *The American Journal*'s new code of ethics to their employees, Thomas and Viola make it clear that top management takes the code seriously— and that employees should do so, too. Support at the top is essential to making any new policy "stick."

Research has shown the many benefits of a serious commitment to ethics and social responsibility. What exactly are these benefits?

Management and quality expert W. Edwards Deming once said, "In God we trust; all others bring data." In this lesson, we will follow Deming's advice, using research data to examine the two sides of the ethical coin: the negative effects of "doing bad" and the positive effects of "doing good." Much of the research cited in this lesson will appear in the training module that *The American Journal*'s employees will complete.

The Negative Effects of Unethical Business Practices

When all is said and done, why should a company be ethical and socially responsible? A close look at the research reveals two conclusions:

1. Unethical or unlawful behavior has negative effects on the company, its stock price, and its public image.

2. Doing what is good and right brings many benefits to the company and its stakeholders.

What Are the Negative Effects of Illegal and Unethical Behavior?

Slippery ethics and dishonest business practices can lead to many negative consequences. As a media website, *The American Journal* needs to be very cautious about maintaining its reputation for ethical reporting. Reporting news that has not been fact-checked and verified opens the company up to potentially expensive judgments.

Potential Impacts of Unethical and Illegal Actions

Diminished Reputation and Profit

In a highly competitive marketplace, a company can build long-term relationships with customers only if it has a reputation for being honest. Accusations or evidence of dishonesty may cause customers to desert the business and transfer their loyalty to another business that they believe is more trustworthy.

Furthermore, companies accused of illegal and/or unethical behavior may find that they are boycotted by customers who seek to impose additional punishment on the company for its illegal or unethical practices.

Investors' perceptions of a company are also essential to a company's profitability. The announcement of unethical practices or illegalities—such as tax evasion, bribery, insider trading, or violations of government contracts—can hurt a company's stock price. Other research shows that investments in unethical firms earn abnormally negative returns for long periods of time.

Employee Fraud

Employee theft costs U.S. businesses $50 billion and disproportionately impacts small- and medium-size businesses. Most commonly, this comes in the form of embezzlement schemes, where employees typically commit small amounts of fraud over a period of time.

Costly Lawsuits

Lawsuits resulting from a company's illegal behavior can clearly hurt its profitability. For example, the executives and directors of former energy company Enron were sued for inflating earnings to drive up the stock price.

Fines and Jail Time

Unethical or illegal behavior can damage not only a company's reputation but its finances as well. Illegal behavior can result in whopping jail sentences and gigantic fines. For example, the U.S. government fined BP $61.5 billion for the 2010 Gulf of Mexico Deepwater Horizon oil spill.

Reaction

Suppose that *The American Journal* develops a reputation for publishing biased, sensationalized, or inaccurate information. What will be the likely result?

Decisions

When all is said and done, why should a company be ethical and socially responsible? A close look at the research reveals two conclusions:

1. Unethical or unlawful behavior has negative effects on the company, its stock price, and its public image.

2. Doing what is good and right brings many benefits to the company and its stakeholders.

The Positive Effects of Doing Good

There are positive—and proven—reasons for a firm to observe sound ethically and socially responsible practices.

Beneficiaries of Ethical Business Practices

Customers

Customers like to do business with companies that have a reputation for honesty and fair dealing. Ethical business practices help companies develop long-term relationships with their customers and develop an increasing customer base.

Suppliers

CSR-conscious companies can benefit society by insisting on the elimination of sweatshop working conditions among suppliers. A sweatshop is a shop, factory, or farm in which employees work long hours for low wages—or no wages, in the case of prison labor, slave labor, and some child labor—usually under environmentally, physically, or mentally abusive conditions. Although these firms do not benefit when ethical practices are followed, suppliers that adhere to such practices benefit from companies that recognize the importance of ethics in the form of new or increased business.

Owners

Owners benefit financially from a reputation for honesty, but they also benefit psychologically from setting high standards for ethical behavior and social responsibility. Additional owner benefits of a reputation for honesty include improved mental and physical health, as well as better branding. This benefits the company by being able to attract and retain talented employees. Studies have found that being ethical also makes financial sense. For example, research has found that companies listed on Ethisphere's World's Most Ethical Companies list did better than large cap sector companies by more than 10% over three years.

Employees

Employees benefit from an ethical workplace. A positive reputation helps a company attract and keep good employees while also increasing productivity. In addition, by fostering a company culture in which employees are encouraged to consistently do the right thing, a happier workplace is created for everyone.

Local and National Communities

When a socially responsible company gives its employees time off for volunteer activities, supports social causes, or donates money, goods, and services, it clearly benefits the local and/or national community. For example, in 2017, Home Depot contributed $3 million to communities in the wake of Hurricane Maria.

The International Community

One important consequence of a worldwide focus on good global corporate citizenship is the **Global Compact,** a voluntary agreement established by the United Nations that promotes human rights, good labor practices, environmental protection, and anti-corruption standards for businesses. For example, the American Red Cross provides disaster relief across the world to countries in need.

Decisions

1. As part of its written commitment to CSR, *The American Journal* has promised to match its employees' contributions to charitable organizations within the United States. Which stakeholders does this policy benefit?

   A. Owners

   B. International community

   C. Local and national community

   D. Suppliers

2. How might *The American Journal* play a role in combating global climate change? Here are a few ideas, can you think of more?

   A. It can publish well-researched, information-filled articles that inform readers about the problem.

   B. It can write and publish editorials about the need to reduce carbon dioxide emissions.

   C. It can develop telecommuting policies that allow workers to not drive as much and work from home.

   Correct Answers: 1. C

Ethical and Social Responsibility in Business: Test

1. Ethics are _____ that influence behavior.

   A. company standards

   B. rules and laws

   C. subconscious emotions

   D. principles of right and wrong

2. Ethan Wong, a student who works at his college bookstore, is often unsupervised and, therefore, has the opportunity to steal merchandise. He needs an expensive anatomy textbook but doesn't even consider taking it without paying for it. This is an example of an individual's behavior being influenced by _____, or ethics.

   A. principles of right and wrong

   B. an understanding of consequences

   C. respect for the law

   D. a fear of negative feedback

3. A U.S. manufacturer makes low-quality furniture that breaks easily. This is an example of something that is _____ but _____.

   A. ethical; illegal

   B. legal; ethical

   C. legal; unethical

   D. illegal; ethical

4. To encourage high ethical standards and support a strong ethical climate, a company's leadership should

   A. establish a code of ethics.

   B. host an employee retreat.

   C. hire only experienced workers.

   D. conduct regular lie detector tests.

5. Jessica Villareal is a manager at Visibility Media. During an interview with Chloe Schwartz, a candidate for the new marketing position, Villareal catches Schwartz in a lie about a fact unrelated to the job. Villareal needs to fill the position quickly, but she also knows that Visibility Media should continually strive to uphold high ethical standards. What is Villareal's best course of action?

   A. She should ask Schwartz to come in for a second interview.

   B. She should inform Schwartz of the company ethics code.

   C. She should not hire Schwartz.

   D. She should check Schwartz's references.

6. One way to make sure that employees understand a company's expectations and guidance for how to act ethically and responsibly is to establish a

   A. code of ethics.

   B. nondisclosure agreement.

   C. corporate responsibility pyramid.

   D. set of laws and regulations.

7. A(n) _____ ethics code attempts to prevent criminal misconduct by increasing control and by punishing violators.

   A. values-based

   B. compliance-based

   C. integrity-based

   D. interaction-based

8. A compliance-based ethics code attempts to prevent _____ by increasing control and by punishing violators.

   A. ethical dilemmas

   B. criminal misconduct

   C. fraud

   D. diversity

9. "Any employees caught stealing from the supply cabinet will be fined and reported to their supervisor for disciplinary action." This statement is an example of a(n) _____ ethics code.

    A. complex

    B. internally-enforced

    C. overly severe

    D. compliance-based

10. Justin Kihana is a hiring manager for Connect, a new social media platform. Connect's customer information is highly confidential, and the company does not share this information with competitors or the general public. Kihana routinely asks new employees to sign nondisclosure agreements. Kihana's action demonstrates that Connect

    A. has a culture of cutting corners.

    B. uses methods that intimidate employees.

    C. has a compliance-based ethics code.

    D. does not foster an ethical environment.

11. Julie Yuen has clearly defined goals for ensuring that her new meal delivery service, Magic Chef, is socially responsible. One goal is to donate a percentage of her profits to local charities. How can Yuen ensure that Magic Chef is implementing its socially responsible goals?

    A. conduct a social audit to assess performance

    B. ask employees to keep her goals in mind

    C. post a list of goals in the employee break room

    D. include a note with each delivery stating her goals

12. Shaun Johnson is a top manager at a construction firm that has been tasked with laying a pipeline through a large section of the state. In some ways the project will help the local community. But in other ways, such as harming the environment, it will hurt the local community. Johnson is concerned about the project's _____, or whether a company's economic development meets present needs without endangering the ability of future generations to meet their own needs.

    A. utility

    B. practicality

    C. sustainability

    D. stability

13. A big company that helps small nonprofit firms working to make a difference in antipoverty, literacy, and the environment by providing them with small loans is an example of

    A. community activity.

    B. cause-related marketing.

    C. financial auditing.

    D. social entrepreneurship.

14. A nonprofit organization that helps the local victims of a hurricane is involved in

    A. a philanthropic effort.

    B. compliance-based ethics.

    C. a social audit.

    D. social marketing.

15. In the long run, a company's unethical or unlawful behavior will have the effect of

    A. lowering its stock price.

    B. attracting quality employees.

    C. generating goodwill.

    D. benefiting the local community.

16. _____ can hurt a company's profitability.

    A. Giving employees time off to volunteer in the community

    B. Lawsuits resulting from illegal behavior

    C. Donating money, goods, and services

    D. Reducing calories and fat to make a food product healthier

17. Not only customers and the community but also owners, employees, and suppliers benefit from

    A. aggressive social media marketing.

    B. price slashing and deep discounts.

    C. ethical behavior and social responsibility.

    D. turning a blind eye to ethics violations.

18. _____ are rules of conduct or action that are formally recognized as binding and are enforced by a controlling authority.

    A. Values

    B. Compliance codes

    C. Laws

    D. Cultural norms

    E. Ethics

19. Julian takes used office supplies from his employer and donates them to underprivileged schools and youth groups in his community. This action can be best described as

    A. legal and ethical.

    B. illegal, but ethical.

    C. legal, but unethical.

    D. illegal, but practical.

    E. legal and socially responsible.

20. MachineWerks Manufacturing wants to encourage responsible conduct for its employees. What would most likely help MachineWerks to meet this goal?

    A. training on the compliance-based ethics code

    B. sharing the principal provisions of Sarbanes–Oxley

    C. building a social responsibility pyramid

    D. creating an integrity-based ethics code

    E. conducting a social audit

3 Essentials of Leadership and Management

What To Expect

By the end of the chapter, you will be able to:

- Differentiate between efficiency and effectiveness.
- Identify examples of the four functions of management.
- Identify examples of managers for each of the three levels of management.
- Implement the four-step decision making process to resolve an issue in a business case.

Chapter Topics

- **3-1** The Essence of Management
- **3-2** Basics of Strategic Management
- **3-3** Management Skills and Building a Company Structure
- **3-4** Foundational Approaches to Leadership
- **3-5** Necessities of Quality Control

Copyright © McGraw Hill   fizkes/Shutterstock

Lesson 3-1
The Essence of Management

Trouble Brewing?

Leading to Grow

Carey and Diane are vice presidents at BrewU—a coffee house that strategically opens stores near college campuses across the United States. BrewU has experienced solid growth over the last few years but business is starting to level off and the CEO is wary of opening too many stores too quickly as a way to show growth. The CEO has called the upper management team together to analyze how the company's management approach is impacting the business

Carey and Diane sit down in the regional corporate office to prepare for the meeting with the CEO.

I am glad our CEO is giving us the opportunity to analyze our approach. Where do you think is a good place for us to start?

I think this is one of those situations where we should get back to the basics and start with analyzing the four cornerstones of management.

That's a great place to start. Then from there we can take a look at our efficiency and effectiveness and see how they impact the company's ability to grow.

Totally! I think from there we look at our tiers of management and see how well they are aligned.

Copyright © McGraw Hill

Yes! That's a fantastic approach, then we can wrap up by looking at our decision-making process and how that may be helping or hindering our teams within the organization.

Awesome, let's grab some coffee and get to work!

Carey and Diane have set up a solid strategy to see if profits can improve by studying their management structure and style.

In this lesson, we'll learn all about management. Managers are needed to make an organization more effective and more efficient. Management has four functions: *planning*, *organizing*, *leading*, and *controlling*. It has three levels: *top*, *middle*, and *supervisory*. Managers make decisions by identifying problems, thinking up alternative solutions, evaluating alternatives, selecting a solution, and implementing and evaluating the solution chosen.

The Need for Management: To Achieve Effectiveness and Efficiency

An organization might stumble along for a while without managers, but eventually it will find it needs them if it is to deliver a quality product on time—that is, to achieve its goals *effectively* and *efficiently*.

- Effectiveness is realizing goals: Effectiveness is about the ends. To be **effective** means to achieve results, to realize the firm's goals by making the right decisions and executing them successfully.

- Efficiency is the means of realizing goals. To be **efficient** means to use people, money, raw materials, and other resources wisely and cost-effectively.

Decisions

Carey and Diane are analyzing some quarterly reports. Help fill in the conversation.

Carey, did you see that last quarter are growth was 110% over goal?

Yes, but our profits were only 90% to goal.

Yes, so in some areas we are achieving results and being _____, yet in others, we are missing the mark.

A. effective

B. efficient

Yes, as I am digging into the results I am seeing some challenges we are having on the people and materials side that are impacting our cost. Let's make note that we need to find ways to be more _____ with our resources.

A. efficient

B. effective

Correct Answers: A; A

The Four Things Managers Must Do

Management is the pursuit of organizational goals effectively and efficiently through (1) planning, (2) organization, (3) leading, and (4) controlling the organization's resources.

What Are the Company's Goals and How Are They to Be Achieved?

Planning is defined as setting goals and deciding how to achieve them. In a for-profit organization, one of these goals is to satisfy customers. Thus, top executives must plan the right strategy to achieve this goal.

How Should Tasks, People, and Other Resources Be Arranged?

Organizing is defined as arranging tasks, people, and other resources to accomplish the work. Thus, the company must design a structure and establish conditions for achieving the goal of satisfying customers.

How to Motivate People to Achieve Important Goals?

Leading is defined as motivating, directing, and otherwise influencing people to work hard to achieve the organization's goals. Leading means establishing a vision and a mission for the company and then communicating and guiding others to realize the organizational goals.

How to Monitor Performance and Compare It to Goals?

Controlling is defined as monitoring performance, comparing it with goals, and taking corrective action as needed. That is, controlling means determining what actually occurs while trying to meet the organization's goals. In the controlling function, managers assess and modify business operations to ensure goals are met.

Decision

Carey and Diane are discussing the needs of the organization based on the four functions of management.

I think we need to work toward doing a better job _____. We need to communicate a more clear vision and mission for the company.

- **A.** leading
- **B.** planning
- **C.** controlling
- **D.** organizing

So, now we need to work as a team to determine how we're going to get where we want to be. We obviously need to spend some time on the _____ function.

- **A.** planning
- **B.** controlling
- **C.** leading
- **D.** organizing

That's a good approach. I think we need to look at the tactics we are using through the _____ process so we know what is working and what we need to correct.

- **A.** planning
- **B.** organizing
- **C.** leading
- **D.** controlling

Yes and by doing that we can best apply the _____ function and arrange tasks, people, and other resources to accomplish the work.

- **A.** planning
- **B.** controlling
- **C.** leading
- **D.** organizing

Correct Answers: A; A; D; D

The Three Levels of Management

In the traditional view of management, managers are arranged in a pyramid-like organization, with one layer sitting at the top and two or more layers of managers beneath. In this model, managers fall into three levels: *top*, *middle*, and *supervisory*. The pyramid is the classic model of management organization, but it is only one of many management models.

Top Managers: Making Decisions for the Long Term

Top managers, the highest level of management, make long-term decisions about the overall direction of the organization and establish the objectives, strategies, and policies for it. These are key executives with titles such as chief executive officer (CEO), chief operating officer (COO), president, and senior vice president.

Middle Managers: Implementing Decisions

Middle managers implement the policies and plans of the top managers above them and supervise and coordinate the activities of the supervisory managers below them. Middle managers have titles such as general manager, division manager, plant manager, and branch sales manager.

Supervisory Managers: Directing Nonmanagerial Employees

Supervisory managers make short-term operating decisions, directing the daily tasks of nonmanagerial personnel. The job titles in this group are on the order of *department head*, *foreman* or *forewoman*, *team leader*, or *supervisor*.

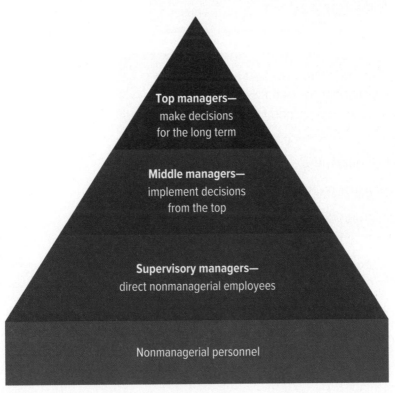

Decisions

Diane and Carey are reading a report that analyzed insights from an employee engagement survey that HR performed a few months ago.

_____ is a solid group of leaders who have created a really great company. I just wish they would get out of HQ and spend more time in the stores.

    A. Top management

    B. A team of supervisors

    C. Middle management

I feel bad for our GM. She constantly is going back and forth between the store and corporate. We really need to get better communication from the top to the bottom of the organization. I am worried we'll lose the best GM I've ever had!

    1. Which level of management is Carey describing?

        A. A supervisor

        B. Top management

        C. Middle management

I feel really fortunate I had worked here only as a barista for four months before I was promoted. It was pretty overwhelming, and I wish we had better training for first time _____.

    A. middle managers

    B. supervisory managers

    C. top managers

Correct Answers: A; 1. C; B

Practical Decision Making

Regardless of level, all managers make decisions. A **decision** is a choice made from among available alternatives. **Decision making** is the process of identifying and choosing alternative courses of action. Typically there are four phases involved in making a practical decision.

Identify the Problem

Managers find no shortage of **problems**, or difficulties, which are issues that impede the achievement of goals: technology glitches, staff turnover, customer complaints, and so on.

Creative managers often find **opportunities**, favorable circumstances that present possibilities for progress beyond existing goals. You need to look past the parade of daily problems and try to actually do better than the goals your boss expects you to achieve. When a competitor's top software engineer unexpectedly quits, that creates an opportunity for your company to hire that person away.

Think of Possible Solutions

Bright ideas are a firm's greatest competitive resource. After you've identified the problem or opportunity and determined its causes, you need to come up with possible solutions. The more creative and innovative the alternatives, the better.

Copyright © McGraw Hill   Roman Samborskyi/Shutterstock

One way to achieve this is through **brainstorming**, wherein individuals or members of a group generate multiple ideas and alternatives to solve problems.

Weigh Alternative Solutions and Select One

In this stage, you need to evaluate each alternative not only according to cost and quality but also according to whether it is effective, feasible, and ethical.

- **Is it effective?** A proposed solution needs to be evaluated to be sure it is effective—that is, not just "good enough" but the best under the circumstances.

- **Is it feasible?** A proposed solution may not be feasible for a variety of reasons: The top decision makers or customers won't accept it. Time is short. Costs are high. Technology isn't available. Company policies don't allow it. The action can't be reversed if there's trouble.

- **Is it ethical?** At times, a proposed alternative will seem to be right on nearly all counts. However, if it isn't ethical, you shouldn't give it a second look.

Implement and Evaluate the Solution Chosen

With some decisions, implementation can be quite difficult. When one company acquires another, for instance, it may take months to consolidate the departments, accounting systems, inventories, and so on.

- **Successful implementation:** For implementation to be successful, you need to do careful planning (especially if reversing an action will be difficult) and you need to consider how the people affected will feel about the change (inconvenienced, insecure, or even fearful, all of which can trigger resistance). This is why it helps to give employees and customers some leeway during a changeover in business practices.

- **Evaluation:** You need to follow up and evaluate the results of the decision. If the action is not working, you need to consider whether to give the new action more time, change it slightly, try another alternative, or start over.

Decisions

Carey and Diane have been preparing for the meeting with the CEO.

1. Which phase of the decision-making process are Diane and Carey currently in?

   A. Implement and evaluate

   B. Identify problems or opportunities

2. Through the course of having extensive conversations, Carey and Diane have began which part of the decision-making process?

   A. Implement and evaluate

   B. Thinking of possible solutions

Correct Answers: 1. B; 2. B

Lesson 3-2
Basics of Strategic Management

By the end of this lesson, you will be able to:

- Differentiate among the three levels of planning in management in terms of time period, managerial level, and key activities.
- Classify examples of statements as vision or mission.
- Summarize the purpose of a SMART goal.
- Perform a SWOT analysis.

Planning for Good Results

Using Planning Strategies to Improve Performance

BrewU's CEO, Raj Kapoor, has just held a company-wide video conference with all the regional managers. Although he felt the actions taken to strengthen BrewU's management approach were successful, the company needs to continue its efforts to maximize growth and increase profits. With that in mind, Kapoor asks the managers to develop goals for growing the business and to come up with a strategy that involves creating new coffee drinks, other beverages, products, and services that appeal to college students while also having attractive profit margins.

Once again, Carey and Diane huddle in the regional corporate office to brainstorm how to meet the CEO's newest challenge.

New beverages with strong profit margins, wow! Good idea but where do we start?

Well, let's think this through. We need to set goals and then achieve them, right?

Yes, absolutely.

Then let's write the goals down for starters.

Copyright © McGraw Hill

Excellent. Then we can apply a SWOT analysis to understand how we might succeed and avoid problems.

Right. And finally we can establish a contingency plan just in case.

Agreed. Funny, I've got a craving for a butterscotch chocolate latte as we speak.

Carey and Diane have put into motion an approach to meet their CEO's challenge. In this lesson we'll learn all about the types of plans managers use.

Managers shape their plans on the basis of vision statements (what the company wants to become) and mission statements (what the company's fundamental purposes are). Top managers develop strategic plans, middle managers develop tactical plans, and supervisory managers develop operational plans.

All these plans specify goals (broad, long-range targets) and objectives (specific, short-term targets). Performing a SWOT analysis—identifying a company's strengths, weaknesses, opportunities, and threats—can help establish strategic planning. Managers should also do contingency planning.

Benefits of Planning

All companies must find ways to respond to rapidly changing markets, and sticking with one business strategy may be a sure path to failure. As a manager, how should you meet this challenge? You could copy competitors or find unexplored niches to exploit. You could produce standardized offerings at low cost (as in fast-food restaurants). You could connect clients to other people (as with eBay). You could apply customized expertise to clients' problems (as law firms do).

Whatever approach you take, all involve planning. We describe:

- Four benefits of planning
- Vision and mission statements
- Strategic, tactical, and operational planning

- Goals and objectives
- Assessing your competitive position with SWOT analysis
- Contingency planning

Why Plan?

As we stated earlier, *planning* is defined as setting goals and deciding how to achieve them. When you make a plan, you make a blueprint for action that describes what you need to do to realize your goals.

You can always hope you'll muddle through the next time a natural disaster strikes, or you could try to plan for it (stock up on flashlight batteries and nonperishable food, for instance). Managers face similar choices. Should you wing it through every crisis or have a plan in place?

Coping with Uncertainty

Don't like unpleasant surprises? Most of us don't. That's why planning for various (including unpleasant) possible events is necessary.

Thinking Ahead

The product you are offering at some point may well achieve maturity, and sales will begin to drop. Thus, you need to plan beyond your present work circumstances, so that you can quickly move to the next stage.

Coordinating Activities

A plan defines the responsibilities of various departments and coordinates their activities for the achievement of common goals—so that the right hand knows what the left hand is doing.

Checking on Your Progress

How well is your work going in an organization? You won't know unless you have some way of checking your progress. You need to have some expectations of what you're supposed to do—in other words, a plan.

The Basis for Planning: Vision and Mission Statements

An organization has a purpose, too—a mission. To accomplish this mission in future years, the organization

Vision statement: "What do we want to become?"

↓

Mission statement: "What are our fundamental purposes?"

↓

Strategic planning: Done by top managers for the next 1–5 years

Goals, objectives

↓

Tactical planning: Done by middle managers for the next 6–24 months

Goals, objectives

↓

Operational planning: Done by supervisory managers for the next 1–52 weeks

Goals, objectives

needs to have a vision. From these, the organization's goals and objectives are derived at each level of planning.

The Mission Statement: "These Are Our Fundamental Purposes"

A **mission statement** is a statement of the organization's fundamental purposes. The mission statement identifies the goods or services the organization provides and will provide and the reasons for providing them. A mission statement answers the basic question of why an organization was created in the first place and why it still exists today.

The Vision: "This Is What We Want to Become"

A *vision statement* describes the company's **vision**, the long-term goal of what the organization wants to become. It outlines the world view of the organization and attracts people—employees, customers, and vendors—who share that vision.

Examples of Mission and Vision Statements

	Vision statements	Mission statements
Amazon	"Our vision is to be earth's most customer centric company."	"To build a place where people can come to find and discover anything they might want to buy online."
Clothing maker Patagonia	"We prefer the human scale to the corporate, vagabonding to tourism, and the quirky and lively to the toned-down and flattened out."	"Build the best product, cause no unnecessary harm, use business to inspire and implement solutions to the environmental crisis."
Marriott Hotels	"Our vision is to be the world's leading provider of hospitality services."	"Our commitment is that every guest leaves satisfied."
Handicrafters website Etsy	"Our vision is to build a new economy and present a better choice."	"To enable people to make a living making things, and to reconnect makers with buyers."

Decisions

Carey and Diane look around the room and see the following statements.

1. "We see BrewU as the coffeehouse for college students to study, work, and connect."

   This is an example of the company's _____.

   A. mission statement

   B. goal statement

   C. vision statement

2. "BrewU is committed to creating a fun, safe, affordable space that provides innovative beverages and food options for college students to work, study, and play."

   This is BrewU's _____.

   A. goal statement

   B. vision statement

   C. mission statement

Centered on this, Carey and Diane start planning!

Correct Answers: 1. C; 2. C

Types of Planning for Levels of Management

Clear, inspirational vision statements and mission statements mark the start of the planning process. Once these are developed, it is top management's job to do *strategic planning*. The strategic priorities and policies are then passed down the organizational pyramid to middle management, which needs to do *tactical planning*. Middle managers then pass these plans along to supervisory management to do *operational planning*. Each type of planning has different time horizons, although the times overlap because the plans are somewhat elastic.

Strategic Planning

Strategic planning occurs when an organization determines its long-term goals for the next one to five years with the resources they anticipate having. It should communicate not only general goals about growth and profits but also ways to achieve them.

Time Period: 1–5 years

Involvement: Top management

Key Activities:

- Top managers make long-term decisions about the overall direction of the organization.
- The CEO, the vice presidents, and the division heads need to pay attention to the competitive environment outside the organization, being alert for long-run opportunities and problems.
- These executives must be future oriented, dealing with uncertain, highly competitive conditions.

Tactical Planning

Middle managers engage in **tactical planning**, which is defined as determining what contributions their work units can make with their existing resources during the next six months to two years. Often the top and supervisory managers will have a hand in developing the tactical plans.

Time Period: 6–24 months

Involvement: Middle management

Key Activities:

- Middle managers implement the policies and plans of the top managers above them and supervise and coordinate the activities of the supervisory managers below them.
- In for-profit organizations, middle managers are the functional managers and department managers.
- Their decisions often must be made without a base of clearly defined informational procedures, perhaps requiring detailed analysis and computations.

Operational Planning

Following the plans of middle and top managers, supervisory managers are responsible for **operational planning**, which involves determining how to accomplish specific tasks with existing resources within the next one-week to one-year period.

Time Period: 1–52 weeks

Involvement: Supervisory managers

Key Activities:

- The supervisory managers are the managers at the bottom of the pyramid who direct the daily tasks of nonmanagerial personnel.
- Some of their decisions may be predictable ones that follow well-defined procedures, but others require using independent judgment.

Contingency Plans

Contingency planning is the creation of alternative hypothetical courses of action that a company can use if its original plans don't prove workable. The scenarios present alternative combinations of different factors—economic, competitive, budgetary, and so on—to anticipate changes in the environment. Because the scenarios look anywhere from two to five years into the future, they are usually written in rather general terms. Contingency planning not only equips a firm to prepare for emergencies and uncertainty, it also gets managers thinking strategically.

Decisions

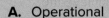

Carey and Diane have been hard at work building out a potential plan for their CEO. Read each piece of the conversation and determine which phase of planning Carey and Diane are discussing.

> I think we should focus on the next year and determine what the leadership team needs to focus on.

> Yes, if we can do this we can have a cascading effect. We really need to be clear about the ways we are going to achieve growth and profit through these steps.
>
> **A.** Operational
>
> **B.** Strategic
>
> **C.** Tactical

Okay, our strategy is to innovate new products that are at a similar price point and renegotiate with our suppliers to see if we can get better pricing based on better margins. We also want to get better training in our stores.

Yes, we need to engage with our regional managers on this and figure out what we can accomplish every month for the next six months to make this happen.

A. Operational

B. Tactical

C. Strategic

We know checklists and easy to follow processes really help our people execute. We know we want to make these systems around product, store aesthetic, and service. We want our folks to be focused on this daily.

Yes, if we get them doing these key activities on a daily basis, we'll create new habits and routines in the store.

A. Operational

B. Tactical

C. Strategic

Correct Answers: B; B; A

Executing Your Strategy

Whatever its type—strategic, tactical, or operational—the purpose of planning is to achieve a goal. A **goal** is a broad, long-range target that an organization wishes to attain. An **objective** is a specific, short-term target designed to achieve the organization's goals.

A goal should be aligned with the S.M.A.R.T. acronym, meaning it should be: specific, measurable, attainable, relevant, and time-bound. As an example, a company may have a goal of increasing revenue by 20% by the end of the calendar year.

Assessing Your Competitive Position for Strategic Planning: SWOT Analysis

Strategic planning often starts with a **SWOT analysis**, which is a description of the company's:

- Strengths (S): What the company excels at and how this differentiates it from the competition

- Weaknesses (W): Where the company needs to improve to remain competitive

- Opportunities (O): Favorable external factors, such as new markets, that the company can use to ensure competitive advantage

- Threats (T): Factors that can potentially harm the company

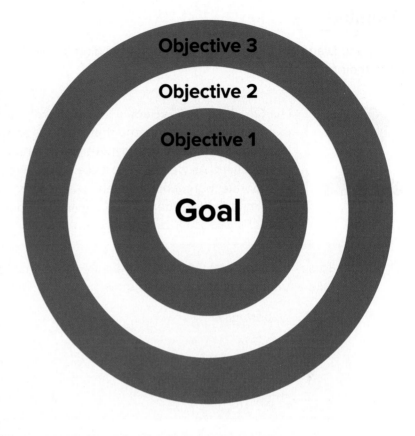

A SWOT analysis should provide senior management with a realistic picture of their organization in relation to its internal and external environments so they can better establish strategy in pursuit of its mission.

The SWOT analysis has two parts: inside matters and outside matters—that is, a picture of *internal strengths and weaknesses* and a picture of *external opportunities and threats*.

Internal Strengths—S	**Internal Weaknesses—W**
Examples: Technology leader, seasoned management, cost advantages, energy-reduction technology, etc.	Examples: Outdated facilities, weak implementation strategy, missing key skills, etc.

External Opportunities—O	**External Threats—T**
Examples: Diversify into related services, compete in new markets, capitalize on complacency of competitors, etc.	Examples: Growing consumer power, government regulatory pressure, changing buyer tastes, spike in fuel costs, etc.

Decision

Carey and Diane are back in the "War Room" building a SWOT analysis for BrewU. Fill in their responses.

I had marketing pull us some information. It turns out that there is a growing trend that students see value in being able to have group meetings in a more social environment. As we build out more stores, we should incorporate more farm-style tables, strengthen our free Wi-Fi, and further extend our early and late hours.

This is definitely a(n) _____ in the market we should take advantage of as we plan to grow.

A. opportunity

B. strength

C. weakness

D. threat

One of our key _____ is our location. Our proximity to colleges give us an ample workforce of students, who encourage their friends to stop in.

A. strengths

B. opportunities

C. weaknesses

D. threats

Further, our ability to build strong community relations with the colleges is helping us drive in-store traffic. We are seeing that our staff is struggling, and the data shows we need to get better at training, developing, and retaining. This is clearly a(n) _____ we need to work on.

A. opportunity

B. strength

C. weakness

D. threat

Just like you and I, we want these students to stay and grow with us. Hopefully someday, they'll be our next generation of company leaders. One of my biggest fears is the stuff that is out of our control.

I know what you are saying. The recent natural disasters have caused issues with our suppliers and for everyone in the industry we need to be concerned about price increases. This is especially tough for us because we either need to reduce margins or increase prices, and our primary customers are so price sensitive.

Definitely put that into the _____ column of our SWOT.

   A. threat

   B. strengths

   C. opportunity

   D. weakness

Correct Answers: A; A; C; A

Lesson 3-3

Management Skills and Building a Company Structure

By the end of this lesson, you will be able to:

- Determine which organizational structure to use for an organization.
- Explain how the three principal skills of management align with the different levels of management.

Why Organizing Matters

Organizing Gets Things Done

In BrewU's ongoing efforts at improving growth and maximizing profits, the CEO has made another announcement at their monthly company-wide meeting. He tasks all upper management to devise a plan that will develop management talent throughout the company but especially in the retail stories where the customers and BrewU workers interact.

Remember when we were BrewU newbies? Being a store manager is a demanding job and I'm glad we are now charged with strengthening our management development plan.

It was fun but such hard work to be a store manager. And yes, my experience was like yours and I felt it was a sort of haphazard process for getting promoted. Not very motivating to the other workers.

Ok, let's get to work then. We'll review our current organizational charts and see where that takes us next.

Excellent. Let's grab some espresso and review our charts.

Copyright © McGraw Hill

Sitting in the regional conference room, Carey and Diane think back to their movement up the corporate ladder and consider how much luck played a part.

Carey and Diane have created a concrete way to begin their review of BrewU's talent pool.

In this lesson, we'll review the organizing function of management. Organizational charts represent traditional hierarchical management arrangements and show both authority (vertically) and specialization (horizontally). To be successful, managers need to develop their skills in three areas: technical, conceptual, and human. A key concern of today's organizations is staffing, which in turn must take into consideration the concept of human capital.

The Organizational Chart and the Skills Managers Need

Though traditional, a pyramid-style hierarchy of top, middle, and supervisory managers need not be unworkable. Many companies are based on this arrangement. Hierarchical organizations are frequently represented in an **organizational chart**, a box-and-lines illustration of the formal lines of authority and the official positions or work specializations.

The organization chart provides two kinds of information about the company's structure:

1. The vertical hierarchy of authority

2. The horizontal specialization

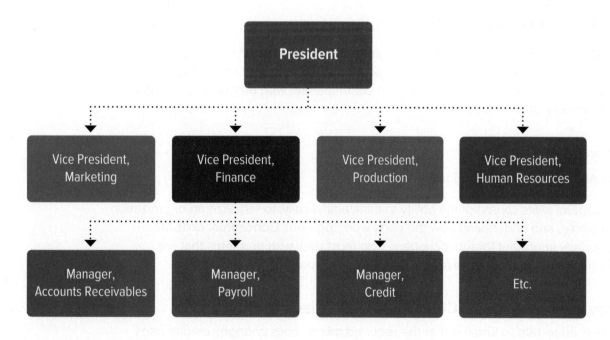

Vertical Hierarchy of Authority: Who Reports to Whom

A top-to-bottom scan of an organization chart shows the vertical hierarchy, the chain of command, who officially communicates with whom. In a simple two-person organization, the owner might communicate with just an assistant. In a complex organization, the president might talk principally to the vice presidents, who talk to the assistant vice presidents, and so on.

Horizontal Specialization: Who Specializes in What Work

A side-to-side scan of the organization chart shows horizontal specialization, the different jobs or work specialization. The husband-and-wife partners in a two-person advertising firm might agree that one is the "inside person," handling production and research , and the other is the "outside person," handling sales, client relations, and finances. A large firm might have vice presidents for each task—production, marketing, finance, and so on.

The Skills That Star Managers Need

In the mid-1970s, one researcher found that through education and experience, managers acquire three principal skills: **technical**, **human**, and **conceptual**.

Technical

The Ability to Perform a Specific Job

Technical skills consist of the job-specific knowledge needed to perform well in a specialized field. Having the requisite technical skills seems to be the most important for supervisory managers.

Human

The Ability to Interact Well with People

Perhaps the hardest set of skills to master, *human skills* consist of the ability to work well in cooperation with other people to get things done. These skills—the ability to motivate, to inspire trust, and to communicate with others—are necessary for managers at all levels.

Conceptual

The Ability to Think Analytically

Conceptual skills consist of the ability to think analytically, to visualize an organization as a whole, and understand how the parts work together. Conceptual skills are particularly important for top managers, who must deal with problems that are ambiguous but that could have far-reaching consequences.

How the Mix of Skills Changes as One Rises to the Top

What is important to know is that *the required mix of skills changes as one rises through the organization, from supervisory manager to middle manager to top manager*—generally from *less technical* to *more conceptual*. Thus . . .

- A supervisor needs more technical skills, a fair amount of human skills, and fewer conceptual skills.
- A middle manager needs roughly an even distribution of each skill.
- A top manager needs more conceptual skills, a fair amount of human skills, and fewer technical skills.

Decisions

Carey and Diane are looking at their talent development plan and are outlining the focus for the next year. They are organizing development into the three areas: technical, human, conceptual

After going through the stores, it is clear that we need to help our baristas. They need better product knowledge and more opportunities to practice creating drinks.

Agreed. This should go in the _____ area.

A. human

B. technical

C. conceptual

I think we can do some really innovative work that will make a major impact in team dynamics and customer experience.

What are you thinking?

I think we should make it a real focus to build a course that helps employees develop emotional intelligence, communication skills, and do more team building.

This sounds good and I can totally see the return on investment. Let's put this in our _____ area.

   A. technical

   B. conceptual

   C. human

What do you think if we started to bring more employees to HQ, make it a real event, there they can get the big picture and connect how they really make it happen for the company. We can then have them engaged in generating new ideas and concepts for our current and future stores?

Wow, that's an awesome idea. I think that belongs in our _____ column.

   A. technical

   B. human

   C. conceptual

Correct Answers: B; C: C

Foundational Approaches to Leadership

By the end of this lesson, you will be able to:

- Differentiate between leaders and managers.
- Propose an appropriate leadership style in a business case.

The Inspiration of Leaders

"Who Are the Best Leaders?"

On the heels of the development of managers process, Diane and Carey decide to explore how effective those in leadership roles are at BrewU.

Leadership is so important in a place like BrewU where our business is dependent not only on quality beverages and food, but on the customer experience. We have distinguished ourselves not only by our signature brew, but also as to how enjoyable the experience is.

I was thinking what if we studied our three top-performing stores and our three bottom-performing stores and just focused on the leadership styles at those stores.

Great idea. We can compare styles with results and see if there is any correlation. Plus, if we learn something tangible, we can mentor employees across our region in following a leadership style.

I'm excited that this may lead us to some important lessons that could really help BrewU grow to full potential

Carey and Diane are using sound business practices in order to determine the best way to foster leadership at BrewU.

In this lesson, we'll explore the leadership function of management. Leaders cope with change, whereas managers cope with complexity. Through exploring leaders, it will become evident that there are three styles of leadership, autocratic, participative, and free-rein, which range from boss centered to employee centered, respectively.

Aside from the three leadership styles, there are two different behaviors that may be present in leaders. Transactional leaders are concerned with getting people to do ordinary things, while transformational leaders are concerned with getting them to do exceptional things.

How Do Managers and Leaders Differ?

When you as a manager *direct* or *order* someone to do something, is that the same as **leading**?

Certainly that has been a time-honored way by which managers got employees to do things. And it's still the preferred way of managing low-skill workers, such as those in farming, fast-food restaurants, and dry cleaning.

Leaders and Managers:
Dealing with Change versus Dealing with Complexity

Although it may seem like the words *leader* and *manager* are used interchangeably, management scholar John Kotter suggests they are different: *Leaders* cope with *change*, he says, whereas *managers* cope with *complexity*.*

How Leaders Cope with Change

Business has become so volatile and competitive that it's no longer enough for a company to survive by making minor improvements. What's required are leaders who can deal with great changes by creating a vision and strategic plan and inspiring others to rally around common goals.

Leaders cope with change in three ways:

> by determining what needs to be done and setting a direction through planning and budgeting;

> by communicating the new direction so that people can align behind it; and

> by motivating and inspiring people by appealing to human needs, values, and emotions to keep them moving ahead in spite of obstacles.

How Managers Cope with Complexity

Today's organizations, especially multinationals, can be incredibly complex. Good management is essential to keep them from slipping into chaos.

Managers cope with complexity in three ways:

> by planning and budgeting, setting targets, and specifying the resources and means for achieving them;

> by organizing and staffing, creating the necessary structure, and hiring the people to fulfill the jobs; and

> by controlling and problem solving, monitoring results, and solving problems as they arise.

You Don't Need to Be a Manager to Be a Leader

In today's business most efforts are *team* efforts: everyone has to work together to achieve common goals.

*J. P. Kotter, "What Leaders Really Do," Harvard Business Review, December 2001, pp. 85–96.

Autocratic Leadership

"Do This Because I Said So!"

Autocratic leaders make decisions without consulting others.

When to use it:

- This "my way or the highway" style tends to work in hierarchical organizations with a militaristic orientation, such as the U.S. Army or some branches of law enforcement.
- This is also effective when employees need direction or are developing skill (e.g., new to the job).

Participative (Democratic) Leadership

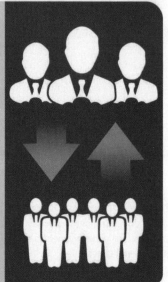

"Let Me Get Your Thoughts on What to Do"

Participative leaders, also called democratic leaders, delegate authority and involve employees in their decisions.

When to use it:

- Most situations, but especially when creating buy-in, a leader needs to leverage expertise from multiple areas or functions of the business.
- This style involves a great deal of communication—requiring the leader to have strong listening skills and empathy—between the leader and the led.
- Although it may not increase effectiveness, it usually enhances job satisfaction.

Free-Rein Leadership Style

"Here's the Goal, Do What You Want to Achieve It"

Free-rein leaders, also known as **laissez-faire leaders,** set objectives, and employees are relatively free to choose how to achieve them.

When to use it:

- This style of leadership is often successful with businesses that use highly skilled professionals who can operate autonomously such as consulting.
- The key for the leader is to remove road blocks and allocate resources for the pros to execute.

But, leadership is really about *motivating* people. Nowadays, therefore, particularly with so-called **knowledge workers**—people who work primarily with information or who develop and use knowledge in the workplace, such as scientists, engineers, and database administrators—managers strive to empower employees.

Empowerment means employees share management responsibilities, including decision making. This means that leading has become a much more subtle process than it was in the days when a manager could simply say "Do this!"

Leadership Styles

Researchers have looked at all kinds of leaders to see what kind of *traits*, or characteristics, they have in common, but most results do not seem to be reliable. Some leaders are kind and empathetic, and some are unkind and arrogant, and both types may get results.

Similarly, there are different *styles*, or ways, authority is used that characterize leaders, although no single type works best for any given set of circumstances. There are three common leadership styles:

1. **Autocratic**

2. **Participative** (democratic)

3. **Free-rein** (laissez-faire)

They range along a continuum from boss-centered leadership to employee-centered leadership.

Decisions

Carey and Diane are going over their observations. Choose the leadership style that would be most effective

When we visited the first store, I noticed the leader was asking everyone how they were doing. Although the staff said, "we're good," it seemed very chaotic, and it was clear they were winging it. The numbers show there are some clear cost issues.

Yes, that leader is very well liked. The challenge is they are a new store and the whole staff is comprised of newbies. They need some more structure until they get the processes and systems down.

1. Which style does this store need to turn it around?
    A. Autocratic
    B. Free-rein
    C. Participative

So, store number two is one of our highest performing stores.

Yes, there are some really seasoned employees, and I really like how the store leader huddled them up, went over the numbers, and asked for their opinions.

Yeah it was great to see them give ideas and the leader not only take them in, but make decisions on tweaks they would make immediately based on the staff's observation.

I think we should use this as a blueprint on where we want to grow our store leadership.

2. Which style is being described in this store?
    A. Autocratic
    B. Participative
    C. Free-rein

You know what I like, Carey?

What's that, Diane?

How our CEO empowers us to run the business. He gives us a framework and necessary resources and then lets us make it happen.

I agree this does take a lot of trust, but the autonomy, ability to grow and master our roles, and the knowledge that we make a difference in the business is pretty awesome!

3. Which leadership style is being described?

   A. Free-rein

   B. Participative

   C. Autocratic

Correct Answers: 1. A; 2. B; 3. A

Transactional Versus Transformational Leaders

Two positive traits of a good leader are what are called *transactional* and *transformational* leadership behaviors. One is concerned with getting people to do *ordinary* things, the other with getting people to do *exceptional* things.

Transactional Leadership: Promoting a Well-Run Organization

Transactional leadership focuses on creating a smooth-running organization, motivating employees to meet performance goals. Transactional leaders are concerned with setting goals, clarifying employee roles, providing rewards and punishments related to performance, and monitoring progress.

If the transactional leader's steady pursuit of order, stability, and performance goals sounds dull, it is nevertheless essential to a well-run organization. Several studies have found that self-effacing, diligent, conscientious types who have good execution and organizational skills make the best managers.

Transformational Leadership: Promoting Vision, Creativity, and Exceptional Performance

Transformational leadership focuses on inspiring long-term vision, creativity, and exceptional performance in employees. It strives to promote high levels of commitment and loyalty that can produce significant organizational change.

Transformational leaders appeal to followers to put the interests of the organization ahead of their own self-interests. Transformational leaders act in four ways to create changes in followers' goals, values, and beliefs.

Inspire Motivation by Promoting a Grand Design

Present an Overarching Vision for the Future

Transformational leaders offer a grand design or ultimate goal for the organization that serves as a beacon of hope and common purpose. The vision attracts commitment and energizes employees by promoting high ideals and creating meaning in employees' lives.

Inspire Trust by Expressing Their Integrity

Show the Importance of Doing What Is Right

Transformational leaders model desirable values by displaying high ethical standards, even making personal sacrifices for the good of the organization, thus inspiring trust in their employees.

Actively Encourage Employee Development

Provide Opportunities to Excel

These leaders encourage their followers to grow and excel by empowering them, giving them more responsibility and challenging work, and providing individualized mentoring.

Communicate a Strong Sense of Purpose

Overcome Challenges Together

Transformational leaders communicate the organization's strengths, weaknesses, opportunities, and threats so that employees develop a strong sense of purpose and learn to view problems as personal challenges to be overcome.

Decisions

Carey and Diane are continuing their leadership analysis by examining transformational and transactional leadership. Choose the best description.

The first leader is doing a great job of communicating our SWOT to people in the store. They also are providing some great coaching and mentoring to their people.

Yes, his team definitely trusts him. I had a chance to hear a few of his ideas and they are awesome!

1. The leader is _____."
   A. transformational
   B. transactional

The second leader knows the goals, leads teams to the goals, and sets very clear performance standards.

Yes, she does a great job of making sure all her team members are clear on their roles and goals. I also like how she holds them accountable and monitors progress to the goals.

2. The leader is _____."
   A. transformational
   B. transactional

Correct Answers: 1. A; 2. B

Necessities of Quality Control

By the end of this lesson, you will be able to:

- Explain why controlling is a necessary management function.
- Analyze the six ways in which managers utilize control.
- Propose a course of action by following the four-step control process.

Lack of Control

Controls and Quality

Diane and Carey just received their sixth e-mail from yet another BrewU location where the manager is reporting problems with quality and performance.

Diane and Carey video conference with Josh and fill him in on their problem.

Gee, another e-mail from a BrewU store in the western part of the region with the same gripe.

Let me guess—the store manager is struggling with beverage quality issues and performance issues with the baristas.

Exactly! This is terrible as it could hurt the two qualities we identify with: quality products and great customer service.

We need a plan and we need it in a hurry.

Maybe we should contact Josh in the eastern region. His region has high volume and he may have had similar experiences.

Why don't you try using the control process to help you uncover the issues that are giving you these problems?

The control process? How will that help us with a quality problem?

The control process can guide you to ask the right questions to find the answers you need.

Thanks Josh!

By contacting a peer in their organization, Carey and Diane are able to discover how the control process can help them.

In this lesson, we'll look at the control function of management. Control is needed for at least six reasons: it can help you deal with changes and uncertainties, become aware of opportunities, detect errors and irregularities, increase productivity or add value, deal with complexity, and decentralize decision making and facilitate teamwork. The four control process steps are (1) establishing standards, (2) monitoring performance, (3) comparing performance against standards, and (4) taking corrective action, if needed.

How Does Control Work?

Controlling involves monitoring performance, comparing it with goals, and taking corrective action as needed. Thus, control—answering the question, "Are we on track?" or making sure that performance meets goals—is concerned with achieving productivity and realizing results.

Deal with Changes and Uncertainties

All businesses must deal with changes and uncertainties: new competitors, changing customer tastes, new technologies, or altered laws and regulations. Control systems can help you anticipate, monitor, and react to these shifting circumstances.

Become Aware of Opportunities

Controls can help alert you to opportunities you might otherwise not have noticed. Some examples: new overseas markets, hot-selling product lines, competitive prices on materials, or changing population trends.

Detect Errors and Irregularities

Customer dissatisfaction, employee turnover, cost overruns, manufacturing defects, accounting errors—all of these matters may be tolerable in the short term, but, if left to fester, can bring down an organization.

Increase Productivity, Cut Waste, Reduce Costs, Add Value

Control systems can increase productivity, eliminate waste, reduce labor costs, and decrease materials costs. In addition, they can add value to products or services, making them more attractive to customers.

Deal with Complexity

Several different product lines, different customer bases, different company cultures—all are complexities that must be dealt with. When one company merges with another, these differences may suddenly become important. Controls help managers integrate and coordinate these disparate elements.

Decentralize Decision Making and Facilitate Teamwork

Managers can use controls to decentralize decision making at the company's lower levels and encourage employees to work as a team.

Decisions

Carey and Diane are applying the concepts to the current situation in the stores.

After talking with the store managers, employees, and some customers. It looks like we need to build some systems that allow the front-line staff to make decisions quicker.

Yeah, the biggest customer complaint was the employees have to go ask their boss. The employees said they feel silly having to do this all the time, and their manager is totally overrun.

1. Which reason for control is most applicable to this situation?

   A. Decentralize decision making and facilitate teamwork

   B. Deal with complexity

   C. Detect errors and irregularities

Okay, so with this store, what is going on is we acquired it from another company. We kept the staff, and they are struggling with the changes.

We need to put a plan together to help them better adjust to the culture and teach them our systems so we can better integrate them into BrewU.

2. Which reason for control is most applicable to this situation?

   A. Decentralize decision making and facilitate teamwork

   B. Detect errors and irregularities

   C. Deal with complexity

We had a lot of customer complaints saying that when they ordered a drink, our staff told them we didn't have the ingredients.

I looked into this and there was a glitch in the inventory system. We need to work with IT to make sure we get this fixed, and I think that should fix it.

3. Which reason for control is most applicable to this situation?

   A. Deal with complexity

   B. Decentralize decision making and facilitate teamwork

   C. Detect errors and irregularities

Correct Answers: 1. A; 2. C; 3. C

Taking Control: Four Steps in the Process

Generally control systems follow the same steps, although they may be modified to fit individual situations. The four-step **control process** follows:

1. Establish standards.

2. Monitor performance.

3. Compare performance against standards.

4. Take corrective action, if needed.

Establish Standards

A **control standard** is the desired performance level for a given goal. Standards can be set for almost anything, although they are more easily measured when they are made quantifiable. For-profit organizations might have standards of financial performance, employee hiring, manufacturing defects, percentage increase in market share, percentage reduction in costs, number of customer complaints, and return on investment. More subjective standards, such as level of employee morale, can also be set, although they may have to be expressed more quantifiably, using measurements such as reduced absenteeism and fewer sick days.

Monitor Performance

The second step in the process is to measure performance—for example by number of products sold or units produced.

Performance measures draw on three sources:

1. Written reports, such as computerized printouts

2. Oral reports, such as subordinates' weekly verbal statements of accomplishments

3. Personal observations, such as those made a manager walking around the factory floor ("management by walking around")

Compare Performance Against Standards

Performance that exceeds standards becomes an occasion for handing out bonuses, promotions, and other rewards. When performance is below standards, managers need to ask whether the deviation from performance is significant. The greater the deviation, the greater the need for action.

How acceptable the deviation is depends on the *range of variation* built in to the standards established in Step 1.

Take Corrective Action, If Needed

There are three possible scenarios:

1. Make no changes.

2. Recognize and celebrate positive performance that meets or exceeds the standards set by bestowing rewards—whether it's giving a verbal "job well done" or more substantial payoffs such as raises, bonuses, and promotions in order to reinforce good behavior.

3. Correct negative performance by examining the reasons why and taking appropriate action. Sometimes the standards are unrealistic and need to be altered. Sometimes employees haven't been given the resources for achieving the standards. And sometimes employees may need more attention and direction from management.

Decisions

Based on Josh's feedback, Carey and Diane have created the BrewU Standards of Excellence Process. Determine the appropriate step of the control process that best characterizes each dialogue.

Our performance goal is to have every drink made to specification with less than 1% waste and 98% satisfaction.

    A. Establish standard

    B. Monitor performance

    C. Compare performance against standards

    D. Take corrective action, if needed

Using our app, customers have the ability to earn free drinks by giving us a thumbs up, down, or neutral. We measure this on a daily basis.

We will run inventory reports daily to monitor or material costs.

    A. Establish standard

    B. Compare performance against standards

    C. Take corrective action, if needed

    D. Monitor performance

At the end of each week we will accumulate the data and benchmark it to our standard.

    A. Compare performance against standards

    B. Establish standard

    C. Monitor performance

    D. Take corrective action, if needed

If we have a gap, we will huddle and identify the challenge and work as a team to improve. If we meet or exceed our goal, then we will celebrate the success by providing a gift card to a team member via a drawing.

    A. Establish standard

    B. Monitor performance

    C. Compare performance against standards

    D. Take corrective action, if needed

Correct Answers: A; D; A; D

Essentials of Leadership and Management: Test

1. Sean Tyson, a new manager, is told by his supervisor that he must enrol in a training course to improve his management skill set. Tyson likes to set goals and figure out how to achieve them, and he excels at deciding how to arrange tasks in the best order to get things done. In addition, he's good at motivating people to do their best, but his supervisor tells him he also needs to focus on monitoring performance outcomes and deciding whether corrective action is needed. The function of management that Tyson needs coaching on is

   A. planning.

   B. controlling.

   C. leading.

   D. organizing.

   E. budgeting.

2. Which step in a manager's decision-making process involves planning for desired outcomes and analyzing actual results?

   A. brainstorming ideas

   B. weighing alternative solutions

   C. implementing and evaluating the decision

   D. identifying the problem or opportunity

   E. sponsoring an employee retreat

3. Selena Rojas is a supervisory manager at Petville. An expensive line of cat toys is not selling nearly as well as expected, and Rojas must decide what to do about the situation. In her morning team meeting with her subordinates, Rojas says, "The Feline Frenzy line is not doing well. Petville wants us to increase its sales. What about rearranging the store display to feature it more prominently? Any other thoughts? All suggestions are welcome." Rojas is engaging in the decision-making step known as

   A. weighing alternative solutions.

   B. identifying the problem.

   C. eliminating alternative solutions.

   D. keeping accurate records.

   E. brainstorming ideas.

4. A company's _____ answers the question, "What do we want to become?"

   A. mission statement

   B. blueprint plan

   C. vision statement

   D. statement of purpose

   E. position report

5. Expressing an organization's fundamental purposes is a key element of its _____ statement.

   A. mission

   B. profit and loss

   C. financial

   D. vision

   E. workflow

6. Rebecca Espinoza, a young entrepreneur, wants to market a new app, What Say You, designed for people who want to learn a new language. She's interested in attracting investors, and she needs a formal way to let them know her company's basic purposes are to help users learn a new language and help them connect with others across the globe as they learn. Espinoza should write a(n)

   A. email to potential investors.

   B. mission statement.

   C. contingency plan.

   D. list of organizational goals.

   E. questionnaire for users.

7. Jesus Reyes, a manager at Singular Financial, wants to inspire and motivate his employees by reminding them of Singular's _____, which expresses what the organization wants to become. To that end, Reyes passes out laminated cards printed with its words, so each employee can carry it and refer to it during the workday. He also considered including Singular's fundamental purposes, or _____ on the card, but he decided to make an inspirational poster out of it instead.

   A. vision statement; mission statement

   B. mission statement; vision statement

   C. aspirational statement; inspirational statement

   D. strategic plan; action plan

   E. business plan; charitable plan

8. On her website, Rula Tariq plans to promote and sell essential oils made from peppermint because peppermint oil is said to relieve headache symptoms. Just in case her supplier has a shortage of peppermint oil, Tariq makes a note to herself to be sure to order a large enough quantity of lavender and eucalyptus oils, also said to relieve headaches, to substitute for peppermint oil if it is unavailable. This is an example of

   A. contingency planning.

   B. brainstorming.

   C. an external threat.

   D. internal weakness.

   E. false advertising.

9. An example of a(n) _____ in a SWOT analysis is when buyers' preferences change.

   A. external threat

   B. internal weakness

   C. external opportunity

   D. integral strength

   E. consumer threat

10. Managers organize people, tasks, and resources. To do so successfully, managers need to develop their skills in three areas: technical, conceptual, and

    A. human.

    B. creative.

    C. strategic.

    D. organizational.

    E. practical.

11. Robert Ochoifeoma is a new supervisory manager at Hearthside Restaurant Supply Company. He wants to know the name and title of his supervisor's supervisor as well as the names and titles of the people whom that person oversees. He needs to look at

    A. the company's telephone directory.

    B. his supervisor's resume.

    C. the company's email contacts list.

    D. the company's organization chart.

    E. the company's emergency contacts list.

12. Matt Snow runs a small office-cleaning business, SnowFlake Services. The company has only two employees, Snow himself and his assistant Jess Thicke. Thicke reports directly to Snow. On an organization chart, Snow's name and position title would appear in what position in relation to Thicke's name and position title?

    A. Snow would appear directly below Thicke.

    B. Thicke would appear directly below Snow.

    C. Snow and Thicke would appear side by side.

    D. Thicke would not appear on the chart because he plays a support role.

    E. Thicke would be next to Snow and connected with a dotted line.

13. Leaders deal with _____, while managers deal with _____.

   A. ideas; people

   B. change; complexity

   C. giving orders; empowering people

   D. conceptual skills; human skills

14. Enrique Linares recognizes that his department needs to go in a different direction. He plans and budgets for this new direction, communicates it to his subordinates, and inspires people to commit to his course of action by appealing to human needs and emotions to keep them motivated despite obstacles. Linares is demonstrating

   A. how managers handle complexity.

   B. how to behave ethically on the job.

   C. how leaders deal with change.

   D. how to use whistleblowing to achieve results.

   E. how to assert authority in a vertical hierarchy.

15. A manager should choose the _____ leadership style in a workplace where employee expertise from multiple areas is needed.

   A. autocratic

   B. relational

   C. free-rein

   D. participatory

   E. group

16. Min-Ji Park is a top manager at a Taskmasters Online, a marketplace that matches freelancers with busy consumers who need jobs and errands done for them. Park sets general objectives for her employees, such as responding to a task request within a certain time period. Because she uses highly skilled professionals who know what they're doing, Park feels comfortable giving her employees freedom to decide on their own how to achieve Taskmasters Online's goals. "I just want to get out of the way and give folks the resources to get the job done," she explains. Park's approach is an example of the _____ leadership style.

   A. easygoing

   B. participatory

   C. free-rein

   D. human

   E. autocratic

17. Supervisory manager Robin Ward won't take "no" for an answer when she gives her employees orders. Drawing from her military background, she takes the attitude, "Do it because I said so." Whenever Ward makes a decision, she rarely asks her subordinates for input. When she heads down the hall, people get out of the way, whispering, "There goes 'My-Way-or-the-Highway' Ward." Ward is a(n) _____ leader.

   A. free-rein

   B. participative

   C. unsympathetic

   D. autopilot

   E. autocratic

18. Of the two leadership behaviours, _____ leadership involves getting people to do ordinary things, while _____ leadership involves getting people to do exceptional things.

A. transactional; transformational

B. human; conceptual

C. free-rein; autocratic

D. autocratic; participatory

19. Quiang Zheng was recently promoted to supervisory manager at Bunk Beds and More. He has read that controlling helps managers be effective. However, the term controlling sounds authoritarian to him. He wants to be a well-liked manager, not a control freak. So far, though, his efforts to be agreeable and easygoing have been met with mixed results. Which choice accurately expresses a way Zheng can use control to be more effective as a manager?

A. Control gives employees free rein.

B. Control involves employees in decision making.

C. Control can improve a manager's human skills.

D. Control can help increase productivity.

E. Control can inspire creative employees.

20. Customer dissatisfaction, employee turnover, cost overruns, and manufacturing defects are some of the issues managers address through

A. conceptualizing.

B. a moral compass.

C. course correction.

D. complaints.

E. control.

Copyright © McGraw Hill

102 Chapter 3 · Essentials of Leadership and Management

4 Operations Management

What To Expect

By the end of the chapter, you will be able to:

- Describe the production/operations process in terms of inputs, transformation, and outputs.

- Recall, in detail, the process through which goods and services are produced.

Chapter Topics

- **4-1** Essentials of Operations Management

- **4-2** Understanding and Improving the Production Process

- **4-3** Operational Planning: Designing and Managing Production Operations

- **4-4** Quality Assurance: Increasing Efficiency and Reducing Defects

© McGraw Hill Yuri_Arcurs/iStock/Getty Images

Essentials of Operations Management

Modular Management

"Keeping our core value while planning for the future."

Owen Sykes and Walker Lewis own Ozark Design, a furniture company that specializes in modular design that allows customers to acquire pieces slowly and at an affordable rate. Customers can start with a dining table and two chairs, for example, and be confident that three years from now they can purchase four more chairs that will match perfectly. Ozark Design employs 12 full-time workers and anywhere from 10 to 30 part-time workers depending on how busy they are.

Each piece of furniture is assembled at their location on the outskirts of Jefferson City. They buy the resources from several different vendors but do their best to support as many businesses in their locale as they can.

Our reputation is built on how modular all our furniture is. But that is presenting challenges as we look to better manage our operations

Right. For the past several years, we've just planned our operations in an ad hoc way. At this stage in our growth, we need to study our options, really understand how we take the resources we use and transform them into our great furniture.

Okay, we agree. But how do we start? Where do we begin?

In this lesson, we'll help Walker and Owen define the nature of their business and how it adds value to the resources it begins with.

Production or operations is any process that takes basic resources and converts them into finished products—inputs into outputs. Operations management is the management of the process of converting resources into goods and/or services. Manufacturing businesses and service businesses differ in their operations management.

Operations Management: How Goods and Services Are Produced

Transforming Resources into Finished Products

Production or **operations** refers to any process that takes basic resources and converts them into finished products—inputs into outputs, whether grapes into wine or electronic parts into cellphones.

Converting Basic Resources into Finished Products

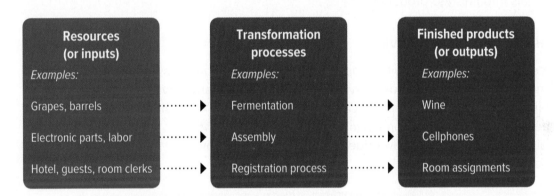

Resources are the factors of production namely, *natural resources*, *capital*, *human resources*, *entrepreneurship*, and *knowledge*. Finished products are goods or services. What the transformation process does, then, is *add value* to the resources.

Adding Value to Resources

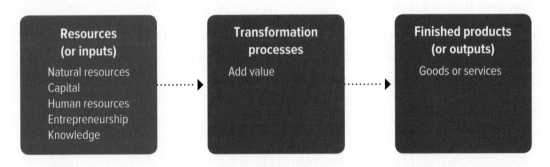

Let's review an example of the value added in the transformation process. Suppose we are building a truck. We add value during (1) the process of shaping metal into the body of the car, (2) the assembly of the parts into a working order (which requires an immense amount of knowledge), and (3) the engineering and R&D required to complete this process.

Production Management Versus Operations Management

Production management is the management of the process of transforming materials, labor, and other resources into goods. Today, businesspeople are more apt to use the term **operations management** to reflect the conversion of resources into services as well as goods. To give a formal definition, then, *operations management* is the management of the entire process related to transforming materials, labor, and other resources into goods and/or services for an organization.

Manufacturing Versus Services: The Differences in Operations Management

There are differences in how operations management works for manufacturing and how it works for services.

Manufacturing Businesses: Producing Goods

Manufacturing businesses, which mainly deal with *things*, produce goods; they convert raw materials into finished products.

Service Businesses: Performing Services

Service businesses, which deal mainly with *people*, perform services; they convert people's unmet needs into satisfied needs. Services are provided in many ways. For example, a laundry service provides clean clothes to the customer. A hospital visit might be needed to set a broken bone. Similar to manufacturing, these activities all require time scheduling, knowledge, machines, and manpower. Yet a new good is not produced.

Decisions

Owen and Walker sit in their small conference room to consider how they can produce higher-quality goods and services to their customers. They decide the first step is to look at how their furniture is developed.

1. Ozark Design begins with the natural resource of lumber and transforms it into finished furniture. Owen and Walker use _____ to oversee this process.

   A. informational transformation

   B. manufacturing process analysis

   C. operations management

2. Ozark Design is a _____ business that produces goods.

   A. service

   B. manufacturing

   C. transformational

3. By taking the raw materials and creating something new, Ozark Design is adding value and engaging the _____.

   A. transformational process

   B. process of being a service business

   C. marginal utility transformation process

Correct Answers: 1.C; 2. B; 3. A

Lesson 4-2

Understanding and Improving the Production Process

By the end of this lesson, you will be able to:

- Analyze a product to determine which kind of form utility transformation it underwent.
- Recommend optimal production processes and technologies to manufacture products.

Transforming Their Design Process

When and How to Upgrade

Walker and Owen are looking to upgrade their tool sets to improve efficiency. Several years ago they invested in CAD/CAM equipment to streamline their design process, which is a central core of their business. They experienced some growing pains, but their CAD/CAM system today helps them be nimble and ensures the constancy of their modular furniture. Now they want to see if investing in a new CIM system will enhance their design process and provide some marketing help too.

We really need to up our game in our entire workflow from concept to delivery.

Agreed. When we updated our CAD/CAM system nearly 10 years ago now, it really improved our efficiency and effectiveness. But I feel as if we are falling behind.

Let's Skype with Jeremy, a workflow guru, to see what he recommends.

Hi to you both. It's been awhile since we last met.

Copyright © McGraw Hill

Yes, and Walker and I realize we could really use your experience to help us figure out how to improve our production process.

I'd love to. My recommendation is that we review your processes and use of technology to see if you are tapping into all the ideas and strategies that can help strengthen a business like yours.

Just what we need. I made a video of the entire process and will upload it to you now. Once you've watched it, let's discuss your recommendations.

Business owners, especially smaller businesses like Ozark Design, should take stock periodically of their workflow and seek specialized help to guide them. In this lesson, we'll analyze these workflows.

Form utility is the value that people add in converting resources into finished products. Two ways of adding value are by breaking down resources or combining resources to create finished products.

Production processes may be continuous (ongoing) or intermittent (as needed). Historically, production processes have been changed by the introduction of mechanization, standardization, assembly lines, automation, and mass production. More recently, production processes have been improved through the use of computerized design and manufacturing, flexible manufacturing, lean manufacturing, and mass customization.

Production Processes: Improving Production Techniques

Most ideas about production processes are based on manufacturing, and have been adapted to service businesses. What are the commonalities of the various production processes? What's required to convert eggs to eggnog, tin to tin cans, newsprint to newspapers? Or indifferent hotel guests to happy guests? Let's show Owen and Walker some concepts to consider.

Form Utility: How Operations Processes Add Value

Form utility is the value that people add in converting resources—natural resources, capital, human resources, entrepreneurship, and knowledge—into finished products. The way that operations processes add value to resources and convert them into products is *by changing their form*. Two ways of adding value are to break down raw materials or combine raw materials. For instance, a cow's milk may be separated out, producing cream. Or it may be combined with sugar and other ingredients to produce ice cream.

Analytic Transformation: Breaking Down Materials

The process in which resources are broken down to create finished products is known as **analytic transformation**. All kinds of materials are made into new forms by breaking the original substance down further, using chemical or mechanical means. Gold ore is crushed, separated, and smelted into pure gold. Chickens are butchered into breasts, legs, and other parts. A new building may be divided into offices, retail shops, condos, and apartments.

Synthetic Transformation: Combining Materials

The process in which resources are combined to create finished products is called **synthetic transformation**. Gold may be combined with silver to make jewelry, for instance. Chicken may be combined with vegetables to make a casserole. Buildings may be combined with streets to make a housing development. (Another term, *assembly processes*, describes the processes in which components are put together, as in electronics and automobile manufacturing.)

Continuous Versus Intermittent Conversion Processes

Whether for manufacturing or for services, production processes are either *continuous* or *intermittent*.

Continuous Processes: Ongoing

A **continuous process** is a production process in which goods or services are turned out in a long production run on an ongoing basis over time. Chemical plants, nuclear plants, and oil refineries, which shut down only rarely, are examples of continuous production processes, but they are not the only ones. Ozark Design is an example of a continuous process manufacturing business.

Intermittent Processes: As Needed

An **intermittent process** is a production process in which finished goods or services are turned out in a series of short production runs and the machines are changed frequently to make different products. Garment makers, for instance, frequently shut down their factories to retool them to handle different clothing styles. Loads of concrete are also made on an on-demand basis, and between orders the equipment and concrete trucks have to be cleaned.

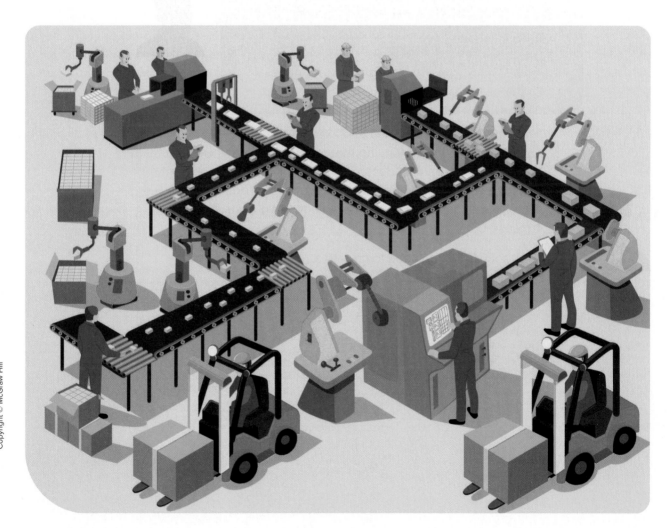

Decisions

Owen and Walker sit down to evaluate their production processes because that is a key component in deciding where to relocate.

So, let's go over our approach. We take this raw material wood, shape it and put it together, and then, we add design elements such as paint stain, wire, or other touches. The result is our awesome furniture pieces. From this aspect, we are engaged in _____.

    A. synthetic transformation

    B. information transformation utility process

    C. material transformation

Yes, and you remember how we built our reputation. We were craftsmen; taking our time and doing everything as a custom product. At that point in our business we used a(n) _____ production process.

    A. continuous

    B. intermittent

    C. batch

The challenge with continuing that type of process is we won't be able to keep up with demand, which will hold us back from scaling. Based on the online comments, if we produce the same piece consistently, we'll be able to keep costs down and increase our volume.

1. It sounds like we need to go with a _____ production process.

    A. continuous

    B. non-stop

    C. batch

Correct Answers: C; B; 1.A

A Short History of Production

The Industrial Revolution in 18th-century England, and later America, introduced a series of technology changes that improved efficiency: (1) *mechanization*, (2) *standardization*, (3) the *assembly line*, (4) *automation*, and (5) *mass production*.

Mechanization: Using Machines to Replace Labor

The first development was **mechanization**, the use of machines to do the work formerly performed by people.

Standardization: Using Uniform Parts

Hand in hand with mechanization was the development of **standardization**, the use of uniform parts that could be easily interchanged with similar parts. This eliminated the need for handcrafting every product, and reduced the need to employ experienced craft workers.

Assembly Line: Series of Specific Tasks

Taking the concept of standardization further, the factory **assembly line** consists of a series of steps for assembling a product, each step using the same interchangeable parts and each being performed repetitively by the same worker.

Automation: Minimal Human Intervention

Gradually, in order to increase output and profits, manufacturers began trying to reduce the role of manual labor on their production lines, striving to use **automation**, using machines as much as possible rather than human labor to perform production tasks. Particularly interesting is the field of **robotics**, the use of programmable machines, or **robots**, to manipulate materials and tools to perform a variety of tasks. Robots are used for everything from building cars to harvesting alfalfa to doing nuclear inspections to fighting oil-well fires.

Mass Production: Production of Great Quantities

Mechanization, standardization, assembly lines, and automation have made possible reduction of production costs and the development of **mass production**, the production of uniform goods in great quantities. Mass production is used all the time to produce goods, of course (such as cars, jeans, and canned soups), but it is also possible for services, where the goal is to produce a predictable experience.

Decisions

Owen and Walker are discussing how they can learn from the past and implement these time-tested approaches in their business.

One of the things we can do in building our inventory is ensure that we stock the same components. This will keep costs low and create better _____.

    A. assembly line

    B. automation

    C. standardization

    D. mechanization

    E. mass production

I think we should also look at deploying some capital to buy more machinery. By doing this, we can apply _____ to our process and better leverage our people.

    A. standardization

    B. mass production

    C. assembly line

    D. automation

    E. mechanization

I agree. When I look at our current approach, we seem to have steps that require too much manual labor as the product moves down the _____ and the team puts it together.

    A. standardization

    B. mechanization

    C. mass production

    D. automation

    E. assembly line

I think we should send some of our high performers to get trained on some different technologies. This will allow us to implement _____ in the process. Then, we can redeploy our people to parts of the company that can be replaced by machines and technology.

    A. standardization

    B. mechanization

    C. automation

    D. assembly line

    E. mass production

Yes! By doing this, we will build a larger sales team, increase our inventory, and be able to get to _____.

    A. standardization

    B. mechanization

    C. automation

    D. assembly line

    E. mass production

Correct Answers: C; E; C; E

Improving Production: Use of CAD/CAM/CIM, Flexible Manufacturing, Lean Manufacturing, and Mass Customization

In recent years, companies have stepped up their production efficiencies by adopting new forms of technology. They are *CAD/CAM/CIM*, *flexible manufacturing systems*, *lean manufacturing*, and *mass customization*.

Owen and Walker are considering purchasing a CIM system that would allow customers to see the furniture they want to order in in their home digitally. The technology is capable of taking a photo from their home and through a CIM process outputting a schematic and photo that shows how the furniture would appear in the home. Customers can move the furniture around, change colors, and get a sense of where everything will fit. This application would also be a great boon to Ozark Design's core principle of encouraging customers to buy furniture in modules over time that has proven to be a budget friendly option many of their customers enjoy.

CAD, CAM, and CIM: Computer-Aided Design, Computer-Aided Manufacturing, and Computer-Integrated Manufacturing

Computers have now become a well-established technology in improving production. Three types of computer technologies are abbreviated *CAD*, *CAM*, and *CIM*:

CAD—Computer-Aided Design: Using Computers to Design Products.

Computer-aided design (CAD) programs are used to design products, structures, civil engineering drawings, and maps. One advantage of CAD software is that the product can be drawn in three dimensions and then rotated on the computer screen, so that the designer can see all sides. CAD programs help architects design buildings and workspaces and help engineers design cars, planes, electronic devices, roadways, bridges, and subdivisions.

CAM—Computer-Aided Manufacturing: Using Computers to Manufacture Products.

Computer-aided manufacturing (CAM) is the use of computers in the manufacturing process. CAM systems allow products designed with CAD to be input into an automated manufacturing system that makes products.

CIM—Computer-Integrated Manufacturing: Uniting CAD with CAM.

Originally, CAD systems didn't have the software to communicate directly with CAM systems. That changed with the introduction of **computer-integrated manufacturing (CIM)**, systems in which computer-aided design is united with computer-aided manufacturing. Often these may be integrated through computer networks linking several departments or contractors.

Flexible Manufacturing Systems: Machines for Multiple Tasks

Flexible manufacturing system (FMS) is a facility that can be modified quickly to manufacture different products. Thus, for example, a manufacturer need not take down an existing assembly line for a certain line of cars and reconstruct it to build other vehicles. Instead, with an FMS, a change in the kind of product can be handled just by sending a few signals to the computer.

Lean Manufacturing: Using the Fewest Resources

Lean manufacturing is the production of products by eliminating unnecessary steps and using the fewest resources, as well as continually striving for improvement. Thus, waste is eliminated to the extent possible, labor is pared to the minimum, machines use the fewest moving parts, rejected products are considered unacceptable, and materials are delivered as closely as possible to the time when they are needed (just-in-time system).

Lean manufacturing was honed by Japanese companies such as Toyota, which identified all the steps in the production process and eliminated unnecessary ones.

The automaker also used teamwork to examine problems and fix them as soon as they appeared. Finally, supplies were obtained from vendors only as they were needed in the factory (just-in-time system).

Mass Customization: Using Mass Production to Produce Individualized Products

Technologies have allowed the development of **mass customization**, using mass production techniques to produce customized goods or services. All kinds of products and services are now being produced to match individual customer needs and tastes.

Decisions

Owen and Walker started their business using their carpentry skills. As they plan the interior of their new building, they discuss how they can enhance operations.

I think we should really look into this JIT approach. If we can reduce waste, increase productivity, and eliminate human struggle, then we should make that happen.

I agree. The Japanese automakers knew what they were doing when they developed _____.

  A. mass customization

  B. flexible manufacturing systems

  C. lean manufacturing

So, I've been thinking what if we give four options in colors, three options in wood, and two stylized options as some of the key pieces. This won't impact our production or costs too much, but it will give them a sense of uniqueness.

I really like that. It's our own version of _____.

  A. a CAD creation

  B. mass customization

  C. fully customizable products

This means that as we purchase equipment, it will need to be a _____ that will allow us to flip a few switches and adjust the machines.

    A. batch creation system

    B. flexible manufacturing system

    C. machine

Lastly, we purchased a license to ensure we have CAD, CAM, and CIM. I think what would help us in our research is purchasing a _____. We can quickly develop prototypes to see what they would look like and determine if they should be in our next line.

    A. 3D printer

    B. design department

    C. CAD machine

Correct Answers: C; B; A

Lesson 4-3

Operational Planning: Designing and Managing Production Operations

By the end of this lesson, you will be able to:

- Recommend optimal facility locations and layouts, supplier strategies, inventory systems, and scheduling tools to manufacture a product for a business case.
- Construct Gantt and PERT charts for simple processes.

Hunting for a Home

Finding the Right Location

As businesspeople, Owen and Walker not only need to design the goods and/or services they are selling, they also need to design the operations for producing them: where to locate their office, store, or factory; what the layout should be; how materials will be purchased and delivered; and so on.

Owen and Walker want to open a new facility that is larger and that offers more technology than they have in their current location.

Think about the advice you would give them to successfully relocate.

Our next appointment with Arielle is in just a minute. Are you ready?

I know. I'm so glad Jeremy put us in touch with Arielle. I'm setting up the Skype call now.

Hi, Owen and Walker. It's a pleasure to meet you.

Arielle, Owen and I aren't sure how to plan the interior of our new space, that is once we find the right location.

Chapter 4 • Operations Management **119**

I'm so glad you got in touch before you settled on a location. What you need inside your space will affect the location you choose.

I've been concentrating on where we should relocate our facility based on public transportation, access to highways, our vendors, and cost of land that the interior design and layout were not in my mind at all.

Let's take some time to review what you should consider as far as the design and layout of the new structure.

Owen and Walker are fortunate they met with Arielle when the did, so they can incorporate the interior needs of their facility into their search requirements.

To effectively design and manage production operations, business organizations need to consider facility location, facility layout, purchasing and supply-chain management, inventory and just-in-time systems for storing supplies, materials requirement planning and enterprise resource planning for purchasing and business organization, and Gantt and PERT charts for scheduling.

What Factors Should a Business Consider for Effective Production Operation?

Facility Location: Selecting a Place for Your Company's Operations

Facility location is the process of selecting a location for company operations, whether it's an office, a store, a gas station, a warehouse, a factory, or a cattle ranch. The kind of location, of course, will depend on the type of business and its special requirements—an apparel factory will have different needs from a cement plant, a gambling casino, a factory-outlet store, an import–export firm, an artichoke farm, and so on. However, there are four factors that often are important business considerations:

Copyright © McGraw Hill

availability and cost of resources, nearness to suppliers, nearness to customers, and *tax relief and local government support.*

Availability and Cost of Resources: Materials, Energy, and Labor

It's clear that the factors that principally influence the production process—materials, energy, labor, money, knowledge, and entrepreneurship—affect a facility's location. Consider materials, energy, and labor:

How Materials and Energy Affect Facility Location.

Obviously, many businesses have to be located where the raw materials exist—silver mines, banana plantations, wind-powered utilities, and so on. Sometimes companies will locate facilities near particular sources of material resources or energy not because they have to but because it makes the most economic sense.

How Labor Affects Facility Location.

Although people seem to readily migrate all over the world to obtain work, businesses still clearly choose to locate their facilities in particular areas and countries—because the labor is inexpensive, because the labor force is highly skilled, because upper-level managers want to live there, or because of the quality of life there.

Nearness to Suppliers

Locating production facilities near suppliers helps reduce the costs of shipping supplies and leads to better communication.

Nearness to Customers: Reducing Time to Market

The benefit of locating a production facility close to customers is that it can reduce **time to market**—the length of time it takes from a product being conceived until it is available for sale.

Tax Relief and Local Government Support

Some states have more favorable tax treatment of companies than other states do. Nevada, for instance, has no warehouse tax, which makes that state a good place for companies storing products for shipment. In order to provide local jobs, many local governments also provide tax benefits, zoning changes, and other financial incentives. Some cities have special enterprise zones.

Laying Out Your Operations

Once Owen and Walker determine the best place to locate their plant, they should consider the layout of the plant to make sure that the location they have chosen will accommodate all their needs.

Facility Layout: Arranging Your Production Resources

Facility layout is the physical arrangement of equipment, offices, rooms, people, and other resources within an organization for producing goods or services. The arrangements can be similar for delivering both goods and services.

The three principal facility layouts for producing goods are *product layout*, *process layout*, and *fixed-position layout*.

Product Layout: The Assembly-Line Arrangement

In the **product layout**, equipment and tasks are arranged into an assembly line—a sequence of steps for producing a single product. This method, of course, is the classic way by which automobiles are manufactured, but it's also used for making household appliances.

| Frame, wheels, and drive train | Install engine | Install steering and seats | Install cab, hood, truck bed | Install doors and windows |

Process Layout: Work Grouped by Function

In the **process layout**, similar work is grouped by function. A cabinet maker or machine shop, for example, might perform work in one room before the product is moved to another department for finishing work. Or a hospital might perform x-rays in one department, patient examinations in another, and surgery in another.

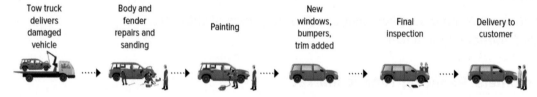

| Tow truck delivers damaged vehicle | Body and fender repairs and sanding | Painting | New windows, bumpers, trim added | Final inspection | Delivery to customer |

Fixed-Position Layout: Equipment and Labor Transported to Production Site

In the **fixed-position layout**, materials, equipment, and labor are transported to one location. This is certainly the case for a nuclear power plant, a dam, or an airport. But, it's also true for most houses and commercial buildings.

(6) Roofing
(5) Electrical work
(4) Plumbing and heating
(3) Rough carpentry
(2) Foundation
(1) Grading

(7) Windows and doors
(8) Finish carpentry
(9) Flooring
(10) Paintaing
(11) Signage
(12) Parking lot paving

Decisions

Owen and Walker have narrowed their choice of location to three. They decide to prioritize the factors involved in facility location to help make their decision. Fill in the term that best fits their list.

1. Since Owen and Walker have retail stores across the entire Midwest, if they choose to locate their operation in Kansas City, MO, they will satisfy which factor?

   A. Tax relief and government support

   B. Availability and cost of resources

   C. Nearness to suppliers

   D. Nearness to customers

2. Owen and Walker have recently discovered that Jefferson City, MO, has an entrepreneurial zone and provides local tax credit for creating jobs. The city also has a small business center that wants to help veterans. Which factor is being considered with this new information?

   A. Tax relief and government support

   B. Nearness to suppliers

   C. Availability and cost of resources

   D. Nearness to customers

3. The local community college in Jefferson City has an awesome trades program, and since Jefferson City is relatively small, the cost of living is not as high and wages are reasonable to allow workers a decent income and quality of life. Owen and Walker are considering _____.

   A. nearness to suppliers

   B. tax relief and government support

   C. availability and cost of resources

   D. nearness to customers

4. For Owen and Walker, certain factors might become more important than others, but what is the most important factor for most all businesses?

   A. Availability and cost of resources

   B. Nearness to customers

   C. Nearness to suppliers

   D. None of these. All factors can be of equal importance to businesses. It all depends on the business and its goals.

Correct Answers: 1. D; 2. A; 3. C; 4. D

Purchasing and Inventory: Getting and Storing the Best Resources

Purchasing is the activity of finding the best resources for the best price from the best suppliers to produce the best goods and services. The Internet, of course, has made it much easier for a company to search for the best suppliers and best price—just as the Internet makes it easier for the suppliers to scout for possible customers.

Dealing with Suppliers: Two Strategies

There are two strategies for dealing with suppliers—use a lot of suppliers or use just a trusted few.

Use Many Suppliers to Ensure Constant Resources

Some companies will deal with many suppliers, reasoning that if one of them fails in some way or charges too high a price, another will be able to deliver the resources needed at the right price.

Use a Few Trusted Suppliers to Ensure Reliability

Companies tend to deal with just a few suppliers, believing there will be more reliability and fewer chances proprietary secrets will be revealed.

Inventory and Inventory Control: Keeping the Goods in Stock

When you buy household supplies—soap, toilet paper, towels, and the like— where do you store them? Businesses face the same problem—only more so, because resources are constantly used up by the production process or by sales to customers. The question of storing supplies (or products resulting from the production process) is known as an inventory problem.

Inventory is the name given to goods kept in stock to be used for the production process or for sales to customers. Makers of acoustic guitars have to store special woods. Shoe stores have to store shoes. In both cases, there are problems with **inventory control**, the system for determining the right quantity of resources and keeping track of their location and use. Guitar woods, for instance, may need to be stored in special climate-controlled conditions. Shoe stores have to cover the widest variety of sizes and fashions.

Decisions

Ozark Design uses the sole supplier strategy for the main supply which is lumber. What other strategies could Owen and Walker consider?

1. Using _____ suppliers might give them more variety but still provide reliability and consistency.

   A. many

   B. a few trusted

2. Using _____ suppliers might give them backup sources in case a fire or other natural disaster affected a supplier.

   A. many

   B. a few trusted

Correct Answers: 1. B; 2. A

Supply-Chain Management and Just-in-Time Systems: Storing the Supplies That Suppliers Supply

Owen and Walker visualize the movement of supplies into a production facility as representing a long chain involving many suppliers—a *supply chain*. In this view, one company's output becomes another company's input.

Supply-Chain Management: Integrating Production from Suppliers to Customers

Many businesses engage in a process known as **supply-chain management**, in which companies produce goods and services by integrating many facilities, functions, and processes, from suppliers to customers. This requires that suppliers be much more involved in the design process.

Just-In-Time: Let Supplies Be Delivered Just as They Are Needed

Holding a storeroom or warehouse full of inventory can be expensive. Many businesses, therefore, now rely on a concept called **just-in-time (JIT) inventory control**, in which only minimal supplies are kept on the organization's premises and others are delivered by the suppliers on an as-needed basis. Once a JIT system is established, all resources should be continuously flowing, with suppliers connected electronically to ensure everyone knows when materials will be needed.

JIT doesn't work for all situations. For instance, it's not effective if demand varies throughout the year, if a firm has a diverse product line, if businesses underestimate the quantities of supplies needed, or if suppliers can't locate close by or make deliveries on time or otherwise meet the whims of their clients.

MRP and ERP: Using Computers to Deliver the Right Resources to the Right Place at the Right Time

Purchasing and supply-chain management has been much enhanced by the use of computers. This has developed into two kinds of systems, *materials requirement planning (MRP)* and *enterprise resource planning (ERP)*.

Materials Requirement Planning: Using a Bill of Materials to Deliver the Right Materials on Time to the Right Place

Like JIT, **materials requirement planning (MRP)** is a computer-based method of delivering the right amounts of supplies to the right place at the right time for the production of goods. It uses what is known as a **bill of materials**, which is essentially a list of materials that go into the finished product. This list is programmed into a computer that already contains the customer's order (for example, 500,000 cellphones) so that the right kinds of materials can be delivered in the right quantities at the right time.

Enterprise Resource Planning: Integrating All Business Processes Across the Entire Company

MRP is concerned with organizing the materials to go into a single product. ERP is concerned with the firm's entire enterprise. **Enterprise resource planning (ERP)** is a computer-based system that collects and provides information about a company's entire enterprise, including identifying customer needs, receipt of orders, distribution of finished goods, and receipt of payment. Most of today's ERP applications are offered by software vendors, which have the applications on their own computer systems and allow companies to access them via the Internet.

Decisions

At Ozark Design, the supply chain is crucial to maintaining a healthy profit margin because the purchase of the main supply—lumber—is so expensive. In order to better control the supply chain, Owen and Walker consider the following strategies.

1. An inventory control strategy in which minimal supplies are kept in the warehouse, which is called _____.

   A. continue near-time approach (CNT)

   B. warehouse management supply

   C. just-in-time (JIT)

2. The concept where companies produce goods and services by integrating many facilities, functions, and processes, from suppliers to customers is known as a _____.

   A. distribution chain

   B. supply chain

   C. supplier management analysis

3. The planning tool that integrates all of a business's processes across the entire company is called _____.

   A. just-in-time (JIT) management system

   B. management

   C. management enterprise resource planning

Owen and Walker decided they should integrate the approaches into a comprehensive strategy.

Correct Answers: 1. C; 2. B; 3. C

Scheduling Tools: Gantt and PERT Charts

Scheduling is the act of determining time periods for each task in the production process. Two tools used by managers in the scheduling process are *Gantt charts* and *PERT charts*.

Gantt Charts: Visual Time Schedules for Work Tasks

Developed by Henry L. Gantt, Gantt charts are useful for graphically indicating deadlines. A **Gantt chart** is a kind of time schedule—a specialized bar chart that shows the relationship between the kind of work tasks planned and their scheduled completion dates.

There is nothing difficult about creating a Gantt chart. You express the time across the top and the tasks down along the left side. Indeed, you could use this device in college to help schedule and monitor the work you need to do to meet course requirements and deadlines (for papers, projects, and tests). A number of personal computer software packages can help you create and modify Gantt charts.

A Gantt chart may be used to compare planned time to complete a task with actual time taken to complete it, so that you can see how far ahead or behind schedule you are for the entire project. This enables you to make adjustments so as to hold the final target date.

Below is a Gantt chart for designing a cellphone app. The visual chart illustrates the tasks done and the plans for remaining tasks.

Stage of development	Week 1	Week 2	Week 3	Week 4	Week 5	Week 6
Review other cellphone apps	IIIIIIIIIIIIIIIIII					
Get content info for your app		IIIIIIIIIIIIIII				
Learn app programming tools		IIIIIIIIIIIIIII	IIIIIIIIIIIIIIII			
Create cellphone app				///////////	////////////	/////
"Publish" app online						////////

IIIIIIIIIIIIIIIIII Done   /////////// To be done

PERT Charts: Identifying Best Sequence of Production Activities

Although a Gantt chart can express the interrelations among the activities of relatively small projects, it becomes cumbersome and unwieldy when used for large, complex projects. More sophisticated management planning tools may be needed, such as PERT charts. A **PERT chart**—*PERT* stands for program evaluation and review technique—is a diagram for determining the best sequencing of tasks. Managers use PERT to analyze the tasks involved in completing a project and estimate the minimum time needed to complete each task, as well as the total time for the project.

Below is a PERT chart for setting up a photography show. This shows the time, in weeks, involved in finding submissions, an exhibit hall, and judges to evaluate the submissions and present awards.

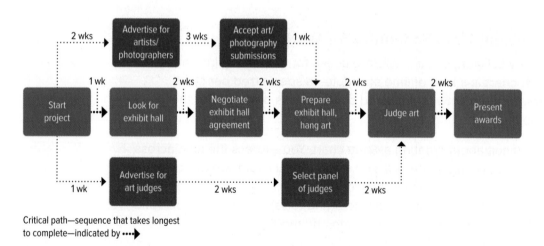

Critical path—sequence that takes longest to complete—indicated by ••••▶

Identify the Tasks

You identify the tasks required in the production process.

Arrange the Tasks in Order

You arrange the tasks in the order in which they must take place.

Estimate Time for Each Task

You estimate the time needed to complete each task.

Diagram the Task Sequences and Times

Using these steps, you draw a PERT diagram (called a PERT network). You can then compute the *critical path*.

Compute the Critical Path

In a PERT chart, the **critical path** is the sequence of tasks that takes the longest time to complete. In other words, the critical path will tell you the time expected to complete the project.

Decisions

Scheduling is such a crucial component to Ozark Design's operations that they have an entire department of three people assigned to these tasks.

1. The workers like using _____ to schedule the production process for dining room tables and chairs because it shows visuals of the tasks and when they need to be completed.

   A. Gantt charts

   B. PERT charts

   C. JIT charts

2. The scheduling staff want to switch to a(n) _____ chart because they believe it will help increase efficiency by identifying, arranging, estimating, and diagraming tasks. This will help them compute the critical path.

   A. Integrated Manufacturing Design (IMD)

   B. Gantt

   C. PERT

Correct Answers: 1. A; 2. C

Quality Assurance: Increasing Efficiency and Reducing Defects

By the end of this lesson, you will be able to:

- Recommend an optimal quality management approach.

The Answers May Be All Around Us

Using Staff Resources to Solve Problems

In the furniture business, quality is a crucial component to ensure happy customers and maintain a firm's reputation.

In this lesson, we'll learn about quality and quality control. Total quality management (TQM) is dedicated to continuous quality improvement, training, and customer satisfaction. It begins with the concept of quality, the total ability of a product or service to meet customer needs, and quality assurance, the strategy for minimizing errors by managing each stage of production. Three quality assurance techniques are the ISO 9000 series, statistical process control, and Six Sigma.

Jeremy recommended that we look into involving our staff even more as part of our quality assurance program.

Well, all our employees contribute a lot already to making sure Ozarks Design has the finest workmanship. What else can they do?

I don't know, but it was one of Jeremy's recommendations from his analysis of our workflow.

I guess you are right. I thought we would be able to act more quickly in moving and upgrading our facility. Every time I think we are ready, another hoop appears that we need to jump through.

Yes, it is hard not to be discouraged, but if our staff can help us have even higher quality, that's a hoop I am willing to jump through.

Good point. Let's get in touch with Jeremy again to find out more.

Eager to move forward, Owen and Walker are smart to make sure they follow the advice they sought. Often business owners decide to go it alone or ignore advice they have sought (and paid for) only to regret it later.

Total Quality Management: Seeking Continual Improvement

Quality refers to the total ability of a product or service to meet customer needs. The term refers to not only giving customers what they want but also reducing defects and errors before and after the product or service is delivered to them.

Whereas once quality inspections were done by a separate department at the end of a production line, today, in a strategy known as quality control, it is implemented throughout the entire process. **Quality assurance** is defined as the process of minimizing errors by managing each stage of production. Among other techniques, it relies on statistical sampling to locate errors by testing some of the items in a production run.

TQM: What It Is

The work of W. Edwards Deming and Joseph M. Juran has led to a strategic commitment to quality known as total quality management. Led by top management and supported throughout the organization, **total quality management (TQM)** is a comprehensive approach dedicated to continuous quality improvement, training, and customer satisfaction.

Continuous Improvement Is a Priority

TQM companies make small, incremental improvements an everyday priority in all areas of the organization. Continually improving everything a little bit of the time enables a TQM company to achieve long-term quality, efficiency, and customer satisfaction.

Every Employee Needs to Be Involved

TQM companies see that every employee is involved in the continuous improvement process. This means that workers must be empowered and trained to find and solve problems. The goal is to build teamwork, trust, and mutual respect.

Companies Learn from Customers, and Their Employees Learn from Other Employees

Successful companies pay attention to the people who use their products or services—the customers. Within the companies, employees listen and learn from other employees outside their own work areas.

Accurate Standards Are Used to Identify and Eliminate Problems

TQM organizations are always alert to how competitors do things better; then try to improve on them—a process known as benchmarking. **Benchmarking** is a process by which a company compares its performance with that of high-performing organizations.

Three Quality-Control Techniques: ISO 9000, Statistical Process Control, and Six Sigma

Companies now use a number of quality-control techniques to continually try to improve products and services. Here we discuss three of them: the *ISO 9000 series*, *statistical process control*, and *Six Sigma*.

ISO 9000 Series: Meeting Standards of Independent Experts

The **ISO 9000 series** consists of quality-assurance procedures companies must install—in purchasing, manufacturing, inventory, shipping, and other areas—that can be audited by "registrars," or independent quality-assurance experts. The goal of these procedures is to reduce flaws in manufacturing and to improve productivity, which requires stringent employee training. Companies also are required to document the procedures and comply with key ISO management standards, such as traceable changes and easy reporting.

Statistical Process Control: Testing with Periodic Random Samples

All kinds of products require periodic inspection during their manufacture: beer, hamburger meat, flashlight batteries, and so on. The method often used for this is **statistical process control**, a statistical technique that uses periodic random samples from production runs to see if quality is being maintained within a standard range of acceptability. If quality is not acceptable, production is halted to allow corrective action.

Six Sigma: Data-Driven Ways to Eliminate Defects

Six Sigma is a rigorous statistical analysis process that reduces defects in manufacturing and service-related processes. By testing thousands of variables in everything from product design to manufacturing to billing, a company using the process tries to improve quality and reduce waste to the point where errors nearly vanish.

Sigma is the Greek letter that statisticians use to define a standard deviation. The higher the sigma, the fewer the deviations from the norm—in other words, the fewer the defects. The attainment of Six Sigma means there are no more than 3.4 defects per million products or procedures. Six Sigma means being 99.9997% perfect.

Six Sigma is not necessarily perfect because it cannot compensate for human error or control events outside a company. Still, it lets managers approach problems with the assumption that there's a data-oriented, tangible way to solve problems.

Decisions

Walker and Owen want to integrate more quality assurance into their business. They discuss how they are going to approach the process.

> I'd like to get our leads together and brainstorm with them about how we can make getting better an everyday priority.

> Yes! This is a component of _____.
>
> **A.** total quality management (TQM)
>
> **B.** Six Sigma engineering
>
> **C.** ISO 14000

> Another key component I would like us to go after is getting every employee involved and have them be part of a process where we learn from customers and each other.

Yes, then we can work together to determine the standards and create _____ that meet our expectations.

    A. benchmarks

    B. new standards

    C. a total quality system

I'd like for us and some of our staff to attend some training to become certified in _____, so we can have nearly flawless production.

    A. Six Sigma

    B. ISO 9000

    C. total quality management (TQM)

Correct Answers: A; A; A

Operations Management: Test

1. Kripa runs a candle-making business where she turns homemade wax into scented candles. The process of creating the candles is best described as

   A. input.

   B. mechanization.

   C. production.

   D. capital.

   E. service.

2. Oscar is a kitchen and bathroom design and construction specialist. Considering his business in the context of operations, the tools, and raw materials he uses would best be classified as

   A. logistics.

   B. services.

   C. outputs.

   D. value.

   E. inputs.

3. Which is the best example of a manufacturing business?

   A. a dairy farm

   B. a computer repair company

   C. a cell phone provider

   D. a car wash

   E. a bookstore

4. Nene is hired by XYZ Auto to oversee the process by which steel, plastic, and other materials are converted into new cars. Nene most likely works in a(n) _____ business.

   A. knowledge

   B. manufacturing

   C. analytic

   D. resource

   E. service

5. Thompson Company creates trailer hitches for cars and trucks as customer orders dictate. At a meeting, the CEO asks the Operations Manager to consider shifting from an intermittent production process to a continuous production process to increase output and profit. Which of the following would be the best response?

   A. This is not a good idea. We are better suited to utilize an intermittent process so that we can continue to manufacture different products as needed.

   B. This is a great idea. If we use a continuous process, it will be easier to utilize a synthetic transformation process.

   C. This is a great idea. Businesses that utilize a continuous production process are nearly always more profitable than those using intermittent processes. This is due to increased output.

   D. This is not a good idea. Continuous production processes take away the ability to maximize the analytic transformation process.

   E. This is not a good idea. Using a continuous production process will require us to add an updated CAM system.

6. Businesses have reached a point where mass production is possible. The primary benefit of mass production is the ability to

   A. implement flexible manufacturing systems.

   B. reduce labor and raw material costs.

   C. produce similar goods in large quantities.

   D. rely solely on robotics to perform assembly operations.

   E. eliminate the need for computer-integrated manufacturing.

7. Using a sole supplier allows a company to

   A. implement just-in-time inventory control.

   B. add a supply-chain management system.

   C. increase their form utility.

   D. reduce the exposure of proprietary secrets.

   E. decrease inventory and the need for warehouse space.

8. Alexis is working on a project to determine how many supplies and resources are needed for her business. She wants to keep track of quantities on hand, each item's location in the warehouse, and which products it is used for. Alexis is analyzing the _____ process.

   A. enterprise resource

   B. trusted supplier

   C. process layout

   D. inventory control

   E. product layout

9. Keen Ear is going to begin manufacturing cellular phones. The company decides to use just two different suppliers for its power cables. Which reason best describes the company's rationale for making that decision?

   A. ability to eliminate their inventory control system

   B. greater reliability in receiving the product

   C. enhance Gantt chart effectiveness

   D. simplify the management of their product and process layouts

   E. ability to easily utilize a backup supplier if needed

10. A successful supply-chain management system will integrate which of the following items?

    A. production managers with ISO 9000 registrars

    B. facilities, functions, and processes

    C. CAD, ERP, and MRP computer systems

    D. internal benchmarking data to external PERT and Gantt analyses

    E. trusted suppliers with one another

11. Forrester Shipping is designing a new supply-chain management system. What would be the most important consideration the company should make as it begins this process?

    A. shift to a sole supplier system for raw materials

    B. reduce fixed-layout processes

    C. begin phasing out current just-in-time inventory controls

    D. ensure that its suppliers are involved in the design process

    E. review and update all ISO 9000 standards

12. Why are Gantt charts and PERT diagrams are useful to companies?

    A. They ensure the correct process layout is implemented.

    B. They simplify the bill of materials for a project.

    C. They help ensure that projects are completed on time.

    D. They create an accurate estimate of project cost.

    E. They help outline project responsibilities.

13. TempStar utilizes a company-wide plan that focuses on regular quality improvement, training, and customer satisfaction. This is best described as an example of

   A. total quality management.

   B. ISO 9000 analysis.

   C. Six Sigma benchmarking.

   D. statistical process control.

   E. supply-chain management.

14. What would be the most important aspect of a successful total quality management program?

   A. a focus on replying to supplier feedback

   B. regular analysis of ERP systems

   C. listening and learning from customers and employees

   D. annual PERT analyses

   E. sole supplier system

15. ISO 9000 procedures are best used for

   A. statistical process control and reporting functions.

   B. inventory and production departments.

   C. auditing and benchmarking services.

   D. enterprise resource and materials requirement planning systems.

   E. external supplier and customer shipping teams.

16. Altomotive is implementing the statistical process control technique at their production facility. The QA Director needs to provide an overview of the testing process. Which of the following would be his best response?

   A. testing a minimum of 3.4 samples and measuring against TQM ratings

   B. hiring registrars to test weekly results and compare with benchmarking figures

   C. random sampling throughout each production run to compare with standard acceptability ranges

   D. scheduled production reviews where samples are compared to Six Sigma standards

   E. constant monitoring of production and comparing with ERP recommendations

17. As a quality control technique, Six Sigma is not a perfect system because it

   A. is not able to compensate for human error.

   B. requires a company to hire independent quality assurance experts.

   C. requires ISO registrars to conduct rigorous inspections on an annual basis.

   D. will render a company's enterprise resource planning system obsolete.

   E. renders current benchmarking calculations obsolete.

18. Shizuka runs a pig farm. She sells the pigs to a butcher who slaughters the pigs and turns them into bacon, pork chops, and ham. This example best describes the _____ process.

   A. continuous transformation

   B. analytic transformation

   C. synthetic transformation

   D. mass customization

   E. flexible manufacturing

19. Vertex Bicycles manufactures a wide variety of bikes, including bikes made for children and for adults, standard to stationary bikes, and bikes with one to three wheels. It can manufacture each bike on the same assembly line by making slight modifications to its production computer. Vertex is most likely using

A. supply-chain management.

B. lean manufacturing.

C. just-in-time inventory controls.

D. flexible manufacturing system.

E. materials requirement planning.

20. Angular Technology holds regular meetings for designated members of the various teams around the company. Members of leadership, finance, human resources, sales, technology, product development, and automation all attend and share recent wins and recent concerns with one another. This example best describes a key component of

A. synthetic transformation management.

B. process improvement review.

C. total quality management.

D. program evaluation review.

E. supply-chain management.

5 Human Resource Management and Labor Relations

What To Expect

By the end of the chapter, you will be able to:

- Apply workplace legislation to a business scenario.

Chapter Topics

- **5-1** Laws and Human Resource Management
- **5-2** Recruiting, Selection, and Onboarding
- **5-3** Training and Development
- **5-4** Performance Appraisal
- **5-5** Reward Systems
- **5-6** Labor Relations

Copyright © McGraw Hill Shift Drive/Shutterstock.

Laws and Human Resource Management

Taking Wing at Seagull

Why Is Human Resource Management Important?

Dylan Silverman is a people person. Fresh out of college with a BA in business management, he's attracted to a career in **human resource (HR) management**, which consists of the activities managers perform to obtain and maintain an effective workforce to assist organizations in achieving goals. HR checks all his boxes—Dylan likes the idea of shaping a company's direction through its employees, welcoming new hires, and helping employees grow.

So, when Seagull Air, a major airline with a great reputation, hires Dylan as its HR department's summer intern, he jumps at the chance to learn about HR management and labor relations in a major industry. Dylan's Seagull Air internship requires him to rotate around departments, shadowing employees as he learns about various aspects of HR at Seagull.

On Dylan's first day, Yuki Kihana, his supervisor, meets with him to discuss his new position.

We're pleased to have you with us, Dylan. Seagull Air has built its reputation on the strength of its employees. Now that you're one of us, we're looking forward to you helping us help them.

I'm ready. Seagull has a great employee culture. The turnover rate here is super low.

You've done your research. So why do you think people keep working at Seagull Air year after year?

I'd say it's the way Seagull's HR management handles employee relations.

In what way do you think we're doing a good job?

Let's see. Some other airlines try to cut corners—slashing the number of crew members on long flights, for one thing. Seagull doesn't do that.

True. If we're going to recruit the next generation of pilots, flight attendants, ground personnel, and customer service reps, we have to show we value our employees.

That's impressive.

To my mind, the key goals of HR management are attracting and developing an effective and engaged workforce. What you learn here will carry over into any HR management job you'll have in the future. So—bad pun alert—get ready to take flight!

Yuki Kihana is happy about having Dylan on board as a summer intern. He demonstrates the people skills and desire to help others that make for a good HR manager. But he wonders: will he still feel the same way about his career choice after exploring the complex HR challenges facing the airline industry?

In this lesson, you'll learn about laws that support employee well-being.

What Laws Protect Employee Well-Being?

Employers and their employees enter into an ongoing relationship. But it isn't built on mutual trust alone. Over the years, laws have been put in place to protect the rights and safety of employees.

Dylan's supervisor Yuki has told him that a major reason he was attracted to a career in HR is that he can help companies support employee rights and safety by staying within the laws designed to protect workers. To get him acquainted with these laws, Yuki gives him information on the four major areas of employment law: labor relations, compensation and benefits, workplace health and safety, and equal employment opportunity.

Labor Relations

Labor relations focuses on employee welfare. This typically refers to the relationship between management and labor unions. Part of working in labor relations involves **collective bargaining**, which consists of negotiations between management and employees in disputes over compensation, benefits, working conditions, and job security. A number of acts relate to labor relations:

- The 1935 Wagner Act created the **National Labor Relations Board**, which enforces procedures allowing employees to vote to have a union and the rules for collective bargaining.
- The 1947 Taft-Hartley Act allows the president of the United States to prevent or end a strike that threatens national security.

Compensation and Benefits

Compensation and benefits typically refers to laws and administration around workers' hours, pay, and benefits. A number of acts relate to compensation and benefits:

- The 1935 Social Security Act created the U.S. retirement system.
- The 1938 Fair Labor Standards Act established a federal minimum wage and a maximum workweek, along with banning products from child labor. Executive, administrative, and professional employees who earn salaries rather than hourly wages are exempt from overtime rules.
- The 1993 Family and Medical Leave Act requires employers to allow employees to take up to 12 weeks of unpaid leave for childbirth, adoption, or family emergencies.

Workplace Health and Safety

Workplace health and safety focuses on ensuring employees have environments to work in that are safe.

- Since 1970, with the passage of the Occupational Safety and Health Act (OSHA), a number of laws have been created that prohibit organizations from forcing employees to endure hazardous working conditions.

- Among the safety regulations brought about by OSHA are required guards on machinery with moving parts; maximum exposure limits to certain chemicals; extended use of personal protective equipment, such as gloves and respirators; and rules regarding exposure to asbestos.

Equal Employment Opportunity

Equal employment opportunity focuses on ensuring that all people have opportunity and are treated fairly in the workplace.

Attempts to reduce **discrimination** in employment based on racial, ethnic, and religious bigotry and gender stereotypes began with Title VII of the Civil Rights Act of 1964. This law created the **Equal Employment Opportunity (EEO) Commission**, which is charged with enforcing antidiscrimination and other employment-related laws. Title VII applies to all organizations or their agents engaged in an industry affecting interstate commerce that employs 15 or more employees, including contractors doing business with the U.S. government. Other laws were added later preventing discrimination against older workers and people with physical and mental disabilities.

Discrimination

Discrimination is judged to happen when people are hired or promoted—or denied hiring or promotion—for reasons not relevant to the job, such as skin color, gender, religion, sexual orientation, or national origin. People who have been discriminated against may sue for back-pay and punitive damages.

Affirmative Action

Affirmative action aims at achieving equality of opportunity within an organization. To try to make up for past discrimination in employment, affirmative action programs actively try to find, hire, and develop the talents of people from groups traditionally discriminated against. Steps include active recruitment, removal of prejudicial questions in interviews, and creation of minority hiring goals, but they do not include hiring quotas, which are illegal.

Sexual Harassment

Sexual harassment consists of unwanted sexual attention that creates an adverse work environment. Offensive acts range from physical nonsexual contact, unwanted touching, suggestive remarks, unwanted dating pressure, and sex-stereotyped jokes to obscene gestures, sexually oriented posters and graffiti, sexual propositions, obscene phone calls, and threats of retaliation unless sexual favors are given.

A term often associated with sexual harassment is *quid pro quo*, which in Latin means "this for that" and often refers to a person being put in a position of having to do or not do something to gain something such as a raise or promotion *or* not lose their job.

Hostile Work Environment

In a hostile work environment, the person being sexually harassed experiences an offensive or intimidating work environment but doesn't risk economic harm.

Another Behavior: Bullying

Another behavior that contributes to a negative work environment is bullying. Bullying itself is not illegal, but it brings down productivity and morale. Committed by supervisors or fellow employees, bullying includes:

- Cursing
- Unwarranted criticism
- Imposing unrealistic deadlines

Decisions

Dylan knows safety is a big concern at Seagull Air. The company is focusing on making the jobs of its ground crews safer. To that end, HR wants to conduct a job hazard analysis, a technique that pinpoints the potential dangers of job tasks.

Windsor Duke is a new HR manager at Seagull. Safety is one of her highest priorities. As a first step in beginning a job hazard analysis, she assigns Dylan to watch a ramp supervisor, Javier Contreras, perform his job tasks, then list each step.

Good luck keeping up with me, kid. I clean the cabin, maintain the ramp, handle the cargo loader. I'm crawling all over that plane.

No problem. I'll try not to get in your way.

Back at Windsor Duke's office, Dylan shares his list of steps the ramp supervisor takes to perform his job tasks.

Did you review the steps with Mr. Contreras and discuss what he sees as possible hazards?

Yes. He also had ideas for solutions. I noted them down.

Great. We want to involve our employees in making their workplace safer. Your work will help me find solutions that will protect our ground crew team.

1. Which law applies to the job analysis Dylan contributed to?

   A. Fair Labor Standards Act

   B. Occupational Safety and Health Act

   C. Family Medical Leave Act

   D. Civil Rights Act

Correct Answers: 1. B

Lesson 5-2

Recruiting, Selection, and Onboarding

By the end of this lesson, you will be able to:

- Differentiate between a job analysis, job specification, and job description.
- Differentiate between internal and external recruiting.
- Summarize the three types of selection tools.
- Summarize the onboarding process.

Who's the Best Fit for the Job?

How Do You Find the Best Employees for the Future?

Dylan Silverman's internship continues with a session in the recruitment department. An organization's value includes its **human capital**, which refers to the productive potential of employee experience, knowledge, and actions. One of the key value-adds of HR is **staffing**, which involves the recruitment, hiring, motivating, and retention of valuable employees.

Part of Judy Sterner's job as an HR specialist at Seagull Air is deciding what kinds of employees will help achieve Seagull's vision and standards for excellence. Currently, she is looking to fill pilot positions. She asks Dylan to come to her office to chat.

I'm curious, Dylan. What do you think it takes to be a good airplane pilot?

I'm guessing pilots have to be calm in stressful situations, just in case something goes wrong.

This is a definite. The safety of our passengers and crew is our number one priority. What else would you put on your list?

I would think they need to be good leaders.

Right. Anything else?

Expertise and knowledge. No second thoughts at 40,000 feet up.

Definitely. Pilots tend to spend a lot of time practicing in real planes as well as in simulators. You see, Dylan, we have an awesome responsibility; we need to recruit, hire, develop, and retain the best pilots in the industry. People who travel every day are counting on us to get them safely to their destination no matter what.

Dylan's internship is entering the phase of HR management he's most interested in: recruitment. In this lesson, you'll learn how Seagull Air attracts, selects, and welcomes aboard its most valuable resource, human capital.

Determining Your Company's Needs

As Dylan works with Judy, he learns that to attract the best employees for the future, managers need to engage in the process of analyzing, describing, and specifying what is required by each position.

Step	Definition	Example
Job Analysis	Determines the basic elements of a job, using observation and analysis	The manager interviews job occupants about what they do, observes the flow of work, and learns how results are accomplished.
Job Description	Outlines what the holders of the job do and how and why they do it	The manager translates the job analysis into a description of the position.
Job Specification	Describes the minimum qualifications people must have to perform the job successfully	The manager goes a bit deeper and carves out the specific requirements for someone to perform well in the position.

Decisions

Dylan is reviewing various employment materials.

1. "We are looking to hire individuals who wake up thinking how we can "WOW" our customer. To be eligible for the role an individual must be able to travel 5 days of the week and have flexibility to work days, nights, weekends, and holidays."

   Which of the following best describes the following from a draft for a Flight Crew Position?

   A. Job analysis

   B. Job specifications

   C. Job description

2. The airline has determined the minimum qualifications for an Airport Customer Representative, which read as follows:

   Three years of customer service experience, the individual may need to lift up to 50 lbs occasionally, they must pocess computer skills, have the ability to communicate effectively with customers, have keen attention to detail, and be excellent at problem solving. These are the minium requirements to be qualified for the position.

   By creating the minium qualifications HR has set the _____.

   A. job specifications

   B. job description

   C. job analysis

3. HR recently spoke with some of their best pilots about their position. They learned the most successful pilots have between 7–10 years of commercial airline experience flying Boeing 747's. They also consistently heard pilot's need to have leadership skills, be able to operate in high stress environment, and be great communicators.

   Which of the following best describes the work HR was engaging in by collecting this information from the pilots?

   A. Job analysis

   B. Job specifications

   C. Job description

Correct Answers: 1. C; 2. A; 3. A

The Recruiting Process: How Companies Look for Qualified Applicants

Recruiting is the process by which companies find and attract qualified applicants for open jobs. Of course, companies want to find people whose characteristics, abilities, and skills are best suited to the organization—who are, in a word, *qualified*. There are two types of recruiting: *internal* and *external*.

Internal Recruiting

Internal recruiting refers to making employees who already work for the organization aware of job openings. The principal avenue by which companies let employees know of job openings is through internal **job postings**—putting information about job vacancies on company intranet websites, bulletin boards, and newsletters. Companies also rely on referrals by current employees.

Advantages

- It fosters greater effort and loyalty because employees realize that staying with the organization and working hard may result in more opportunities.

- It is less expensive than the standard recruiting process (which involves advertising, interviewing, and so on).

- Internal candidates are already known to the organization and so there is less risk they won't work out.

Disadvantages

- It limits the pool of fresh talent and different viewpoints.

- It leads employees to assume that longevity and seniority alone will lead to promotion.

- When a job is filled, the person filling it leaves another job to be filled within the organization.

External Recruiting

External recruiting refers to attracting job applicants from outside the organization. Job vacancies are often listed through career websites such as indeed.com, professional networking sites like LinkedIn, employment agencies (for both full and temporary employment), executive recruiting firms (so-called *head hunters*), media ads, job-placement offices, technical training schools, job fairs, and union hiring halls.

Advantages

- Applicants may have needed specialized knowledge and experience.

- Applicants may have fresh viewpoints that they can bring to the organization.

Disadvantages

- Hiring from outside is more expensive and takes longer than internal recruiting.

- The risks are higher because the persons hired are less well known.

Decisions

Dylan and Judy are discussing a recruiting plan for a couple of positions. Fill in the dialog with the best term.

Judy, I'm looking at our job descriptions and I know we have to hire a number of customer service reps in a short amount of time. I think an _____ recruiting strategy would be best as it would promote some people from within, strengthening their commitment to the company while keeping our cost low, and allowing us to quickly fill the spots.

   A. internal

   B. external

I agree, Dylan. What do you think about some of these senior-level positions in marketing?

For those, I think we should use an _____ strategy because in creative areas it may be good to get fresh eyes and a solid pool of candidates with specialized marketing knowledge.

   A. internal

   B. external

Even if it takes a bit longer and costs a bit more?

Yes, I think it's the right move.

I think you're right too.

Correct Answers: A; B

Choosing the Best from the Rest: From Selection to Onboarding

Based on a company's recruiting efforts, the next phase is the **selection process**, which screens job applicants to hire the best candidate. There are three types of selection tools: background information (such as résumés), interviews, and employment tests. It's important for HR professionals to ensure that the selection tools they are utilizing are both **valid** and **reliable**.

Background Information: Résumés

Background Information: Résumés, Applications, Reference Checks, Credit Checks, and Checks on Legal Status

Résumés and application forms provide basic background information about job applicants, such as citizenship, education, work history, and certifications. Some companies resort to computer prescreening, which job seekers must pass before obtaining an in-person interview.

Interviewing

Interviewing: Unstructured or Structured

Once applicants have cleared all the foregoing hurdles, they face the commonly used selection technique known as interviewing, which may take place face to face, by videoconferencing, or via phone. To help deter bias, interviews can be designed, conducted, and evaluated by a committee of three or four people. Interviewing may be either *unstructured or structured*.

In an **unstructured interview**, the interviewer simply asks applicants probing questions in a conversational way; there are no identical, fixed questions asked of all applicants and no systematic scoring of answers.

In a **structured interview**, the interviewer asks each applicant the same identical, fixed questions and rates their responses according to some standard measure, such as a five-point rating scale ranging from "excellent" to "poor."

Employment Tests

Employment Tests: Performance, Ability, Personality, and Other

From a legal standpoint, **employment tests** consist of any procedure used in the employment selection decision process. This includes not only traditional paper-and-pencil, performance, and physical-ability tests but also application forms, interviews, and educational and experience requirements.

Among the most common employment tests are the following:

Performance tests: These measure performance on actual job tasks, such as typing.

Ability tests: These measure physical abilities, such as strength and stamina or mechanical abilities.

Personality tests: These measure personality traits, such as sociability, adjustment, independence, and need for achievement.

Other tests: Examples are tests for lies (using polygraphs) and for drugs (a new test is the hair test, which can detect drug use for a period of up to 90 days).

Onboarding Activities

Working with Judy, Dylan learns that at most companies, including Seagull Air, once an employee is hired, the first 30 to 90 days of the initial socialization period is designed to give new employees the information they need to be effective.

This includes the process of of **onboarding**, which is designed to help the newcomer fit smoothly into the job and the organization.

Judy tells Dylan that company onboarding includes a discussion of the following:

- The **job routine**—what is required in the job for which he or she was hired, how the work will be evaluated, and who the immediate coworkers and managers are.

- The **organization's mission and operations**—including the purpose, products, operations, and history of the organization.

  ▶ The **work rules**—procedures and matters of law (such as those prohibiting sexual harassment) affecting work operations that every employee should be made aware of.

  ▶ The **employee benefits**—the benefits to which employees are entitled, such as a health insurance plan.

Decisions

Judy and Dylan are going over several applicants who are at different stages in the selection process. Choose the stage that best fits the description in the conversation.

> Okay, Dylan. First we have Sam. We need to get her scheduled to come in and meet with the hiring manager.

I can reach out to her and see if we can get her in Tuesday or Wednesday afternoon.

    A. Background information

    B. Interview

    C. Employment test

Great. Then reach out to Aaron—he is the hiring manager—and make sure he has our company-approved questions and scoring measurements.

    A. Employment test

    B. Structured interview

    C. Background information

    D. Unstructured interview

Got it!

Next we have this stack of applicants. These folks have gone through the process. We just need to reach out and talk to a few of their former employers to validate what they told us.

    A. Interview

    B. Background information

    C. Referral

    D. Employment test

Lastly, we have the results from our pilot simulation test, so we need to enter those into the applicant tracking system

    A. Structured interview

    B. Background information

    C. Unstructured interview

    D. Employment test

Correct Answers: B; B; B; D

Training and Development

By the end of this lesson, you will be able to:

- Summarize orientation, training, and development strategies.

Filling in Knowledge Gaps

Employees as Lifelong Learners

A change in how Seagull Air's ground crews service the airline's ramps has resulted in an uptick in accidents. HR management believes additional safety training will help.

Majid Patel in HR is in charge of employee training and development. He asks to meet with Dylan.

I'd like you to write an e-mail to our ground crew employees announcing our new training on ramp maintenance.

Happy to help. What are the top issues you'd like me to focus on?

Basically, when a procedure changes, more accidents tend to occur. I'd like your e-mail to focus on Seagull's desire for employees to slow down as they get used to the new methods—no short cuts. I'd also like you to make clear that our training doesn't mean employees are doing something wrong. Training gives employees tools for getting things right. Finally, remind people that the training's main goal is keeping workers safe. Does that make sense?

Yes. Will do. I'll get a draft ready for you to review ASAP.

Dylan is excited about presenting the new training program in the e-mail he will be crafting. He hopes it will improve safety.

Employees can miss out on knowledge that could help them do their jobs. In this lesson, we'll learn about the training and development programs that bridge gaps and improve employee performance, productivity, and safety.

Training and Developing the Team

Interning in HR management at Seagull Air has Dylan thinking about his future in the field. He's already been *shadowing* HR employees. He wonders whether he should also look for a mentor among the people he's been shadowing. **Mentoring** describes the process in which an experienced employee, the *mentor*, supervises, teaches, and provides guidance for a less-experienced employee, the *mentee* or *protégé*.

Dylan has also quickly learned the necessity of strong company **training and development**, which are the steps the organization takes to increase employee performance and productivity. As he has learned, training can come in several forms including **on-the-job training** and **off-the-job training**.

On-the-Job Training

On-the-job training takes place in the workplace while employees are working on job-related tasks. Three types of on-the-job training are *shadowing*, like that Dylan has experienced, *apprenticeship*, and *job rotation*.

Type of Training	Definition
Shadowing	An employee being trained on the job learns skills by watching more experienced employees perform their jobs
Apprenticeship	A training program in which a new employee works with an experienced employee to master a particular craft
Job Rotation	Consists of rotating employees through different assignments in different departments to give them a broader picture of the organization

Off-the-Job Training

Off-the-job training, on the other hand, consists of training that employees receive when they are not in the workplace. This includes such things as:

- Classroom programs
- Videos
- Workbooks
- Online distance learning programs

One specific type of off-the-job training is **vestibule training**, training that occurs in a simulated environment. This type of training would be particularly helpful for pilots, for example, as they are learning how to fly aircraft.

Decisions

Now that you know a bit more about training and developing a team, match the correct type of training and development with its example at Seagull Air.

1. A new flight attendant works with a more experienced flight attendant to master the job requirements, including helping customers find their seats and stow their bags efficiently and without conflicts.

    A. Shadowing

    B. Job rotation

    C. Online learning

2. A new customer service rep takes a course from her desktop computer on good customer relations in the airline industry.

    A. Online learning

    B. Shadowing

    C. Job rotation

3. A new HR manager follows different employees, from ground crew members to pilots, and documents their daily tasks to gain insight into how to recruit and to write job descriptions for various positions at Seagull Air and get a broader picture of the company.

    A. Online learning

    B. Job rotation

    C. Shadowing

Correct Answers: 1. A; 2. A; 3. B

Performance Appraisal

By the end of this lesson, you will be able to:

- Determine the appropriate type of performance appraisal for a business case.
- Apply the steps of a performance appraisal to a business case.
- Describe effective ways to deliver and receive performance feedback.

How Am I Doing?

Performance Appraisals Can Help

Interning for Seagull Air's HR department means Dylan's performance will be reviewed. Yuki Kihana has a creative approach to his performance appraisal.

Dylan is thrown off by being asked to evaluate his own job performance. But the more he thinks about it, the more he appreciates the opportunity to think critically about his work. It will help him become a better employee. And who knows, it might help future interns at Seagull Air, as well.

In this lesson, we'll explore performance appraisals. A performance appraisal is a manager's assessment of an employee's performance. As a manager, how should you handle employee evaluations, and how should you handle receiving

You're serious? I can review my own performance?

Absolutely. We'd like you to rate your own job performance as our summer intern thus far. I'll also evaluate your performance, but a self-appraisal will get you more involved in the evaluation process.

Wow. I've never rated my own job performance before. I promise not to give myself stellar marks in every category. I'll try my best to be objective.

Just try to be as accurate as possible. And it's certainly OK if you give yourself a favorable review after careful consideration. This is just a tool to get you thinking about your job in general, including any areas that might need improvement.

evaluations of your own work performance? Giving evaluations requires tact, while dealing with negative reviews from your manager requires a positive mindset. Human resources can assist managers companywide with the delicate process of appraising an employee's performance.

Types of Performance Appraisals

After asking Dylan to do a self-appraisal, Yuki spends some time telling him about the purposes of performance appraisals and the different kinds they conduct at Seagull Air.

A **performance appraisal** (or **performance review**) is a manager's assessment of an employee's performance. Performance appraisals have two purposes:

1. They help employees understand how they are doing in relation to objectives and standards; here the manager must *judge* the employee.

2. They help employees in their training and personal development; here the manager must *counsel* the employee.

Note that each organization may develop its own performance appraisal process. However, the key elements include:

1. Choosing a performance appraisal format

2. Executing on the format

3. Ensuring timely feedback

4. Staying consistent with the process

Performance Appraisal Formats

A number of different kinds of performance appraisals exist.

Formal Versus Informal

Formal appraisals are conducted at scheduled times of the year and are based on pre-established performance measures.

Informal appraisals are conducted at unscheduled times and consist of less rigorous indications of employee performance.

Objective Versus Subjective

Objective appraisals are based on facts and are often based on numbers related to employees.

Subjective appraisals represent a manager's perceptions of a subordinate's traits or behaviors.

Benefits

- They measure results.
- They are harder to challenge for bias.

Approaches

- *Trait appraisals* look at subjective attributes such as "attitude" and "initiative."
- *Behavioral appraisals* measure specific, observable aspects of performance—on-time attendance, for instance—although making the evaluation is still somewhat subjective.

Self-Assessments

In a **self-assessment**, employees rank their own performance, as Yuki asked Dylan to do. Such appraisals can serve to motivate employees to become involved in the evaluation process and may make them more receptive to feedback about areas needing improvement.

360-Degree Assessments

In a **360-degree assessment**, employees are appraised not only by their managers but also by their coworkers, subordinates, and sometimes customers or clients, thus providing several perspectives.

Typically in this kind of assessment, an employee chooses 6 to 12 other people to fill out anonymous forms, the ratings are tabulated, and the employee and his or her manager go over the results to develop a long-term plan for the employee's performance goals.

Forced Ranking Performance Review Systems

Forced ranking performance review systems are those in which all employees within a business unit are ranked against one another, and grades are distributed along some sort of bell curve. Top grade earners are then rewarded with bonuses and promotions, and low grade earners are warned or dismissed.

Giving Effective Performance Feedback

As they discuss performance reviews, Yuki gives Dylan some tips for managers giving a performance appraisal should he ever become a manager:

Think of Yourself as a Counselor or a Coach

Managers who must give feedback to employees on their job performance can overcome their hesitation to appear critical and fault-finding if they think of themselves as counselors, or even as athletic coaches. The purpose is not to find fault, which may only undermine employee confidence. Instead, the goal is to show them how to improve.

Be Respectful

When giving feedback, treat the employee with respect and avoid criticism. Describe to the employee how he or she is performing well and not well and give evidence.

Use Facts Rather Than Impressions and Be Specific

Facts should always be used rather than impressions. Be specific in describing performance and desired improvements. Managers are sometimes advised to keep diaries about specific incidents so they won't have to rely on their memories (and so that their evaluations will be more lawsuit-resistant).

Get the Employee's Ideas

Don't make it a one-way conversation; get the employee's own ideas. Employees are more satisfied with their performance appraisal when they are allowed to state their opinions during their appraisal.

Receiving Performance Feedback

Yuki also provides Dylan with some tips on how to handle criticism during a performance review:

Take Time to Think about the Review before You React

Give yourself time to process the review and how you want to respond to it.

Ask Your Managers for Details

Also ask about specific ways that you can improve your performance in the future.

Create an Action Plan and Provide Status Reports

Demonstrate to your manager that you are taking the feedback seriously and are actively improving your performance.

Decisions

Dylan is sitting in on an appraisals with several managers to see how they use the different approaches. Choose the approach being described in each scenario.

1. In the first session, Carl, a pilot, is being evaluated using the company's standard system for rating pilots based on numbers related to their performance. He has such an evaluation every quarter. Which kind of appraisal is this?

   A. Informal

   B. 360

   C. Formal

   D. Forced Ranking

2. Carl's appraisal is employing which approach?

    A. Objective

    B. Subjective

    C. 360

    D. Forced Ranking

3. Next, Dylan sits in on a performance review of Carla, who leads the advertising and sales team. She is responsible for selling advertisements to sponsors for their in-flight magazines as well as other advertising efforts. Her manager evaluates her performance by talking to her subordinates, coworkers, managers, and customers. She is receiving what type of evaluation?

    A. Self Review

    B. Informal

    C. 360

    D. Forced Ranking

4. The HR team is discussing whether they should use a performance review system that grades employees based on their customer service, with the bottom 5% of performers being automatically fired. They ultimately decide against this approach. What is the approach they are discussing?

    A. Informal

    B. 360

    C. Self Review

    D. Forced Ranking

Correct Answers: 1. C; 2. A; 3. C; 4. D

Lesson 5-5
Reward Systems

By the end of this lesson, you will be able to:

- Implement a compensation and/or reward strategy for an employee that relies on appropriate motivation.

- Determine which of the four types of employee movement is the most appropriate action in a business case.

Compensating, Promoting, and Disciplining

Tough Go or Grow Decisions

Gus Cintra, a marketing manager, pays a visit to the HR department. He needs Yuki's assistance with his department.

Hi Gus. I understand you have a few items you wanted to discuss about your department.

Yes, I've got a number of employees asking about their pay and about whether we're going to get bonuses and incentives this year.

I totally understand. I'm going to send out updated information about this year's program in the next week. If we keep getting great results, your team will reap the rewards of their hard work.

Let's schedule a time for me to come in and we'll talk to each person about them.

Great. I've also got a few employees asking about job sharing, and a couple more on the support team wondering about our flextime and telecommuting options.

Copyright © McGraw Hill

Great! Also, I just wrapped up my performance evaluations. I've got some folks who I think are well suited for promotion, I had one request a transfer, and unfortunately I've got a couple that need to go through the discipline process, we may even need to let them go.

Well that is the good, the bad, and the ugly of HR. Let's tackle those cases one at a time and see what's the best approach.

Dylan is impressed by his boss's ability to handle so many HR situations. He knows that if he wants a career in HR, he needs to understand compensation and benefits, as well as be able to help managers address employee issues, both positive or negative.

The main reason most people work, of course, is for *compensation*. In this lesson, we'll recognize that compensation is more than money. An HR manager, needs to understand compensation, which includes base pay (wages or salaries), benefits, and incentives. HR managers must also deal with the movement and replacement of employees, such as promoting, transferring, suspending, demoting, laying off, or firing.

Compensation Is More Than Money

After Gus leaves, Yuki and Dylan discuss various aspects of compensation and motivation. He explains that compensation consists of three categories: *base pay*, *benefits*, and *incentives*.

Base Pay: Wages or Salaries

Base pay consists of the basic wage or salary workers are paid for doing their jobs.

The base pay is arrived at by looking at the prevailing industry pay levels, what competitors are paying in a given location, whether the jobs are unionized, whether the jobs are hazardous, and the employees' rank and experience.

Benefits: Nonwage or Nonsalary Compensation

Benefits, or *fringe benefits* or *perquisites* ("perqs" or "perks"), are nonwage or nonsalary forms of compensation paid for by the organization for its employees.

Examples are paid holidays, vacations, sick leave, family leave, insurance (health, dental,

life), and pension plans, as well as discounts on company merchandise, country club memberships, and so on.

Incentives: Inducements to Employee Productivity

Incentives, such as commissions, bonuses, profit-sharing plans, and stock options, induce employees to be more productive and attract and retain top performers.

Pay for Performance

Pay for performance bases pay on the employee's work results.

Different salaried employees might get different pay raises, promotions, and other rewards depending on their overall job performance.

- One standard pay-for-performance plan is payment at a **piece rate**, in which employees are paid according to how much output they produce.

- Another is the **sales commission**, in which salespeople are paid a percentage of the earnings the company made from their sales.

Bonuses

Bonuses are cash awards given to employees who achieve particular performance objectives.

Unlike commissions, bonuses are not computed simply as a percentage of sales but also may be calculated according to the employee's rank in the organization and years of employment.

Profit Sharing

Profit sharing is sharing a percentage of the company's profits with employees.

Shares are apportioned to individual employees according to such criteria as performance, attendance, and lateness.

Stock Options

With **stock options**, key employees are given the right to buy stock at a future date for a discounted price.

The motivator here is that employees holding stock options will supposedly work hard to make the company's stock rise so that they can make a larger profit when they sell their shares obtained at a cheaper price.

Gainsharing

Gainsharing is the distribution of savings or "gains" to groups of employees that reduced costs and increased measurable productivity.

The idea with gainsharing is when the organization wins, the group wins.

Noncompensation Strategies

So far, we have discussed compensation-based strategies to compensate and motivate employees. But employees are motivated by more than just a good salary and benefits. They also feel motivated by other rewards employers offer, such as bonuses for superior work, flexible hours, or the chance to work from home. Companies have found that what is good for morale is also good for the organization.

Part-Time Work

Part-time work is any work done on a schedule less than the standard 40-hour workweek.

Flextime

Flextime (or **flexible time**) consists of flexible working hours or any schedule that gives an employee some choices in working hours.

- This can help organizations attract and keep employees who need to take care of children or elderly parents or who wish to avoid heavy commuting times.
- The main requirement is that the employee be at work during certain "core" hours, so as to be available for meetings and consultations.

Compressed Workweek

In a **compressed workweek**, an employee works a full-time job in less than five days of standard 8- or 9-hour shifts.

- The most common arrangement is a 40-hour week performed in four days of 10 hours each, which can offer employees three (instead of two) consecutive days off.
- Although this can offer employees more leisure time, the disadvantages are possible scheduling problems, unavailability of an employee to coworkers and customers, and fatigue from long workdays.

Job Sharing

With **job sharing**, two people divide one full-time job.

- Usually, each person works a half day, although there can be other arrangements (working alternate days or alternate weeks, for example).
- As with a compressed workweek, job sharing provides employees with more personal or leisure time.
- The disadvantage is that it can result in communication problems with coworkers or customers.

Telecommuting

With **telecommuting**, employees work at home with telecommunications between office and home.

- Some employees have always been allowed to work at home, away from the office, but modern technology (e-mail, computers, the Internet) and overnight-delivery services now make this arrangement much more feasible.

- The advantages to employers are increased productivity because telecommuters experience less distraction at home and can work flexible hours.

Decisions

Dylan is listening to Yuki speak at a managers' meeting about compensation benefits and motivation. Choose the term that best describes what Yuki is discussing.

We are in the process of developing new policies that will allow our contact center employees to begin working from home. This will help motivate employees while reducing facility costs and employee commute times.

- **A.** Compressed workweek
- **B.** Stock options
- **C.** Telecommuting
- **D.** Profit sharing

To help motivate and reward our employees, we are going to allow certain staff to work four 10-hour days and take Fridays off. Our hope is they'll get to maximize the summer.

- **A.** Profit sharing
- **B.** Compressed workweek
- **C.** Job sharing
- **D.** Telecommuting

We will continue taking our quarterly earnings and sharing those with our employees.

- **A.** Job sharing
- **B.** Stock options
- **C.** Telecommuting
- **D.** Profit sharing

There has been talk about us going public. If this is the direction the company goes, employees will be compensated with the opportunity to purchase stock at discounted prices.

A. Job Sharing

B. Stock Options

C. Telecommuting

D. Profit Sharing

Moving: Up, Lateral, and Out of the Organization

Within organizations, employee movement occurs in four main ways: promotion, transfer, disciplining, and dismissal.

Promotion: Moving Upward

Apart from awarding raises and bonuses, one of the principal ways managers recognize a person's superior performance is through **promotion**—moving the employee to a higher management job within the company.

Before this can take place, however, managers must ask three questions:

1. *Is the promotion fair?* The step upward must be deserved, not the result of favoritism, as through nepotism (favoring relatives) or cronyism (favoring friends).

2. *Is the promotion nondiscriminatory?* The new position cannot discriminate against other employees similar in rank for reasons of race, gender, age, physical ability, religion, or pregnancy.

3. *Will nonpromoted employees be resentful, and how should they be handled?* Some workers left behind may resent the promotion and need to be counseled about their performance and their future opportunities.

Transfer: Moving Sideways

Transfer is movement of an employee sideways within the company to a different job with *similar responsibility*.

Three reasons for transferring an employee are as follows:

1. The transfer broadens an employee's experience.

2. The transfer solves an organizational problem.

3. The transfer keeps an employee motivated.

Disciplining: Suspensions and Demotions

Disciplining is punishing an employee, often for a poor performance appraisal, usually by suspending or demoting that employee.

The employee might be given a warning or a reprimand and then **suspended**—temporarily removed from the job (with or without pay) while the company investigates the situation and figures out what to do.

Or the employee might be **demoted**—have their current responsibilities and pay taken away.

Dismissal: Laying Off, Downsizing, or Firing

Cutting jobs might seem to be the fastest and easiest way to get a company through economic hard times, but the costs can be high, including loss of morale among surviving employees, loss of future leaders, and reduced ability to attract top talent.

Still, sometimes companies may have to resort to dismissals, in which employees are temporarily or permanently made to leave the company.

There are three categories of dismissals:

- **Layoff: Temporary Dismissal, Possible Rehiring Later:** The phrase *being laid off* tends to suggest that a person has been dismissed temporarily—as when an appliance manufacturer doesn't have enough orders to justify keeping its production employees—and may be recalled later when sales improve.

- **Downsizing: Permanent Dismissal, No Rehiring Later:** A *downsizing* is a *permanent* dismissal; there is no rehiring later.

- **Firing: Permanent Dismissal "for Cause":** The phrase *being fired* tends to mean that a person was dismissed *permanently "for cause,"* the cause being unsatisfactory performance as documented in the performance appraisal, absenteeism, sloppy work habits, breaking the law, and the like.

Note: In all states except Montana, employers operate under the legal doctrine of ***at*-will employment** (or **employment at will**) in which the employer is free to dismiss any employee for any reason at all—or no reason—and the employee is equally free to quit work. (Exceptions are some whistleblowers and people with employment contracts, such as a union's collective bargaining agreement. Dismissals are also prohibited for discrimination on the basis of gender, skin color, and so on.)

Decisions

Dylan and Yuki are discussing what they should do about several employee situations. Choose the most applicable approach to each employee's situation.

This employee's manager really doesn't want to lose him, but she says that he is a superstar and would make a great addition to our operations management team.

A. Transfer

B. Discipline

C. Promotion

What about this person, they have attendance issues, should we fire them?

Not quite yet, we want to give them a chance to change their ways.

A. Promotion

B. Discipline

C. Transfer

This is an interesting one. This person has let her manager know that she needs to move to Atlanta. We do have an opening in Atlanta. Can we help her out?

Yes, our policies definitely allow for that. I am sure it will ease the move as well.

A. Discipline

B. Transfer

C. Promotion

Correct Answers: C; B; B

Lesson 5-6
Labor Relations

By the end of this lesson, you will be able to:

- Summarize the relationship between unions and management and their respective roles in labor relations.
- Summarize the tactics used by unions and management to exert pressure on one another.

Bargaining in the Workplace

Negotiating Working Conditions

On his lunch break at Seagull Air headquarters, Dylan finds that the lunchroom is crowded and the only spot available is across from a young woman in a flight attendant's uniform.

Is this seat taken?

No, please go ahead.

They introduce themselves. Minette LeBrun mentions that she has just come from a union meeting where they were talking about an issue.

You know, it's not fair. We've been fighting for better rest provisions for flight attendants for a long time now with no results.

By rest provisions, you mean how many hours of rest you get after you work overtime?

If pilots get a certain amount of rest before they have to go back to work, so should we. We're on the same plane and working the same schedule, after all. But they get more hours of rest than we do.

Copyright © McGraw Hill

What has the union done so far?

They're going to schedule a meeting with management to discuss the issue as well as put it into our negotiation strategy for the upcoming collective bargaining.

Dylan's conversation with Minette helps him gain insight into a labor union issue. In this lesson, we'll learn more about maintaining labor relations between employees and companies.

Organized **labor unions** are concerned with representing employee well-being in a wide range of issues: fairness in hiring policies and work assignments, compensation, employee benefits, job security, and work rules. They also handle the mediation of employee grievances.

Conducting Labor Relations

Dylan is shadowing an HR rep in the labor relations department. He learns that unions grew out of terrible working conditions, such as 90-hour workweeks, use of child labor, and filthy and dangerous workplaces. During the Industrial Revolution, they played a major role in improving workplace conditions and wages.

HR professionals working in labor need to understand:

- The process that must be followed for a group of employees to unionize
- What is involved in the collective bargaining process
- What a grievance is
- The difference between mediation and arbitration
- The tactics used by management and unions

Dylan decides to spend some time researching each of these topics.

Steps to Organizing a Union

There are four main steps involved in organizing a union:

1. First, 30% or more of the workers must sign an authorization card, designating a certain union as the bargaining agent with the employer.

2. The National Labor Relations Board (NLRB) may consider which union is the right bargaining unit.

3. The NLRB holds an election to see whether workers want representation.

4. If 50% or more of the votes agree to unionization, the NLRB certifies the union to represent workers.

Collective Bargaining

Once a union is formed, it has the right to bargain with management. This bargaining is on behalf of and binding for all members. It is called **collective bargaining**. The steps in collective bargaining—the process of labor and management meeting to negotiate pay, benefits, and work terms—include:

1. Preparing for negotiations

2. Meeting and negotiating

3. Striking a deal

4. Ratification (voting) by union members on the proposed contract

5. Signing the negotiated labor-management contract.

The objectives organized labor attempts to address during collective bargaining include:

Hiring Policies

Should the union or management control hiring policies and work assignments? Should the workplace be a **closed**, **union**, **agency**, or **open shop** (depending on state law, because some states have right-to-work laws that prohibit employees from being forced to join a union)?

Compensation

What kind of compensation will employees get? Will new workers doing the same job be paid less (two-tier wage contracts)? Will there be a cost-of-living adjustment clause that ties wage rates to the government's cost-of-living index? Will there be givebacks that surrender previous wage and benefit gains in return for other gains?

Benefits

What kind of employee benefits, such as health insurance, pensions, paid time off, and the like, will employees have?

Job Security

Employees want to understand how they will be rated, reviewed, and what processes will be utilized in the event of a layoff or downsizing. They also want to understand what protections will be extended to them to protect their jobs. The larger question at play is will jobs be made secure?

Work Rules and Conditions

What are the standards for the work conditions? What are the key policies, related to the workplace? Who is accountable for handling complaints? What happens if these standards are not met? What are the work rules about who may work and under what conditions?

Grievances, Mediation, and Arbitration

When employees believe the agreement is not being followed or someone has violated a term of the agreement, they can file a **grievance**. Employee grievances, or complaints about violations in the labor-management agreement, may be handled by a union official (a union steward).

If the issue is not resolved, it can be submitted to a third party for **mediation**, a process in which a neutral third party, a *mediator*, listens to both sides in a dispute, makes suggestions, and encourages them to agree on a solution.

If that does not work, the grievance can be sent to **arbitration**, a process in which a neutral third party, an *arbitrator*, listens to both parties in a dispute and makes a decision that the parties have agreed will be binding for both sides.

Management and Union Tactics

The goal for both management and union members should be to act as partners for the good of both employees and the organization. However, if negotiations or relationships deteriorate, both unions and management utilize various tactics to deal with challenges in their relationship:

Union tactics may include:

1. *Slowdowns* (working more slowly) and *sickouts* (calling in sick)
2. *Strikes* or temporary work *stoppages*, along with picketing
3. *Boycotts*, in which members and sympathizers refuse to buy a company's products

Management tactics may include:

1. Closing the company and not paying workers (referred to as a *lockout*)
2. Obtaining *court injunctions* requiring strikers to return to work
3. Hiring *strikebreakers* to cross picket lines and fill the jobs of strikers

Good Labor Relations Are Important to Both Sides: Employees Are People, Too

As an intern in the HR department of Seagull Air, Dylan Silverman has learned that the airline industry offers its employees an exciting work environment with lots of variety. But it can be challenging, even dangerous for them. They are subject to working long hours under conditions that can be hazardous.

Labor unions protect the rights of workers, but their tactics when negotiations fail, including slowdowns, strikes, and boycotts, can have a negative impact on companies. And when companies strike back with anti-labor tactics of their own, such as lockouts, court injunctions, and hiring strikebreakers, workers can be harmed. Thus, good labor relations are important to both sides.

Dylan will be leaving his summer internship with Seagull Air soon. He's learned a lot, and he is thinking of applying to HR departments at other companies that use unionized employees.

Decisions

Dylan is shadowing HR personnel in the labor-relations department. Which of the terms best applies to each scenario?

1. An employee has recently shared with his shop steward that management isn't following the rules related to breaks outlined in the collective bargaining agreement. The steward will file a(n) _____.

   A. arbitration report

   B. collective bargaining notification

   C. grievance

2. The contract for flight attendants is about to end and representatives from both management and the union are working to ensure they reach a new deal that addresses wages and working conditions, including the rest time that Dylan heard about in the lunch room. What are they working on?

   A. Arbitration

   B. Filing a grievance

   C. Collective bargaining

3. Unfortunately, a dispute between the ground crew's union and management could not be resolved. After trying to work it out among themselves, they are now going to a third party who will make a decision for them. What are they engaged in?

   A. Filing a grievance

   B. Collective bargaining

   C. Arbitration

Correct Answers: C; C; C

Human Resource Management and Labor Relations: Test

1. The employees at Bluey Company are planning to vote on whether to unionize. Their right to do so is protected by the _____ Act and is enforced by the _____.

    A. Taft-Hartley; Equal Employment Opportunity Commission

    B. Wagner; National Labor Relations Board

    C. Fair Labor Standards; Title VII Commission

    D. Equal Employment Opportunity; National Labor Relations Board

    E. Wagner; Affirmative Action Commission

2. Ahnalee is a recent retiree and is going to be collecting retirement benefits through the United States government. Which law established the system responsible for her benefits?

    A. Family and Retirement Leave Act

    B. Fair Labor Standards Act

    C. Equal Employment Opportunity Act

    D. Taft-Hartley Act

    E. Social Security Act

3. Dante works for Rondon Metals and is preparing to adopt a newborn baby with his husband. Which statement is accurate regarding Dante's situation?

    A. FLSA would lower the maximum hours Dante is required to work.

    B. FMLA would allow Dante to take 12 weeks of unpaid leave.

    C. OSHA would protect Dante's position if he takes time off from work.

    D. NLRB would require Dante's role be exempt from overtime rules.

    E. EEOC would ensure that Dante is paid his full salary while away from work.

4. Patton is the HR Manager for Shady Lane Manufacturing. He knows there is often a lot of dust particles floating around the assembly line due to the production process. How can he ensure that the company is compliant with OSHA requirements?

    A. He should ensure that employees working on the assembly line are exempt from overtime rules.

    B. He should request an EEOC audit of the production process and ask for suggestions.

    C. He should provide individual respirators to employees working on the assembly line.

    D. He should allow employees to take 1–2 weeks of unpaid time off each year to clear their lungs.

    E. He should institute a maximum number of hours that employees can work each week

5. Vella's mother is diagnosed with a serious health condition and Vella needs time off from work to drive her to and from her treatments. Which legislation serves to protect employees going through a situation like this?

    A. Fair Labor Standards Act

    B. Civil Rights Act

    C. Family and Medical Leave Act

    D. Equal Employment Opportunity

    E. Wagner Act

6. Colton breaks his hand while using a press at Wharton Company. His manager determines that the machine was missing a safety guard due to some repair work that had been completed during the previous shift. This is most likely a violation of which law?

    A. OSHA

    B. WARN

    C. EEO

    D. NLRB

    E. FLSA

7. Irie worked as a machine operator at Tyborg Company while she went to school for accounting. After earning her degree, she is promoted into a professional role as an accountant. After reviewing her first paycheck as an accountant, she is surprised to notice that she no longer receives overtime pay. What statement would best explain what happened in Irie's case?

   A. The EEOC eliminated overtime pay for salaried employees.

   B. The FLSA made professional employees exempt from overtime rules.

   C. The NLRB required companies to eliminate overtime pay for non-union personnel.

   D. The SSA replaced overtime pay for professional employees with entry into the U.S. retirement system.

   E. The CRA implemented anti-discrimination rules regarding pay for salaried employees.

8. The collective bargaining process consists of negotiations between _____ and _____.

   A. management; the NLRB

   B. the U.S. president; union stewards

   C. management; employees

   D. the EEOC; union stewards

   E. the NLRB; employees

9. Management at PAK Enterprises is actively trying to block employee efforts to unionize. The _____ would most likely step in as this is illegal under the _____ Act

   A. EEOC; Wagner

   B. NLRB; OSHA

   C. NLRB; Taft-Hartley

   D. EEOC; Taft-Hartley

   E. NLRB; Wagner

10. The Fair Labor Standards Act is responsible for

    A. restricting the maximum hours in a workweek.

    B. creating the Equal Employment Opportunity Commission.

    C. requiring unpaid leave for employee childbirth or adoption.

    D. reducing employee discrimination in the workplace.

    E. establishing guidelines for collective bargaining.

11. Which action would enable a company to remain compliant in regard to the Occupational Safety and Health Act?

    A. providing gloves to employees working with battery acid

    B. ensuring that employees are paid at least the federal minimum wage

    C. allowing union members to meet during work hours

    D. requiring antidiscrimination training for supervisors

    E. enhancing overtime rules for exempt employees

12. Title VII of the Civil Rights Act of 1964 was one of the first pieces of legislation that

    A. required a business to provide protective equipment for its employees.

    B. required a business to provide 12 weeks of paid leave for employee family emergencies.

    C. allowed a company to ignore overtime rules for its professional employees.

    D. punished a business for refusing to negotiate with its appointed union representative.

    E. attempted to reduce discrimination in companies that had regularly denied promotions to minorities.

Copyright © McGraw Hill

13. The CFO at Air Central Company wants to create an updated job description for her staff accountants. Where should she begin?

   A. conduct a job analysis

   B. review job specifications

   C. create validity tests

   D. perform a forced ranking

   E. complete a job rotation

14. The CEO at FSG Company has asked Madelyn to provide a suggestion for a new on-the-job training solution to enhance their current program. What would be the best place for her to start?

   A. reviewing vestibule training options

   B. considering apprenticeship options

   C. learning about networking opportunities

   D. looking at online distance learning programs

   E. researching mentorship programs

15. JJ works as a benefits consultant at HOU Company. He has been asked to create a presentation that he can share with new employees hired into the company. Which option would be the most appropriate venue for JJ to use for his presentation?

   A. during a mentorship session

   B. during new employee onboarding

   C. during vestibule training

   D. during a job shadowing session

   E. during a structured interview

16. The management team at Bushwood Manufacturing wants to improve productivity (and profitability) for the company by reducing overhead costs for the production team. How can they best motivate their production employees to help reduce overhead costs?

   A. by providing limited stock options for the team

   B. by implementing a compressed workweek option for the team

   C. by increasing base pay for the team

   D. by creating a gainsharing program for the team

   E. by adding a commissions program for the team

17. Employees at Wolf Metals receive a small payment based on their attendance record for the year. The amount varies in proportion to their actual attendance in comparison to other employees and the total profits Wolf Metals made for the year. Wolf Metals is using a _____ plan for its employees.

   A. profit sharing

   B. fringe commissions

   C. perk sharing

   D. pay for performance

   E. gainsharing

18. A(n) _____ is a union tactic used to put pressure on management during collective bargaining. They are often accompanied by union-organized _____.

   A. strike; picketing

   B. boycott; lockouts

   C. grievance; picketing

   D. sickout; strikebreaking

   E. strike; grievances

19. Kyia works for Thielen Metals. Last month, she filed a complaint against her manager claiming he had violated the terms of the labor-management agreement. The case made its way from Kyia's shop steward through mediation. Unfortunately, management and union personnel were unable to come to an agreement. What is most likely to occur next?

A. The company and union will go to arbitration.

B. The union will vote on whether decertify the current labor agreement.

C. The company will terminate Kyia or she will be forced to quit.

D. The NLRB will lead efforts to file a court injunction against the company.

E. The union will issue a call to boycott the company.

20. In which assessment are employees appraised not only by their managers but also by their coworkers, subordinates, and sometimes customers or clients?

A. behavioral assessment

B. 360-degree assessment

C. formal, structured assessment

D. at-will assessment

E. multilevel assessment

6 Organizational Behavior

What To Expect

By the end of the chapter, you will be able to:

- Infer the way(s) organizational culture may be impacting a firm in a business case.

- Diagnose an organization's placement within the process of institutional decline in a business case.

- Ascertain the area of need for organizational change.

- Apply the three steps to implementing positive change in a business case.

Chapter Topics

- **6-1** Organizational Culture
- **6-2** Hierarchical and Structural Approaches
- **6-3** Building a Team
- **6-4** Motivation in the Workplace

Copyright © McGraw Hill   Pressmaster/Shutterstock

Organizational Culture

Ecodrive: A Company Buys into Rapid Change

"How Do We, as an Organization, Adapt to Change?"

Ecodrive is a U.S. automaker specializing in hybrid and electric cars. The company was founded several years ago by Wang Cheng and Ellie Hiashi.

The company has faced many challenges in research, development, and marketing, but Ecodrive is now a global force that is highly competitive with other car manufacturers. However, this rapid expansion has caused problems with its organizational culture, structure, and employee motivation.

Wang and Ellie are committed to maintaining a strong corporate culture and to motivating their employees. To help work on these issues, Ecodrive has retained the services of Russ Imelda from Company Support Advisors, a consulting group.

Hi Wang and Ellie. It's great to meet with you.

Thanks, Russ. We're glad you're here. We'd like to get some input on the changes our company is going through.

Yes, we're both engineers, but we've worked closely with our human resources VP to better understand how to manage our growth.

We've been so focused on the products and the bottom line that we feel we've lost track of our people—and that's our most important resource.

It's not unusual for companies that grow as quickly as Ecodrive to experience changes in their corporate culture. And that, of course, impacts all employees in the organization.

We've certainly been aware of some changes and want to be sure we don't lose what's made us a special place to work—the creativity and the camaraderie.

In this lesson, we will introduce the concepts of organizational culture and change. Just as a human being has a personality—such as fun-loving, warm, disorganized, competitive, hard-working, uptight, or frantic—an organization has a "personality" too, only it's called its *culture*. In order to know what changes to make to their organization and to avoid organizational decline, Wang and Ellie need to understand their company's culture.

What Is the Meaning of Organizational Culture?

 We're committed to keeping our growth trajectory, but we're seeing some changes in the organization.

And we're not comfortable with those.

 It's great that you're paying attention. When companies don't heed those warning signs, it can be the start of major problems.

Such as?

 Well, let me talk to you a bit about the relationship between "organizational culture" and what we call "institutional decline."

The study of **organizational culture**, sometimes called **corporate culture**, is the study of the shared beliefs and values within an institution. Culture gives employees an organizational identity, facilitates collective commitment, promotes stability, and shapes behavior by helping employees make sense of their surroundings. It is the "social glue" that binds members of the organization together.

Organizational culture can differ considerably from one organization to the next, with varying emphases on treatment of employees, teamwork, rewards, rules and regulations, and conflict and criticism.

Organizational culture is communicated to employees in many ways. For example, culture can be communicated through how people in the organization dress (for example, casually or formally), by how the office is laid out (for example, with an open plan or many separated offices), by how top management interacts with employees (for example, asking for input or unilaterally making decisions), and by the slogans and other company materials displayed around the office. In addition, the culture may be communicated through the organization's heroes, symbols, stories, and rites and rituals.

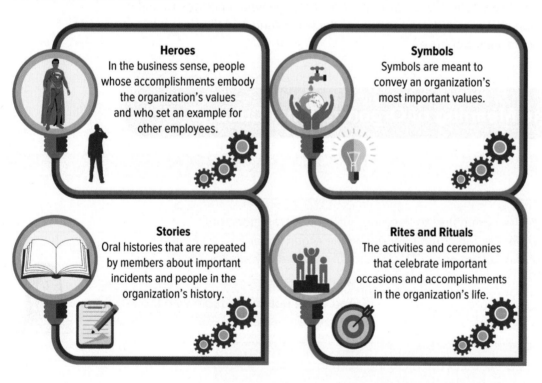

Heroes
In the business sense, people whose accomplishments embody the organization's values and who set an example for other employees.

Symbols
Symbols are meant to convey an organization's most important values.

Stories
Oral histories that are repeated by members about important incidents and people in the organization's history.

Rites and Rituals
The activities and ceremonies that celebrate important occasions and accomplishments in the organization's life.

After meeting with Russ, Wang and Ellie sit down to discuss what elements of their organizational culture they feel they need to do a better job of communicating.

Why does organizational culture matter? Because the culture of the organization you work for can have a powerful influence on employees' behavior and happiness and can thereby affect the organization's success.

I feel like we need to work harder at letting our new employees know what our company's history and values are. Do you remember how we started this company?

Of course. It was all about doing good for the environment . . .

. . . while meeting people's needs.

For years we celebrated that, but we've been so focused on growth that I'm not sure all our employees know the real story. All those ideas and sketches . . .

That's exactly what I'm talking about—the "real story" of Ecodrive! We need to do a better job at communicating that and focusing on what really matters to us.

Goal Understanding

"I Understand What the Organization Does"

An organization's culture helps employees understand what the organization does and, second, how it intends to accomplish its long-term goals.

This is typically communicated by organizational leaders and aligns an organization's strategy with its mission.

Organizational Identity

"I Know What the Company Wants to Do"

An organization's culture helps employees understand what the company's mission and vision are, such as being a technological innovator or helping to solve ecological problems.

Organizations bring this to life through their processes, actions, and organizational decisions from the ground floor to the C-suite. This also shows up in office spaces, online, and other imagery bringing the identity to life.

Collective Commitment

"I'm Proud to Be Part of This Company"

By providing employees with role models and inspiring stories, an organization's culture helps employees feel committed to its goals.

Companies bring this to life by sharing e-mails of great customer and employee experiences that demonstrate and epitomize what success looks like when goals and the mission are being accomplished. Further, this inspires, motivates, and celebrates individual and collective employee accomplishments.

Social-System Stability

"I Feel I'm Treated Fairly Here"

Social systems within organizations are more stable when conflict and change are managed so that employees feel they are in a positive work culture.

Organizations who construct systems, processes, and policies that are transparent and embody fairness and equality while including employee engagement in the process can foster a positive work environment.

Decisions

We've just discussed how the culture of an organization affects its employees. Now read the following situations going on at Ecodrive and determine which effect is reflected in each.

1. As an innovator in the auto industry Ecodrive is pushing to have an affordable totally 100% carbon free SUV in production in the next 24 months.

    A. Organizational identity

    B. Collective commitment

    C. Social-system stability

    D. Goal understanding

2. Ecodrive is striving to build innovation into its culture by encouraging employees to spend 20% of their time on personal research interests. As a result, they have been able to develop unique features that set them apart from competitors.

    A. Goal understanding

    B. Organizational identity

    C. Collective commitment

    D. Social-system stability

3. Ecodrive currently has 3% employee turnover in its production facility because it consistently offers employees advancement opportunities as well as the ability to try out different positions.

   A. Collective commitment

   B. Organizational identity

   C. Social-system stability

   D. Goal understanding

4. One of the strategies Ecodrive manages is through offering clear road mapping for career development and promotions. As a result, employees feel they are treated fairly while knowing how to advance in the organization.

   A. Organizational identity

   B. Social-system stability

   C. Collective commitment

   D. Goal understanding

Correct Answers: 1. D; 2. B; 3. A; 4. B

What Are the Five Stages That Organizations Tend to Go through When They Go into Decline?

Russ, the consultant working with Wang and Ellie, recommends that they read a bit about organizational decline to better understand the issues their company may be facing. He sends Wang and Ellie the following information.

Jim Collins, researcher of enduring great companies, identifies five stages of organizational decline. These stages—which are largely self-inflicted—are depicted here.

Hubris Born of Success

Employees begin attributing the company's success to their own superior qualities and lose understanding about the underlying factors that created that success.

"We're so great we can do anything".

Undisciplined Pursuit of More

More of whatever those in power define as "success," such as more growth or more acclaim. Here companies begin overreaching, making undisciplined leaps into areas where they cannot be great, taking actions inconsistent with their basic values, or outstripping their resources, leading them to ignore their core business.

"Let's apply our genius to areas beyond our core business."

Denial of Risk and Peril

Internal warning signs begin to increase, but managers explain away disturbing data by suggesting that difficulties are "temporary" or "not that bad." In this stage, says Collins, "leaders discount negative data, amplify positive data, and put a positive spin on ambiguous data."

"Our setbacks are just temporary."

Grasping for Salvation

The perils of the previous stage reach the point of throwing the company into a sharp decline that is visible to all. At that point, managers may begin desperate reaches, such as "a bold but untested strategy, a radical transformation, . . . a hoped-for blockbuster product, a 'gamechanging' acquisition, or any number of other silver-bulleted solutions." Usually these don't work. "Leaders atop companies in the late stages of decline," says Collins, "need to get back to a calm, clear-headed, and focused approach."

"We need a magic-bullet solution to keep us going."

Capitulation to Irrelevance or Death

In this final stage, the company may be sold, left to shrivel into utter insignificance, or allowed to die—go bankrupt.

"It's the end of the line."

Organizational decline is "harder to detect but easier to cure in the early stages; easier to detect but harder to cure in the later stages," says Collins. But the scary part, he says, is that companies don't visibly fall until Stage 4. That is, "companies can be well into Stage 3 decline and still look and feel great, yet be right on the cusp of a huge fall."

Decisions

After reading about organizational decline, Wang and Ellie get back together to discuss.

> Ellie, I think we may be guilty of some of these.

> Well, we certainly think we're great . . . and we've been talking about that new robotics project.

> That doesn't sound like a core business for us, does it?

> No, but it does tie in with our environmental focus.

> Sort of . . . but perhaps it's something we need to rethink. We have to be careful to protect our company.

1. Ellie and Wang feel they have been sure of their future success based on their past successes. Which stage of decline is most applicable?

   A. Undisciplined pursuit of more

   B. Hubris of success

   C. Denial of risk and peril

2. Ellie and Wang seem very centered on growth being a metric of success. As they discuss growth and going after new products, what stage of decline could they most likely slip into?

   A. Denial of risk and peril

   B. Hubris of success

   C. Undisciplined pursuit of more

3. If Ellie and Wang were to dive deeper with Russ about the organization and Russ heard them consistently discounting troublesome data or consistently saying this was just a temporary setback, they would be heading to what stage of decline?

   A. Denial of risk and peril

   B. Undisciplined pursuit of more

   C. Hubris of success

Correct Answers: 1. B; 2. C; 3. A

What Four Areas Tend to Need Organizational Changes?

Wang and Ellie call Russ back into the office to discuss strategy and how they can focus on making organizational changes to ensure a long and happy life for their company.

Russ, to help us get centered again, what do you think we need to focus on?

Yes, I know our employees have been concerned that we're spreading ourselves too thin focusing on sales growth as well as sticking our toes in the robotics market.

Well, there are several things you can do to change direction. Let me explain them to you.

Successful change to avert decline doesn't just happen. Organizations committed to bringing their culture to life need to also ensure the organization can adapt and evolve through initiating changes. Companies who want to make organizational culture changes must also align these four main areas:

People: Changing Employees' Minds and Performance

Even in a small organization, changes may be required in employee perceptions, attitudes, skills, or performance.

Technology: Changing Machines and Processes

Technology—computerized or other—is a major area of change for many organizations.

Strategy: Changing Company Direction

Shifts in economics, popular tastes, or other factors may force companies to have to change their strategy.

Structure: Changing the Management Hierarchy

One way to stimulate performance is to change an organization's structure. The recent trend is to eliminate several middle layers of management—"flatten the hierarchy"—and use electronically linked work teams.

Decisions

Wang and Ellie evaluate areas they want to change. Choose the most applicable area for cultural change based on their conversation.

I think it starts with re-engaging our employees and ensuring we establish the appropriate mindset, communicating with them about how we want them to be a part of changing and growing the company.

Yes, and I think we need to meet with HR and construct a survey to better understand the current hearts and minds of our team.

A. People

B. Technology

C. Strategy

D. Structure

I think we also need to meet with marketing and see exactly where we are making the biggest impact. We need to determine what we are truly best at and really target it.

This is a shift in our direction, but I think if we hone our focus, make it a priority, and do it with purpose we will get the best results.

A. Technology

B. Structure

C. Strategy

D. People

This may mean we need to make some capital investment into machinery and/or other systems to help our teams.

A. People
B. Technology
C. Structure
D. Strategy

As we go through this process, we may also need to realign our people so we can be more effective and successful as an organization.

A. Strategy
B. Technology
C. Structure
D. People

Correct Answers: A; C; B; C

How Are Positive Changes Implemented?

Wang and Ellie continue to talk with Russ about how they want to change their organization and its culture.

It is pretty clear we aren't here *just* to avert decline. We want to move forward with our employees behind us—as a real team—with a solid organizational culture that everyone understands.

I agree. We need to focus on making positive changes to our organization. Russ, do you have any suggestions?

If you're going to not just survive but *prevail* as a company, it's important to know how to make positive change happen. There are three main steps.

Step 1: Recognize Problems and Opportunities and Devise Solutions.

Change begins when you recognize a problem that needs solving or an opportunity.

Step 2: Gain Allies by Communicating Your Vision.

Once you've decided how you're going to handle the problem, you need to develop and communicate your vision to key allies. This means painting a picture of the future and painting in broad strokes how the change will benefit the organization and its employees.

Step 3: Overcome Employee Resistance and Empower and Reward Them to Achieve Progress.

Along the path to change, you may need to overcome some employee resistance to change. You'll need to ensure that you focus on maintaining a positive culture. Part of this may mean offering periodic rewards—recognition, celebrations, and bonuses—for goals met.

Decisions

Let's assume that Wang and Ellie are most focused on employee concerns that Ecodrive is spreading itself too thin dealing with expansion as well as delving into the robotics market.

After hearing data back from their marketing team, they see they have the best opportunity by solely focusing on electric automobiles.

1. This decision demonstrates which step in the process?

    A. Recognize problems and opportunities

    B. Gain allies by communicating your vision

    C. Overcome employee resistance

2. Russ begins advising Wang and Ellie on constructing a communication strategy that paints a picture for upper management on how this will benefit people, planet, and profits. Ellie and Wang feel confident they can convince the company managers that this change will inspire, energize, and motivate employees. This demonstrates which step in the process?

    A. Gain allies by communicating your vision

    B. Recognize problems and opportunities

    C. Overcome employee resistance

3. Russ warns Ellie and Wang that with any change there will be some people who don't like the change and may even try to sabotage it. He suggests they work to develop some outcomes for "wins" when achievements occur during the change period to celebrate advancement of the initiative while hopefully moving those struggling with the change to embrace it.

   A. Recognize problems and opportunities

   B. Overcome employee resistance

   C. Gain allies by communicating your vision

Correct Answers: 1. A; 2. A; 3. B

Lesson 6-2

Hierarchical and Structural Approaches

By the end of this lesson, you will be able to:

- Explain how an organization's structural characteristics impact success and efficiency.
- Differentiate among organizational structures.

Ecodrive: Constructing a Structure to Excel

Designing an Organization for Excellence

Ellie, Wang, and their organizational development consultant Russ are striving to help Ecodrive determine an organizational culture and structure that will help the organization innovate, grow, compete, and succeed in the competitive auto industry. The company leaders have learned about organizational culture. Now they must turn their attention to how they will organize and structure their company.

As you grow, you also have to consider the organizational structure of your business. You're not a mom-and-pop store; you're a company with more than 3,500 employees.

So we need to ensure we are structured in a way that's clear and productive for our employees

And we need to make sure we know who has accountability and ownership for key functions without creating too much bureaucracy! That doesn't sound doable.

Sure it is. It's not easy, but you just need to take a multi-faceted approach. Remember, you're not doing this alone. By involving your employees you'll be able to design a structure and hierarchy that will work for your employees and your business.

Copyright © McGraw Hill

Chapter 6 · Organizational Behavior **193**

I think a good place for us to start is with production and HR.

I agree, then we can help determine how to design our organization chart for other key areas of the company.

Wang and Ellie realize they have a lot to think about with regard to the structural characteristics of their organization. In this lesson, we'll discuss the formal side of an organization's structure.

What Are the Structural Characteristics of an Organization?

Russ, Wang, and Ellie are discussing their current organizational structure and whether any changes are needed to help them continue on a path to success. Russ gives them a brief review of the five basic structural characteristics of an organization and how each characteristic can affect an organization's success and efficiency:

Accountability, Responsibility, and Authority

Accountability and responsibility go along with authority.

Accountability: Managers must report and justify their work results to managers above them.

Responsibility: The obligation to perform the tasks assigned to you.

Authority: The legitimacy an organization confers on managers in their power to make decisions, give orders, and utilize resources.

Division of Labor

Work Specialization

Specialists can perform different parts of complex work, resulting in greater efficiency.

Span of Control

This refers to the number of people who report to a particular manager.

Narrow span of control: Limited number of people reporting to a manager.

Wide span of control: Many people reporting to the manager.

Narrow and wide spans of control: benefits and drawbacks.

	Narrow span of control	Wide span of control
Benefit		
	More managerial control	More employee freedom to make decisions
	Closer supervision	More responsive to customers
	Greater specialization	Faster decision making
Drawbacks		
	Less employee freedom to make decisions	Less managerial control and input
	Less responsiveness to customers	Loss of supervision
	Delayed decision making	Less specialization

Delegation

This refers to the assignment of work to subordinates.

Staff personnel: Have advisory duties; they provide advice, recommendations, and research to line managers.

Line managers: Involved directly in an organization's goals, have authority to make decisions, and usually have people reporting to them.

Line and staff: *Line* positions are identified with solid lines, *staff* positions with dashed lines.

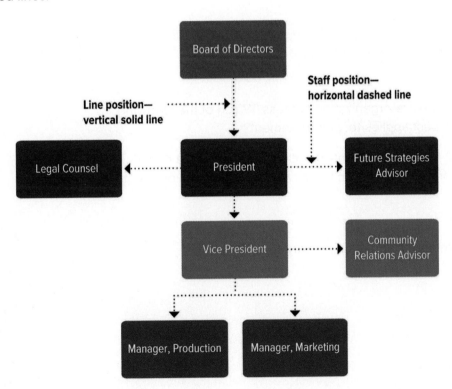

Centralization Versus Decentralization of Authority

Centralization versus decentralization of authority focuses on: Who makes the decisions in an organization?

Centralized authority: Important decisions are made by higher-level managers.

Decentralized authority: Decisions are made by middle-level and supervisory-level managers.

Centralization and decentralization: benefits and drawbacks

	Centralization	Decentralization
Benefit		
	More control by top management	More decision autonomy by lower managers
	Less duplication of effort	Faster decision making
	More efficient procedures	More responsive to customers
	Greater specialization	Higher employee morale
Drawbacks		
	Less decision authority by lower managers	Less control by top management
	Delayed decision making	More duplication of effort
	Less responsiveness to customers	Fewer streamlined procedures
	Lower employee morale	Less specialization

Decisions

As Wang and Ellie begin their re-organization process. Which of the following structural characteristics best applies to each statement?

1. Ellie and Wang want to give more control back to those who are directly involved with the work. However, with this new power there will be greater expectations.

    A. Division of labor

    B. Authority, accountability, and responsibility

    C. Span of control

2. Because of the complex work involved in developing next generation automobiles, Ellie and Wang realize they need to have a clear _____ so each specialist can perform their function effeciently and effectively.

   A. division of labor

   B. decentralized authority

   C. authority, accountability, and responsibility

3. They believe the employees on the floor need to be able to make more decisions and then feed them back up the chain of command. Doing this will create more autonomy and better morale.

   A. Decentralized authority

   B. Span of control

   C. Centralized authority

Correct Answers: 1. B; 2. A; 3. A

Organizational Structures

Organizations can be arranged into four basic types of structures. These groupings are used to form some sort of organizational structure, called **departmentalization**.

There are four principal departmental arrangements:

1. **Functional structure:** In this structure, the employees are grouped by occupational specialties.

2. **Divisional structure:** In this structure, the employees are grouped by purpose.

3. **Hybrid structure:** In this structure, the employees are grouped both by occupational specialties (functional) and by purpose (divisional).

4. **Matrix structure:** In this structure, the employees are grouped vertically and horizontally in a grid.

See the following for more information on the four principal departmental arrangements.

Functional Structure

Grouping by Occupational Specialties

In a functional structure, production, marketing, and similar departments are each headed by a vice president (VP), who reports to the company's president. This arrangement has many benefits, which is why so many companies use it, but it also has some drawbacks.

Divisional Structure

Grouping by Purpose

Employees may be grouped by common

- customers or customer groups,
- geographic division (regional sites or areas);
- process divisions (work specialization, product divisions);
- industry divisions (the conglomerate structure).

Hybrid Structure

Both Functional and Divisional

Owing to "the difficulty of working globally with a centralized functional structure and the communication gaps that come from working in divisional" structures, says one analysis, "most modern companies employ a hybrid structure that combines elements of each." By using both, companies hope to balance the economies of scale (cost savings) that come from centralization with the local efficiency that comes with decentralization.

Matrix Structure

Vertical and Horizontal Command Structures in a Grid

Here the *functional* structure remains the organization's normal divisions (marketing, finance, and so on). The *divisional* structure is usually by product (although it could be by customer or other arrangement).

Organizational Structure Design

The needs of the company and the importance of organizational components drive structure selection. Each of the four main types of organizational structures can be visualized, which helps to explain the designs and differences among them.

Functional Structure

Functional divisions are arranged by occupational specialties.

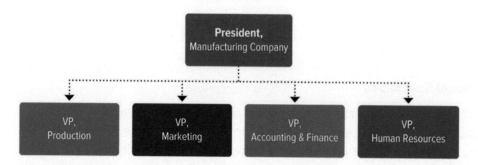

This structure has many benefits, which is why it is widely applied, but it also has some drawbacks.

Functional Departmentalization: Benefits and Drawbacks

Benefits	Drawbacks
• Workers grouped by specialization—for example, skill or resource use	• Employees in a department may tend to think alike
• Specialization saves costs, improves efficiency	• Employees may become narrow specialists
• Employees able to develop skills in depth	• Department's priorities may be put before firm's priorities
• Resources and expertise centralized in one place	• Departments may not communicate well with one another
• Specialists can easily coordinate within the department	• Company may respond less quickly to outside changes
• Management able to more easily direct department activities	• Development of well-rounded managers more difficult

Divisional Structure

In a divisional structure, the firm is organized by purpose. There are five types of divisional structures, which are explained below.

Customer Division

The firm is grouped by common customers or customer groups. This method centralizes people around a particular customer type or focus.

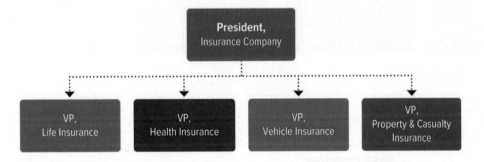

Geographic Division

The firm is grouped by region or area. Divisions are structured via a specific geography or set territory.

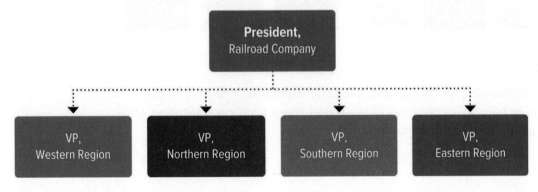

Process Division

The organization is structured by work specialization. The process of the work is what places people into particular groups.

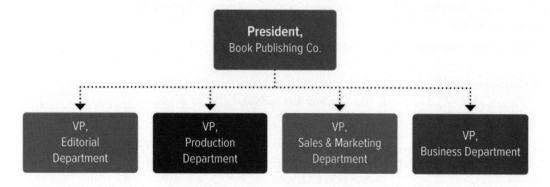

Product Division

The firm is structured around a particular product or service. Organizations group their people based on the products or service offerings.

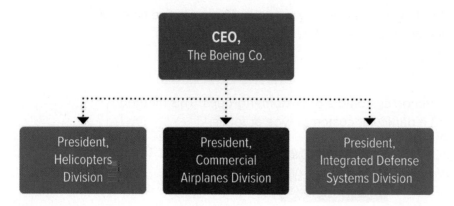

Industry Division

The firm is structured by companies or conglomerates that own and operate other companies in diverse industries.

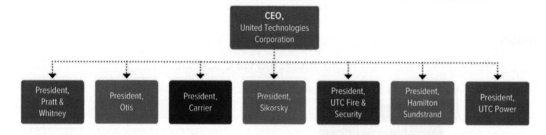

Hybrid Structure

This approach combines the functional and divisional structures. The goal of the hybrid structure is to balance economies of scale that come from centralization with the efficiencies gained through decentralization.

A Hypothetical Example of the Ford Motor Company

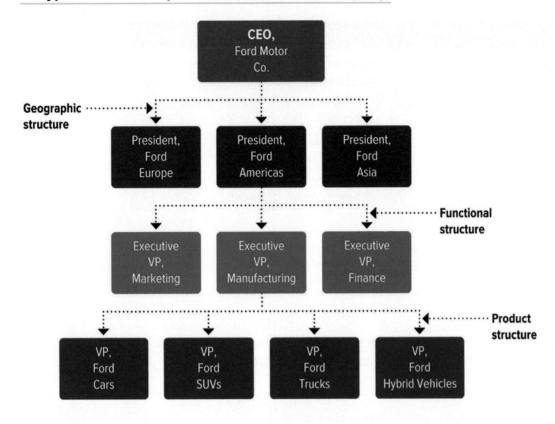

Matrix Structure

In this structure, companies apply the functional chain of command (horizontal) and build this around a product (vertical). This allows companies to organize themselves for special projects and product development.

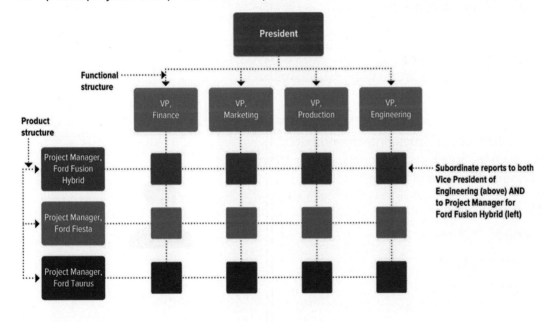

Matrix Structures: Benefits and Drawbacks

Benefits	Drawbacks
• Allows managers to use firm's resources more effectively	• May not be a long-term solution to development problem
• Gives managers flexibility in assigning right workers to projects	• Can be expensive and complicated to execute
• Can lead to innovative solutions in product development	• Employees may be confused about who they report to
• Encourages cooperation among different specialists	• Project members may have communication problems

Decisions

Ecodrive is looking at a number of options for their new organizational structure. Based on the descriptions, choose the most applicable structure.

We could organize around these core areas: Manufacturing, Marketing and Sales, Admin Operations, and Research and Development.

    A. Product

    B. Customer division

    C. Functional division

    D. Hybrid structure

What do you think about structuring around our segments, such as: Young Professionals, Family, Urban, Rural, Economic, Sporty, and Luxury?

    A. Customer division

    B. Product

    C. Hybrid structure

    D. Functional division

It might be wise for us to look at organizing around our models: Sedan, SUV, Crossover, Truck, Van/Minivan, and Sports.

- **A.** Hybrid structure
- **B.** Functional division
- **C.** Customer division
- **D.** Product

These are all great options. Have you considered integrating the ideas? At one level you could leverage the key areas Ellie hit on as they oversee your different segments, and then you could build teams around your different lines?

- **A.** Product
- **B.** Customer division
- **C.** Hybrid structure
- **D.** Functional division

I think you might be on to something!

Correct Answers: C; A; D; C

What Is Distinctive about a Virtual Organization?

A **virtual organization** is a networked entity that is extremely flexible. The core company can outsource various processes or functions to outside companies—any one of which can be changed when necessary.

A company operating as a virtual organization is called a *virtual corporation* or even a *hollow corporation* because its core company retains processes essential to its operation (such as strategic decision making and marketing) while outsourcing other processes (such as design or distribution), thus appearing to "hollow out" the organization. To its customers and others, however, the virtual corporation appears to be a single, unified organization, perhaps operating from a single location.

A variation on the virtual organization is the **modular structure**, one in which the organization is outsourcing pieces of a product rather than, as is true in virtual organizations, outsourcing certain *processes* (such as design or distribution).

You know, production is based in several facilities while marketing, sales, and research are located in lots of different areas. I never realized how "virtual" we actually are.

With all the new technology, as a company we're actually traveling less and doing more online.

Those staff meetings at all levels . . . sometimes I look at my calendar and can't see any time to just think!

Remember though, we're still controlling production. But we've been outsourcing several human resource and marketing functions.

Decisions

1. Based on the information provided, what types of organization structures are currently in use at Ecodrive? (Check all that apply.)

   A. Virtual organization

   B. Modular structure

   C. Flat structure

   D. Matrix

2. What are the benefits of virtual structures? (Check all that apply.)

   A. Saves time and travel

   B. Limits employees to one team

   C. Allows for the best people to be put on a team, regardless of location

   D. Makes team meetings easier to organize

Correct Answers: 1. A & B; 2. A & C

Copyright © McGraw Hill

Building a Team

By the end of this lesson, you will be able to:

- Summarize the types of teams and benefits of each.

Building a Team for Impact

Leveraging Teams for Organizational Success

Together with Russ, Ellie and Wang have learned about the role culture and structure play in an organization. They are now realizing the way they structure and build their team plays a crucial role in being able to execute the company's vision and strategy.

I can see we have some work to do. But Ellie and I have always been team players, and from the beginning we've worked to instill that feeling into our culture.

Absolutely, but as we deal with these changes, we have to make sure we're still using the right team strategy.

Teams are teams, Ellie. We need to be sure everyone has a voice.

Of course, Wang, but Ellie is correct. There are different types of teams.

Ellie and Wang discuss with Russ how to deal with quickly changing conditions and eliminate organizational functional barriers. They find that they may need to resort to different forms of organization involving networks and/or teamwork. In this lesson, we'll explore the importance of teamwork in organizations.

What Is the Definition of a Team?

If different drivers stop at the scene of a car accident and try to interact with each other to offer assistance, what do you call them? And when an ambulance crew arrives, what do you call it? The first is a group; the second is a team.

"The essence of a team is common commitment," say management consultants Jon R. Katzenbach and Douglas K. Smith. "Without it, groups perform as individuals; with it, they become a powerful unit of collective performance."

Increased Productivity

American Apparel sewing workers trained in teamwork and paid by number of garments produced by their team instead of individually tripled output from 30,000 to 90,000 pieces a day, with only a 12% increase in workers.

Increased Speed

Guidant Corp., maker of life-saving medical devices, halved the time it took to get products to market.

Reduced Costs

Boeing used teamwork to develop the 777 at costs far less than normal.

Improved Quality Outcomes

Training surgery personnel in teamwork at 74 Veterans Administration hospitals resulted in 18% fewer surgery-related deaths.

Reduced Destructive Internal Competition

Men's Wearhouse fired a salesperson who wasn't sharing walk-in customer traffic with other salespeople, and total clothing sales volume among all salespeople increased significantly.

Improved Cohesiveness, Reduced Absenteeism

Isola Fabrics restructured production into a teamwork system that resulted in decline of absenteeism rates of 28% for the summer and 39% for the winter.

There are many kinds of **teams** engaged in collective work requiring coordinated effort. In virtual teams, for instance, members interact with one another via computer network to collaborate on projects. Basically, however, there are four types of teams, whose names reflect their basic purpose: action, production, project, and advice.

Action Team

We are quite accustomed to thinking of teams in terms of sports. Sports teams are called action teams, because they work on tasks (winning games) that require a high degree of coordination among people with specialized training (such as the pitcher, catcher, or outfielder). Other examples of action teams: hospital surgery teams, airline cockpit crews, police homicide investigation teams.

Production Team

Production teams are charged with performing the day-to-day operations in an organization. Examples: include flight crews, maintenance crews, data processing groups, manufacturing product-assembly teams.

Project Team

Project teams work to do creative problem solving. Often this is done by temporary teams of knowledgeable workers who meet long enough to solve a specific problem and then disband, such as the Ford truck engine team. Other examples: include task forces, planning teams, engineering teams, development teams, research groups. Any of these could be a virtual team—one that does all work online.

Advice Team

Advice teams give managers a broader base of information on which to make decisions. Examples include committees, review panels, and research teams.

To give you an idea of how teams work, consider **cross-functional self-managed teams**, with routine activities formerly performed by supervisors now performed by team members. Cross-functional means the team is made up of workers with different specialties and expertise. Self-management means the traditional clear-cut distinction between manager and managed is blurred as nonmanagerial employees are delegated greater authority over planning, scheduling, monitoring, and staffing and

granted increased autonomy. The idea, of course, is to increase productivity and employee quality of work life.

Cross-Functional Self-Managed Teams: Benefits and Drawbacks

Benefits	Drawbacks
• Bring more expertise	• More training required
• Boost innovation and productivity	• Possible conflicts, disorganization
• Higher employee morale, less boredom and apathy	• Unclear leadership roles

Decisions

Which kind of team are Ellie and Wang describing?

I'd like to develop a specialized team of experts who could come into some of our projects and really blow them out of the water. The team could be something for our employees to aspire to, like making the dream team.

- **A.** Action teams
- **B.** Project teams
- **C.** Production teams
- **D.** Advice teams

What if we had a team of leaders from throughout the entire company and they were tasked with developing ideas as well as making some key decisions related to our culture and strategy?

- **A.** Production teams
- **B.** Advice teams
- **C.** Action teams
- **D.** Project teams

Correct Answers: A; B

Motivation in the Workplace

By the end of this lesson, you will be able to:

- Summarize the importance of motivation.
- Apply motivation theories to address organizational challenges in a business case.
- Differentiate among key aspects and examples of motivation theories.

Ways to Boost Motivation in the Workplace

Igniting Effort at Ecodrive

Ellie and Wang are striving to build a workplace that is designed for people to be highly productive and give their best effort. They are talking to Russ about which strategies and theories they can apply to motivate and reward their workforce.

As they continue to talk, Wang and Ellie learn more about the different theories of motivation and which of those are most applicable to Ecodrive.

In this lesson, we'll see that motivation is important in every facet of life. In the workplace, there are a number of ways managers can increase the motivation of their employees.

We sure want to move our company ahead successfully.

But I think the most important focus is how best to motivate our employees. And I would assume different types of motivation work in different situations.

That's true. And it's why it's important to understand the different theories of motivation.

What Is Motivation, and How Does It Work?

Motivation consists of the psychological processes that inspire people's goal-directed behavior. Although its actual operation is complex, the basic model of motivation is simple: you have certain *needs* that *motivate* you to perform specific *behaviors* to try to attain a certain *goal* for which you receive *rewards* that feed back to and satisfy the original need.

Extrinsic Versus Intrinsic Motivators

Motivators are of two types—extrinsic and intrinsic. An **extrinsic motivator** comes from outside; for example, it is the money you get when you build and sell a boat. An **intrinsic motivator** comes from within yourself; for example, it is the feeling of accomplishment you get from building the boat. Both extrinsic and intrinsic motivators are used to encourage employees to improve their performance.

The Importance of Motivation

Motivation is important for organizations of every size. For example, for Ecodrive Wang and Ellie want to stimulate interest in working for their company. They want the people they hire to show up for work—and to show up on time. They want good employees to stay committed to their organization. They want employees who will be happy and therefore highly productive. Finally, they want employees who will be good organizational citizens and represent the company well in the community. These motivations are summarized below.

Extrinsic Motivators

Money

Pay Raise

Promotion

Intrinsic Motivators

Accomplishment

Purpose

Join

You want to motivate talented prospective workers to hire on with you.

Show up

You want employees to be motivated to come to work—to show up on time.

Stay

You don't want good people to leave.

Perform

You want them to be motivated to be highly productive.

Do Extra

You hope they will be good organizational citizens and perform extra tasks beyond the regular call of duty.

What Are the Different Motivation Theories?

There are numerous motivational theories that offer different perspectives that may help organizations. But first, let's look at some research that was done early on to discover how factory owners could improve productivity.

Improving Productivity

Scientific Management

Theory: Emphasized the scientific study of work methods to improve the productivity of individual workers.

Researcher/Scientist: Engineer Fredrick Taylor, known as the "Father of Scientific Management"

Notes: Engaged in time-motion studies: Breaking down each worker's job into basic physical motions and then training workers to use the methods of their best-performing coworkers.

Believed managers could increase worker productivity by applying four principles:

1. Evaluate a task by scientifically studying each part of the task.

2. Carefully select workers with the right abilities to perform the task.

3. Give those workers the training and incentives to do the task and to use proper work methods in doing so.

4. Use scientific principles to plan the work methods and to help workers to do their jobs.

Principle of Motion Economy

Theory: Every job can be broken down into a series of elementary motions.

Researcher/Scientist: Frank and Lillian Gilbreth

Notes: A husband-and-wife team of industrial engineers who expanded on Taylor's time-motion studies by developing their **principle of motion economy**. By analyzing each motion in a task, you can increase efficiency.

Motivational Theories

Research in this area began to evolve and social scientists wanted to see what additional variables impacted worker productivity and behavior, which lead to a series of additional studies and theories.

The Hawthorne Effect

The **Hawthorne Effect** is the name given to a Harvard research group's conclusion that employees worked harder if they received added attention—if they thought managers cared about their welfare and that supervisors paid special attention to them.

Researchers succeeded in drawing attention to the importance of *motivation*—of how managers using good human relations, not just offering money, could improve worker productivity. This in turn led to the so-called *human relations movement* in the 1950s and 1960s, which focused more on psychological motivation rather than work steps in increasing productivity.

Maslow's Hierarchy of Needs

Abraham Maslow, in 1943, put forth a theory of motivation called the **Hierarchy of Needs** in which he suggested that needs are never completely fulfilled, that our actions are aimed at fulfilling the unsatisfied needs higher in the hierarchy.

He proposed that people are motivated by five levels of needs, ranging from low to high: (1) physiological, (2) safety, (3) social, (4) esteem, and (5) self-actualization.

Maslow's Hierarchy of Needs

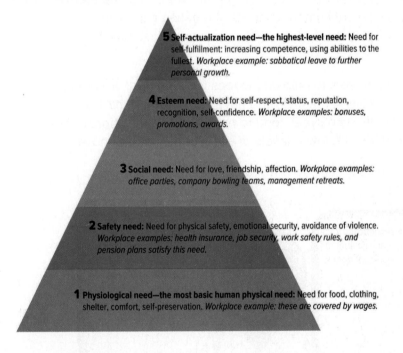

5 Self-actualization need—the highest-level need: Need for self-fulfillment: increasing competence, using abilities to the fullest. *Workplace example: sabbatical leave to further personal growth.*

4 Esteem need: Need for self-respect, status, reputation, recognition, self-confidence. *Workplace examples: bonuses, promotions, awards.*

3 Social need: Need for love, friendship, affection. *Workplace examples: office parties, company bowling teams, management retreats.*

2 Safety need: Need for physical safety, emotional security, avoidance of violence. *Workplace examples: health insurance, job security, work safety rules, and pension plans satisfy this need.*

1 Physiological need—the most basic human physical need: Need for food, clothing, shelter, comfort, self-preservation. *Workplace example: these are covered by wages.*

Herzberg's Two-Factor Theory

Frederick Herzberg interviewed 203 accountants and engineers to determine what made them happy and unhappy about their jobs.

Job *satisfaction*, he found, was more frequently associated with achievement, recognition, characteristics of the work, responsibility, and advancement. Job *dissatisfaction* was more often associated with working conditions, pay and security, company policies, supervisors, and interpersonal relationships.

From survey results came Herzberg's **two-factor theory**, which proposed that work dissatisfaction and satisfaction arise from two different factors—work satisfaction from higher-level needs he called *motivating factors*, and work dissatisfaction from lower-level needs he called *hygiene factors*.

Herzberg's factors for job satisfaction and dissatisfaction.

Motivation factors can be used to create more work satisfaction. Hygiene factors can cause work dissatisfaction, but changing them may have little motivational effect.

Motivating Factors (Causing Work Satisfaction)	Hygiene Factors (Causing Work Dissatisfaction)
• Achievement	• Pay and security
• Recognition	• Working conditions
• The work itself	• Interpersonal relationships
• Responsibility	• Company policy
• Advancement and growth	• Supervisors

Job Enrichment Theory

Job enrichment is the practical application of Herzberg's motivator-hygiene theory of job satisfaction. Specifically job enrichment consists of creating a job with motivating factors such as recognition, responsibility, achievement, stimulating work, and advancement.

By doing this the goal is for employers to help employees feel that they are doing meaningful work, take responsibility for results, and have knowledge of how their results impact others. As a result, employees tend to have higher motivation, better performance, greater satisfaction, and lower levels of absenteeism and turnover.

The following represent the key elements to how companies can fit jobs and people.

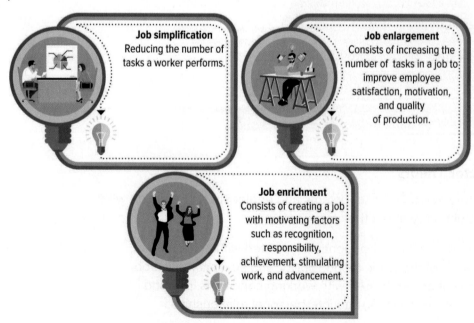

Job simplification
Reducing the number of tasks a worker performs.

Job enlargement
Consists of increasing the number of tasks in a job to improve employee satisfaction, motivation, and quality of production.

Job enrichment
Consists of creating a job with motivating factors such as recognition, responsibility, achievement, stimulating work, and advancement.

McGregor's Theory X and Theory Y

Douglas McGregor realized that it was not enough for managers to try to be liked; they also needed to be aware of their attitudes toward employees. Basically, McGregor suggested in his classic book, *The Human Side of Enterprise*, these attitudes could be either "X" or "Y."

Theory X represents a pessimistic, negative view of workers. It assumes workers are irresponsible, resistant to change, lacking in ambition, hating work, and preferring to be led rather than to lead. It also reflects the need for extrinsic rewards.

Representing the point of view of the human relations movement, **Theory Y** makes the positive assumption that workers are capable of accepting responsibility, self-direction, and self-control and of being imaginative and creative. Thus, Theory Y supports the notion of offering intrinsic rewards for good performance.

Ouchi's Theory Z

Developed by UCLA management professor William Ouchi, who studied management approaches in Japan and the United States, **Theory Z** considers how employees view management. It assumes that employees value a working environment supporting family, culture, and traditions and that they have a desire to work hard, are competent to make informed decisions, want to have cooperative relationships, and are knowledgeable about various issues in the company.

Characteristics of Theory Z

1. Long-term employment
2. Collective decision making
3. Collective responsibility (individual responsibility within a group context)
4. Slow evaluation and promotion
5. Implicit, informal control with explicit, formalized control measures
6. Moderately specialized career paths
7. Concern for the total person, including his or her family

Thorndike and Skinner's Reinforcement Theory

Developed by Edward Thorndike and B. F. Skinner, **reinforcement theory** suggests that behavior with positive consequences tends to be repeated, whereas behavior with negative consequences tends not to be repeated. The use of reinforcement theory to change human behavior is called *behavior modification*. It can be through positive reinforcement, negative reinforcement, extinction, or punishment.

- Positive reinforcement: when a desirable behavior is exhibited, an employee receives a positive reinforcement such as pay or praise.
- Negative reinforcement: there is a removal of an unpleasant consequence. When an employee completes a task correctly, the boss stops yelling.

- Extinction: Either the withholding or withdrawal of positive reward for undesirable behavior (making it less likely to occur in future). Employees have their pay docked for errors they make that cost the company money.
- Punishment: A negative consequence to stop or change undesirable behavior. Employees are written up with the potential of losing their job for being late to work.

Vroom's Expectancy Theory

Victor Vroom's **expectancy theory** proposes that people are motivated by (1) how strongly they want something, and (2) how likely they think they are to get it. That is, assuming they have choices, people will make the choice that promises them the greatest reward if they think they can get it.

Vroom suggests that motivation—how willing someone is to work hard at tasks—involves three assessments or calculations:

1. Expectancy: "Will I be able to accomplish the task?"

2. Instrumentality: "If I accomplish the task, what kind of reward do I get?"

3. Valence: "How much do I want the reward?"

Expectancy Theory: The Three Assessments or Calculations

Adam's Equity Theory

J. Stacey Adam's **equity theory** focuses on employee perceptions as to how fairly they think they are being treated compared to others. It is based on the idea that employees are motivated to seek fairness in the rewards they expect for task performance.

The following are the key elements of equity theory:

- Contribution: "What am I putting into the business?" (e.g., time, effort, and skills)
- Return: "What am I getting out of the job?" (e.g., pay, recognition, and status)
- Comparison: "How do my contribution and returns compare to others?"

Based on these elements, employees make a judgment on fairness, which in turn impacts their satisfaction and behavior.

Equity Theory: How Employees Try to Reduce Inequity
- **They will reduce their contributions:** They will do less work, take longer breaks, leave early on Fridays, and call in "sick" on Mondays.

- **They will try to change the returns or rewards they receive:** They will lobby their supervisor for a raise or they will steal company supplies or equipment.
- **They will distort the inequity:** They will exaggerate their work efforts and complain they're not paid what they're worth.
- **They will change the object of comparison:** They may compare themselves to another person instead of the original one.
- **They will leave the situation:** They will quit, transfer, or shift to another group.

Locke and Latham's Goal-Setting Theory

Locke and Latham's **goal-setting theory** proposes that employees can be motivated by goals that are specific and challenging but achievable. Locke and Latham assert that the goal-setting process is certainly natural, but that it is useful only if two things happen—people understand the goals and accept them. What's needed, then, is to set the right goals in the right way.

Drucker's Management by Objectives

Peter Drucker's **Management by Objectives (MBO)** is a four-stage process in which a manager and employee jointly set objectives for the employee, the manager develops an action plan for achieving the objective, the manager and employee periodically review the employee's performance, and the manager makes a performance appraisal and rewards the employee according to results. The purpose of MBO is to motivate, rather than control, employees.

The Four Stages of Management by Objectives (MBO)

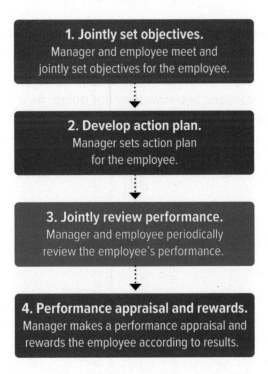

1. **Jointly set objectives.**
Manager and employee meet and jointly set objectives for the employee.

2. **Develop action plan.**
Manager sets action plan for the employee.

3. **Jointly review performance.**
Manager and employee periodically review the employee's performance.

4. **Performance appraisal and rewards.**
Manager makes a performance appraisal and rewards the employee according to results.

Ways to Create Role Empowerment

Researchers have found a number of ways to create role *empowerment* using workers' motivation and performance:

1. Skill variety: "How many different skills does my job require?"

2. Task identity: "How many different tasks are required to complete the work?"

3. Task significance: "How many other people are affected by my job?"

4. Autonomy: "How much discretion does my job give me?"

5. Feedback: "How often do I find out how well I am doing?"

The Impact of Empowering Your Workforce

There are a number of benefits to an organization when it empowers its workforce:

- High motivation
- High performance
- High satisfaction
- Low absenteeism and turnover

Decisions

Ellie and Wang are reading about motivational theories. Choose the term that best applies.

1. Ellie and Wang create a new policy called "Walk the Floor" where managers make a special effort to check on employees and how they are doing. As a result, they see an increase in productivity.

   A. Expectancy Theory

   B. Hertzberg's Two-Factor Theory

   C. Hawthorne Effect

   D. Theory Z

   E. Goal Setting

   F. Maslow's Hierarchy

   G. Job Enrichment

2. Ellie and Wang are committed to their team and have created a new standard that all employees will be paid a wage that ensures every employee can put a roof on their head, food in their bellies, and clothes on their backs. As a result, they see employees feeling secure and that more highly talented applicants want to work for them.

   A. Goal Setting

   B. Theory Z

   C. Hertzberg's Two-Factor Theory

   D. Expectancy Theory

   E. Hawthorne Effect

   F. Maslow's Hierarchy

   G. Job Enrichment

3. After instituting the policy, they see an uptick in job satisfaction. They want to make a bigger impact in motivation, so they work with leaders on a new program in which managers write handwritten notes of gratitude expressing their appreciation and recognizing hard work from their teams. It is a hit and motivation is through the roof!

   A. Expectancy Theory

   B. Goal Setting

   C. Maslow's Hierarchy

   D. Hertzberg's Two-Factor Theory

   E. Job Enrichment

   F. Hawthorne Effect

   G. Theory Z

4. Ellie and Wang want to build a leadership program for employees that helps them grow and develop. Their hope is that it creates purpose, accountability, and and an evironment for better feedback.

   A. Maslow's Hierarchy

   B. Hawthorne Effect

   C. Goal Setting

   D. Theory Z

   E. Expectancy Theory

   F. Hertzberg's Two-Factor Theory

   G. Job Enrichment

5. Ecodrive wants to have a culture that has long-term employees, centers on collective decision making, and demonstrates concern that extends beyond the employee to include their family.

   A. Hawthorne Effect

   B. Job Enrichment

   C. Expectancy Theory

   D. Theory Z

   E. Hertzberg's Two-Factor Theory

   F. Maslow's Hierarchy

   G. Goal Setting

6. Recently, the production team shared that the production goal is not realistic, and they don't believe with current staffing they'll be able to meet it. Even if they did, they think their current wages do not match the work they'll need to put in. They are asking to either increase the staffing or create a worthwhile bonus.

   A. Maslow's Hierarchy

   B. Expectancy Theory

   C. Goal Setting

   D. Hertzberg's Two-Factor Theory

   E. Hawthorne Effect

   F. Job Enrichment

   G. Theory Z

7. The biggest improvement in motivation and performance has come from the "Yes we can" initative in which each team and employee creates some specific, measurable, and challenging plans for the quarter. If the goals are accomplished, employees will be rewarded. The organization is quickly finding these to be a great motivator.

   A. Job Enrichment

   B. Expectancy Theory

   C. Hawthorne Effect

   D. Theory Z

   E. Hertzberg's Two-Factor Theory

   F. Goal Setting

   G. Maslow's Hierarchy

Organizational Behavior: Test

1. The management at Craftmine Company wants to analyze the company to make positive improvements each year. They should start by

    A. creating a plan for increasing production.

    B. conducting a review to analyze problems.

    C. updating its current list of stories.

    D. reviewing its departmental span of control.

    E. obtaining a buy-in from leadership.

2. Which is the best example of organizational identity?

    A. Your employer is adding a uniform performance rating system to fairly evaluate employees.

    B. Your coworkers all feel a sense of pride and commitment towards your employee.

    C. Your employer is planning a series of groundbreaking product launches in the next year.

    D. Your coworkers will be treated to annual picnics and recognition ceremonies by your employer.

    E. Your employer puts a limit on the number of people who can report to a manager.

3. The president of Seeger's Soda company wants to optimize the organizational chart to ensure that the company's managers do not have too many people reporting to them. By doing this, the president believes that the company will be well-positioned to meet its annual financial goals. This demonstrates the concept of

    A. responsibility.

    B. decentralized authority.

    C. narrow span of control.

    D. authority.

    E. work specialization.

4. Windy is a manager with Olly's Plastic Tote Company. Each morning he comes in and writes a list of tasks for each of his direct reports to complete that day. This best describes the concepts of

    A. matrix of control.

    B. centralization.

    C. accountability.

    D. delegation.

    E. span of control.

5. The senior leadership team at Brigsby's Clock Emporium prefers to make all important decisions regarding the company's operations. Brigsby's is most likely using a _____ authority.

    A. centralized

    B. staff personnel

    C. decentralized

    D. line management

    E. functional

6. What is a benefit of departmentalization?

    A. It widens the span of control.

    B. It enhances a firm's rites and rituals.

    C. It improves collective commitment.

    D. It simplifies management.

    E. It eliminates the need for staff personnel.

7. Which category is not one of the four divisional structure groupings?

    A. geographic region

    B. work process

    C. industry

    D. occupational specialty

    E. customer group

8. Neo Speaker Company has functional teams that report up to CEO. The product management team also directs different specialists from these functional teams on various projects throughout the year. Which structure best describes the one used by Neo Speaker?

A. narrow

B. modular

C. cross-functional

D. matrix

E. line

9. Channel Sales Company wants to review its market for new product opportunities and potential threats to the company. The Board asks for volunteers to form a team to analyze the market and provide feedback at the next quarterly meeting. The team that the Board created can best be described as a(n) _____ team.

A. project

B. action

C. advice

D. virtual

E. hybrid

10. Tre's Toy Company implemented a new network to connect itself to its supply and shipping vendors. The company is considering outsourcing its accounts payable processing to a vendor and adding the vendor to the network as well. Tre's Toy Company is most likely using a

A. modular structure.

B. virtual organization.

C. hybrid organization.

D. self-managed authority.

E. matrix structure.

11. What is the end result in the basic model of motivation?

A. goals

B. behaviors

C. output

D. needs

E. rewards

12. JCB Company wants to motivate its assembly team to by providing a bonus each time they exceed established production goals. _____ represents the behaviors definition included in the model of motivation.

A. Employee needs

B. Base salary

C. Production output

D. The bonus

E. Production goals

13. The leadership team at Recon Production Works makes it a point to regularly compliment and thank employees for their accomplishments and achievements. Which type of reward is the leadership team utilizing?

A. extrinsic

B. valence

C. expectancy

D. enrichment

E. intrinsic

14. Timbre Pharmaceuticals wants its employees to believe that their work is making a difference to the organization. Senior leadership holds weekly employee meetings where they share stories about how their products positively impact and enrich the lives of customers. This is an example of _____, a(n) _____ reward.

    A. purpose; intrinsic

    B. valence; extrinsic

    C. needs; extrinsic

    D. motivation; extrinsic

    E. promotion; intrinsic

15. The Human Resources Manager at Oddball Sports has been reading up on motivational theories. She begins asking Oddball Sports managers to spend time in one-on-one meetings with employees. She wants them to ask about their well-being and solicit feedback about their role and the company. The HR Manager has most likely been reading about _____ theory.

    A. Thorndike and Skinner's Reinforcement

    B. Vroom's Expectancy

    C. Herzberg's Two-Factor

    D. The Hawthorne Effect

    E. Adam's Equity

16. Antoine recently graduated from college and relocated from Wisconsin to Texas. He was worried about joining a new company in a new state. Antoine was pleased to learn that his new employer sponsored a company softball team. By joining the team, he made friends and found out more about the company and the city. The job most likely satisfies the _____ level of Maslow's Hierarchy of Needs.

    A. social

    B. physiological

    C. self-actualization

    D. safety

    E. enrichment

17. Lali is the director of operations with Seeksme Corporation. She has been updating the jobs held by her direct reports to include additional responsibility while also providing regular recognition to her employees. Lali is most likely a believer in _____ theory.

    A. Two-Factor

    B. Job Enrichment

    C. Reinforcement

    D. Expectancy

    E. Equity

18. Which theory assumes that workers are irresponsible and lacking in ambition and, therefore, require extrinsic rewards to motivate?

    A. McGregor's Theory Y

    B. Ouchi's Theory Z

    C. Vroom's Expectancy Theory

    D. McGregor's Theory X

    E. Adam's Equity Theory

19. Which theory assumes that workers value a working environment supporting family, culture, and traditions and is characterized by long-term employment and collective responsibility and decision making?

A. McGregor's Theory Y

B. Ouchi's Theory Z

C. Vroom's Expectancy Theory

D. McGregor's Theory X

E. Adam's Equity Theory

20. According to Locke and Latham's goal-setting theory, goals are useful only if they are

A. broad in nature.

B. easy-to-meet.

C. challenging, but attainable.

D. mandated by management.

E. flexible and easily changed.

7 Introduction to Marketing

What To Expect

By the end of the chapter, you will be able to:

- Recall how marketing adds value to an organization's goods and services.
- Differentiate among products, product lines, and product mixes.

Copyright © McGraw Hill   angellodeco/Shutterstock

Lesson 7-1
The Basics of Marketing

Marketing: America's Pastime

"How Can We Take Advantage of Marketing Opportunities?"

Mark is about to start a summer marketing internship program with the minor league baseball team, The Great Falls Golden Doodles. "The Doods," as they are affectionately known around town, plan to engage Mark in several marketing tasks as they prepare for the upcoming season.

It is Mark's first day of work, and although he is a little anxious, he is also excited to get started and help the team however he can!

> Welcome to the minors, Rookie! I'm Jim, the general manager. We are thrilled you are joining us for this season. This is Ginger; she is our marketing manager.

> Yes, Mark, we're excited to work with you. Because our business is primarily based on the season, we HAVE to make sure we capitalize on our key marketing opportunities.

> So, before the season is literally in full swing, we think it's important for you to gain an understanding of our "value-add" and the products we sell here at the ball park—or as our fans affectionately call it "The Dog House."

> Let's get your stuff put away and get you started.

In this lesson, we'll help Mark add value to the team.

What Is Marketing and How Does It Add Value?

Marketing is a core function of business. It helps businesses understand the needs, wants, and desires of customers. This understanding is then used to develop, price, distribute, and promote value-added products and services in the marketplace. Marketing evolved over four eras: the production, selling, marketing concept, and customer relationship eras. Value is an important part of marketing. Companies market products, product lines, and a product mix.

Understanding Marketing

According to the American Marketing Association, **marketing** is the activity, set of institutions, and processes for creating, communicating, delivering, and exchanging offerings that have value for customers, clients, partners, and society at large. Marketing is practiced by both:

For-Profit Organizations	Nonprofit Organizations
We see marketing being practiced everywhere by profit-oriented firms to deliver goods (Tide, Chipotle, and Chevrolet) and services (Hilton, Verizon, and Netflix).	We also see marketing used more and more by nonprofits, whether private-sector organizations such as Harvard University, the Presbyterian Church, the Red Cross, or the American Cancer Society, or public-sector organizations such as the University of Nebraska, the U.S. Postal Service, or the U.S. Marines.

Companies strive to use a **marketing concept**, which focuses on customer satisfaction, service, and profitability.

Customer Satisfaction: "We Need to Give Buyers What They Expect from Us."

Learning what customers want and giving it to them isn't a unique idea, but it's surprising how many firms emphasize promotion or sales instead. **Customer satisfaction** is the concept of offering a product to please buyers by meeting their expectations. The most successful American businesses consistently stay aware of what customers want and provide it to them.

Focus on Serving Customers: "Everyone, from CEO to Stock Clerk, Should Focus on Customer Service."

Firms that successfully employ the marketing concept integrate their approach so that everyone in the organization—from top management to entry-level associates—focuses on the same goal of satisfying the customer. This is why you may see managers at local supermarkets step up and help with bagging groceries during busy periods at the checkout counters. The "not my job" attitude doesn't work here.

Emphasis on Profitability, Not Sales: "We Need to Concentrate on the Products That Are Most Profitable."

Successful firms focus on offering the goods and services that are most profitable, not on offering the entire range of products and not on total sales. For example, a restaurant may have only a handful of menu items that drive revenue and profitability, therefore they may choose to revise their menu to focus on what items keep them in business.

The marketing concept combined with the advent of digital marketing and social media has led to a further refinement known as the relationship management concept. **Customer relationship management (CRM)** emphasizes finding out everything possible about customers and then using that information to satisfy and even exceed their expectations in order to build customer loyalty over the long term.

Delivering Value and Building Relationships with Customers

Companies focus on utilizing marketing to produce and deliver offerings that have value—for customers, clients, partners, and society at large. **Value** is defined as a customer's perception that a certain product offers a better relationship between costs and benefits than competitors' products do.

Note that we used the word *perception*—it is not the actual value of one product compared to another, but rather how the customer perceives that value.

Decisions

Jim and Ginger meet to help Mark get more acquainted with the role marketing plays in the organization. Ginger explains to him the role marketing plays on the team.

Mark, our strategy is to utilize _____ to focus on customer satisfaction, service, and profitability.

A. a marketing concept

B. the value-added process

C. the profitability concept

D. the customer relationship process

Because season ticket holders are very important to our success, we utilize a _____ system to find out as much information as we can about them to ensure we are exceeding their expectations and building long-term loyalty.

A. marketing

B. CRM

C. production-era

D. value

We've heard that we need to enhance our food menu and have better apparel options for our fans. We believe this will help us increase the perceived _____ of the fan experience.

A. marketability

B. value

C. profitability

D. marketing concept

Correct Answers: A; B; B

How to Distinguish Products, Product Lines, and Product Mixes

Whatever the type of marketing, the point is to get consumers to buy or use the organization's products. Product-oriented organizations may carry some sort of product(s), have product lines, have a product mix, or some combination of the three. As a company grows and evolves they may go from a single product to offering a number of products so as to better survive wide swings in demand.

Product: A Good or Service That Can Satisfy Buyers' Needs

A **product** is a good (which is tangible) or service (intangible) that can satisfy customer needs.

Examples: A product can be almost anything: goods such as tomato soup, motorcycles, hearing aids, or houses, or services such as auto insurance, plumbing repair, Internet connection, hotel stay, or college education.

Product Line: A Group of Products Designed for a Similar Market

A **product line** is a collection of products designed for a similar market or that are physically similar.

Examples: Campbell Soup Company sells not only tomato soup but also a product line of other condensed soups: mushroom, minestrone, and so on. State Farm offers not only auto but also life, home, and health insurance.

Product Mix: The Combination of All Product Lines

A **product mix** is the combination of all product lines that a firm offers.

Examples: Campbell offers condensed soups, Supper Bakes meal kits, Prego Italian sauces, Swanson broth, and Pepperidge Farm cookies.

Decisions

Mark, you're learning very quickly. And I could really use your help with a few tasks today. In my upcoming meeting with Jim, he wants us to understand what our core products, product lines, and product mixes are going to be for the season. I've written them down, and I'd like for you to go through the list and put each in the appropriate category.

1. Which of the following lists best represents a product line?

    A. Hot dogs, hats, tickets, baseball bats, big foam fingers

    B. Party planning or Uber rides to and from events

    C. Regular Coke, Coke Zero, Diet Coke, Coke Life, and Cherry Coke

    D. Hot dogs, burgers, nachos, and our specialty items

    E. Tickets as single-game, small packages, and season tickets

2. Which of the following best represents a product mix? Choose all that apply.

    A. Hot dogs, brats, and polish sausages

    B. Hot dogs, burgers, nachos, and our specialty items

    C. Tickets as single-game, small packages, and season tickets

Correct Answers: C; B; C

Consumer Buying Behavior

By the end of this lesson, you will be able to:

- Categorize customer behaviors into the steps of the consumer buying process with which they are associated.

- Differentiate among the factors that influence buying behavior.

Consumer Buying Behavior: Ball Game or Movie?

Mark is quickly learning that marketing plays a major role in the success of an organization. He understands that it is imperative for the business to add value to its customers. Therefore, marketers must learn as much as they can about customers and how they make their purchasing decisions.

You've seen some of the ways we generate revenue beyond ticket sales. Now, we'd like to get your help in better understanding our fans.

We want you to utilize the consumer buying behavior process to help us understand how we can better serve our fans. Last year, we noticed a dip in attendance, concessions sales, and revenue from our team gift shop.

Yes, we have a crucial goal to increase the revenue that's generated.

Let us know what you find based on some of this data we collected from fans.

For this task, Mark will need to help the Doods better understand their customers. In this lesson, we'll help him learn a few things about how consumers make decisions and what influences their buying behavior.

Deciding What to Purchase: The Consumer Buying Process

Consumers don't automatically make a purchasing decision. In fact, they typically work through a process to determine whether they will ultimately make a purchase. By understanding how the consumer thinks and what influences their process, marketers can more effectively communicate and assist consumers in that decision-making process.

How Does the Consumer Buying Process Work?

The **consumer buying process** consists of five steps by which consumers make decisions: problem recognition, information search, evaluation of alternatives, purchase decision, and postpurchase evaluation.

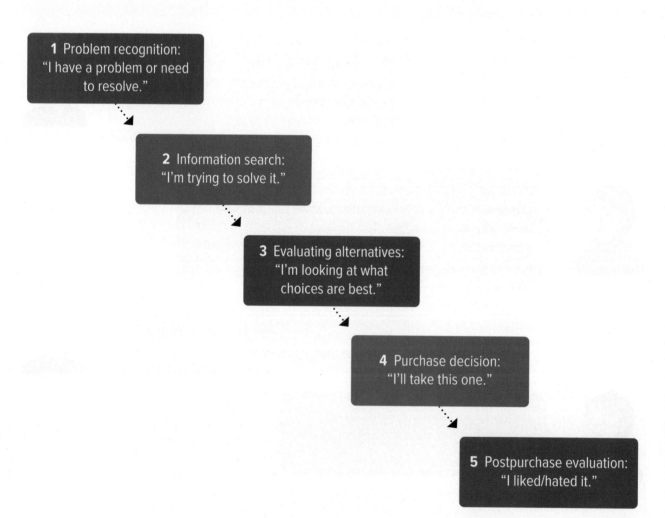

1 Problem recognition: "I have a problem or need to resolve."

2 Information search: "I'm trying to solve it."

3 Evaluating alternatives: "I'm looking at what choices are best."

4 Purchase decision: "I'll take this one."

5 Postpurchase evaluation: "I liked/hated it."

Problem Recognition: "I Realize I Have a Problem to Resolve."

Here you discover you have a problem or a need that needs to be addressed, such as hunger.

Example: You are wrapping up a long day of work, and you know there are limited food options in your fridge at home.

Information Search: "I Need to Find a Solution to My Problem."

Here you do some sort of search for a solution to your problem. For example:

- You could go to the store and buy ingredients, or a premade meal.
- You could stop at a fast-food or quick service restaurant on your way home.
- You could eat at a restaurant.
- You could put in an order to a restaurant through an app such as UberEats and have food brought to you at home.

Evaluating Alternatives: "I'll Weigh the Pros and Cons of the Products Available."

After gaining information on competing products, you consider the benefits and drawbacks of each. For example:

- You are pretty tired and don't necessarily have the energy to stop at the store, buy ingredients, and make something, nor do you really feel like going to a restaurant and sitting down.
- You want something a bit higher quality than fast food.
- You don't mind spending a little extra today to get something you'll enjoy.
- You want to get home and enjoy your meal while you relax and watch Netflix.

Purchase Decision: "I'll Choose This One or Not Choose at All."

Finally, you make your decision. You decide you'll order food from one of your favorite restaurants through UberEats. You don't mind spending a few extra dollars on the service because you know you'll get a good quality meal from one of your favorite restaurants, and you'll be able to time the delivery to arrive shortly after you get home from work.

Postpurchase Evaluation: "I'm Happy/Unhappy with My Purchase and Will/Will Not Buy a Similar One in the Future."

Marketers hope you will be satisfied with your purchase and might be inclined to repeat your choice in the future.

On the other hand, you might suffer unhappiness, *buyer's remorse*, for having bought something that you perceive later to be too expensive, too shoddy, lacking other products' features, not delivering on its promises, and so on.

You may decide while this was a good decision for this particular situation, having food delivered more than once a week would be too expensive and not a good use of your income.

Decisions

Mark, did you have a good weekend?

I guess it was okay. Nothing spectacular, but come to think about it, I'm not really sure what I did to tell you the truth.

Haha, same here. It got me thinking about why so many people like coming to the watch the Doods. They are probably bored with life, and this is a way to make them feel connected to something. This is the concept of _____, and at least they are taking steps to resolve it.

    A. personal satisfaction

    B. evaluation

    C. problem recognition

You know, if you think about it, you're right! What if we try to work that into our advertisements? What if we try to give people a sense of belonging here at the park watching *their* Doods play each week?

Great idea! It's almost like you are getting inside the heads of our customers and figuring out _____.

    A. customer buying behavior

    B. the product life cycle

    C. psychological factors

That's exactly what I'm doing, I think? Yeah, that's what I'm doing! When customers start _____ of what to do with their time, what else do they have to choose from that is even close to what the Doods can offer them on a weekly basis?

A. recognizing the problem

B. evaluating alternatives

C. taking corrective action

Haha, well, Mark, you might be overinflating the impact of a minor league baseball team on a person's life, but you really are making a point about why consumers desire certain products. They want to feel like they are solving a problem they have at the moment, and maybe we should think about making people want to feel part of something cohesive here at the ball park. The Doods might just be what they need!

Correct Answers: C; A; B

Factors That Influence Buying Behavior

Throughout the buying process, consumers are influenced by various factors, from global to personal, from general to specific. It is important for marketers to learn and become aware of these factors as they impact what consumers may or may not purchase.

Culture and Subculture

The Influence of Values and Attitudes

Consumers' ideas about ways of doing things are passed along to us from earlier generations of whatever nationality we are (culture) and the ethnic, religious, age, education, gender, and other groups we belong to (subculture). These influence our buying decisions.

Consumers may want to come to a baseball game because it is considered the national pastime, because they were once part of team, or because the community around them supports the team.

Examples of culture and subculture: nationality, gender and age, ethnicity and race, and religion

Social Class

The Influence of Our Socioeconomic Group

Our choices are also affected by our social class, whether lower, middle, or upper. The cars and houses people buy, for instance, reflect their income levels.

In minor league baseball, we can create an experience at a price for different income levels allowing fans at all socioeconomic levels to enjoy coming to a game. We do that through our ticket pricing, price of apparel, concessions offerings, and a wide variety of products and services.

Examples of social class: income level, profession, educational level, social status, and political status

Reference Groups

The Influence of Groups We Identify With

We are also affected by those special groups we belong to or identify with: family, friends, fellow students, coworkers, music lovers, fraternity/sorority members, and so on.

If you're an athlete, for example, you may favor the kind of footwear worn by other athletes, rather than, say, those in country music bands. This is one of the great parts of being a fan, you feel connected to the team and can feel like you are part of the team by cheering with other fans, wearing the apparel, and joining friends, family, and coworkers at a game.

Examples of reference groups: family, friends, fellow students, college groups, and coworkers

Personal Image

The Look We Wish to Project

A lot of us want to project a certain image, based on the products we buy.

This is why marketers often recruit sports stars and other celebrities to promote products. As an organization, teams want to project an image that plays to a wide array of people so that coming to a game is the thing to do!

Examples of personal image: physical look, profession, lifestyle, and fashion

Situational Matters

The Effects of Timing, Moods, Impulse, and Expectations

All kinds of other things affect our buying decisions: timing, moods, impulse, expectations, advertising, pricing, and beliefs about a product.

Teams try to create situations with special promotions, incentives for coming to the game such as discounts and giveaways from sponsors. It also helps when the team is winning!

Examples of situational matters: timing, coincidence, mood, and impulse

Decisions

Mark, our _____ here at the ballpark has been on higher-level income fans, but I think we need to find a way to attract a larger fan base including people with lower incomes.

    A. subculture

    B. geographic

    C. reference group

    D. socioeconomic focus

I noticed that while being at the first couple games. It seems to me that if the Doods are only appealing to one type of person, then we have an opportunity to attract the _____ they identify with, but we will probably miss out on others.

    A. classes

    B. marketing mix

    C. reference groups

    D. people

Yes, and that concerns me too, since we could be appealing to a much larger group of people in general. Let's run a few targeted promotions based on social media by offering a deep discount if the tickets are purchased within 10 minutes of the ad running. Maybe this will entice certain groups of people to buy the tickets on a whim, and maybe these _____ will attract them.

    A. situation matters

    B. subcultures

    C. consumer preferences

    D. reference groups

I'll get right on it! I'm curious to see if this will work.

Correct Answers: D; C; A

Lesson 7-3
Marketing Strategy

By the end of this lesson, you will be able to:

- Differentiate among the three approaches to market strategy.
- Differentiate among the types of consumer segmentation.
- Differentiate among the types of business segmentation.

Building a Winning Marketing Strategy

As the season approaches, the front office team needs to build a winning marketing strategy that will help them target the right customers. Mark, Ginger, and Jim huddle to discuss how to create a marketing strategy.

Wow, Mark, you are proving yourself to be an MVP in the marketing department!

We've been really impressed with the work you've done so far. You're definitely ready for your next task.

Last season, we were able to capture some great information about our fans. This season, we want to use that information to develop a target market profile and to help us better understand our key market segmentation.

Once we know this information, we'll be able to develop a better marketing strategy for the upcoming season.

And we'll have the right marketing mix to deliver value to our fans!

In this lesson, we'll help Mark execute this task with the team, by learning about how markets are classified, what constitutes a marketing strategy, and the different ways to segment a market.

Developing a Strategy for a Target Market

A marketing strategy is a plan for identifying the target market among market segments (groups), creating the right marketing mix, and dealing with the external environment. Marketers targeting consumers may market to geographic, demographic, psychographic, benefit, or user-rate segments and may also resort to niche marketing and one-to-one marketing. Business-to-business marketers classify business markets into geographic, customer-based, and product-use-based segments. Nonprofit marketers draw on five types of marketing approaches: people, place, event, cause, and organization.

Marketing, which begins with learning who your customers are and what they need and want, may be of three types:

- For-profit marketing to consumers
- For-profit marketing of businesses to other businesses
- Nonprofit marketing

How Do You Begin to Develop a Marketing Strategy?

It starts with—this is important!—having a **marketing strategy**, a plan for (1) identifying the target market among market segments, (2) creating the right marketing mix to reach that target market, and (3) dealing with important forces in the external marketing environment. Buyers or users of a product fall into all kinds of groups, or segments.

A particular need that the firm can serve
Have access to the product
Not already served by too many competitors
Attributes
Have decision-making power to buy the product
Have enough money to afford the firm's product

Thus, a marketing strategy relies on

- **Market segmentation**, dividing a market into groups whose members have similar characteristics or wants and needs.
- **Target marketing strategy**, consisting of marketing directly to such segments—the target market. Marketers don't have endless resources.

Thus, they need to direct their efforts toward people who are most likely to buy their products.

Marketing professionals look to create a well-defined target market strategy by defining the following consumer attributes.

Decisions

Mark, since you've been at many of the games, what are your thoughts about the type of customer the Doods appeal to the most?

You know, I have been thinking about this, and I have noticed a large part of our audience seems to be women in their 20s and 30s. It's strange because I thought I would notice more men.

Good eye, Mark! You have nailed our _____.

A. target market

B. marketing strategy

C. mass market

D. attributes

Really? Well, I guess I'm that good!

The Doods seems to be attracting a younger female audience, so we have been thinking about developing a full _____ to target this group.

A. marketing strategy

B. for-profit marketing concept plan

C. checklist

D. market attribute plan

True, and I think we could _____ the market even more with a bit more research to help us really narrow down on this group.

A. mass

B. divide

C. segment

D. attribute

I think you're right! Grab your notebook and binoculars, and let's meet at the game tonight at 7:00 PM!

Correct Answers: A; A; C

Market Segmentation

The **consumer market** consists of all those individuals or households that want goods or services for their personal use. These are all the products you buy every day, from toothpaste to insurance to watching Netflix.

Consumers are divided into five segments by **geographic segmentation**, **demographic segmentation**, **psychographic segmentation**, **benefit segmentation**, and **user-rate segmentation**.

Geographic

Dividing the Market by Location

Geographic segmentation categorizes customers according to geographic location.

Examples: A nationwide retailer of hiking boots would tend to advertise more in Colorado (with its Rocky Mountain trails) than in New York City. Makers of tortillas would promote their products more in Texas (with its large Hispanic population) than in Minnesota.

Demographic

Dividing the Market by Age, Gender, or Income

Demographic segmentation consists of categorizing consumers according to statistical characteristics of a population, such as gender, age, income, education, social class, ethnicity, and so on.

Example: Clothing is segmented first by gender, then by age, then by income level.

Psychographic

Dividing the Market by Psychological Characteristics, Values, and Lifestyles

Psychographic segmentation consists of categorizing people according to lifestyle, values, and psychological characteristics.

Examples: Frugal versus free spending, or rebel versus conservative.

Benefit

Dividing the Market by Benefits That People Seek in a Product

Benefit segmentation consists of categorizing people according to the benefits, or attributes, they seek in a product.

Examples: Style versus economy, or safety versus speed, or high-tech versus low-tech features.

User Rate

Dividing the Market by Frequency of Customer Usage

User-rate segmentation consists of categorizing people according to volume or frequency of usage, as with heavy users versus light users.

Example: 60% of U.S. adults purchased wine in 2013; however, the Wine Market Council reported that just over one-third (35%) of adults aged 21 years and older consumed wine in 2013.

Taking Segmentation Even Further: Niche Marketing and One-to-One Marketing

Segmentation can be taken even further through two other processes: (1) niche marketing and (2) one-to-one marketing.

Niche Marketing: Dividing Marketing Segments into Microsegments

Niche marketing consists of dividing market segments even further to microsegments for which sales may be profitable.

For example, men who grow long beards may be actively seeking and purchasing grooming products for their beards, but those products would not necessarily have appeal outside the niche.

One-to-One Marketing: Reducing Market Segmentation to Individual Customers

One-to-one marketing consists of reducing market segmentation to the smallest part—individual customers. Marketers need to do intensive research to gain a deep understanding of a customer's preferences and keep detailed records on customer interactions.

For example, common uses are online recommendations for books and movies by Amazon.com based on consumers' previous purchasing or viewing histories. High-end applications are sales of expensive real estate, boats, and cars, where a salesperson may collect all kinds of information about a wealthy prospect, then craft a custom sales pitch.

For-Profit Marketing to Businesses: Goods and Services for Business Use

The **business market** or **business-to-business (B2B) market**, also known as the industrial or organizational market, consists of those business individuals and organizations that want business goods and services that will help them produce or supply their own business goods and services.

What Are Three Market Segments That Businesses May Target in Marketing to Other Businesses?

Business markets can be classified into three categories: geographic, customer-based, and product-use-based.

Category	Description	Example
Geographic	As with the consumer version, the business version of geographic segmentation consists of categorizing customers according to their geographic location. Industries are often grouped in certain geographical areas.	The part of the San Francisco Bay area near Palo Alto that has been dubbed Silicon Valley hosts such well-known information-technology companies as Google, Yahoo, Facebook, Apple, Intel, Oracle, and Sun Microsystems.
Customer-based	Resembling demographic segmentation for consumers, in the business market, customer-based segmentation consists of categorizing business customers according to specific characteristics.	Examples might include size, industry type, and product/service-related attributes.
Product-use-based	Product-use-based segmentation categorizes business customers according to how they will use the seller's product.	A manufacturer of GPS (global positioning system) devices might divide its target market into, say, long-haul trucking companies, taxi-cab companies, delivery companies (pizza, flowers), home health care services, security companies, and so on.

Decisions

Mark, were you able to make any sense of the information about our fans that I gave you last week?

That was a lot of information, and I tried my best to break it down into categories just to get a grip on it.

Good! That is actually called _____, and it is the first step in the right direction.

    A. market segementation

    B. mass marketing

    C. niche marketing

    D. customer breakdown

See, my schooling is paying off, right?

I would say it has! Did you use _____ segmentation to divide the market up by things such as age, gender, religion, and so on?

    A. geographic

    B. psychographic

    C. demographic

    D. personal

I sure did, and then I also dove into where most of the fans are driving in from to go to the games.

Excellent, I was just about to ask you if you
_____ segmented your results.

   A. categorically

   B. psychographically

   C. demographically

   D. geographically

When I compared the two together, I see we have our largest fan base coming from within 10 miles of the stadium, and they are women, who are about 28 to 40 years old.

Fantastic! I have been trying to figure out who our primary target actually is, and I do believe we are getting close to being able to find a better way to market directly to this group!

Correct Answers: A; C; D

Lesson 7-4
The 4 Ps

By the end of this lesson, you will be able to:

- Recall the reasons a firm may develop a new product.
- Recall the four key strategy considerations (the 4 Ps) of a marketing mix.

The Marketing Mix

"Let's Explore Product, Price, Place, and Promotion."

A marketing plan comes together when marketers deploy the 4 Ps of marketing: product, price, place (distribution), and promotion around their target market. Ginger will need Mark's assistance to begin to construct what is known as a marketing mix that applies all 4 Ps to a target market ensuring the right products are offered at the right price, and distributed and promoted to the customer in the optimal manner.

"Don't look back," said legendary ballplayer Satchel Paige. "Something might be gaining on you." This sentiment also reflects an important reason to produce new products, but it is only the first of four reasons.

And those are?

Don't worry, Mark. We'll discuss those in more detail later on. But understand that this information becomes the basis for determining the marketing mix, which consists of four key strategy considerations—the "4 Ps" of product, pricing, place, and promotion.

Copyright © McGraw Hill

In this lesson, we'll help Mark and Ginger create marketing mixes for the Doods.

The 4 P Marketing Mix Starts with New Products

Companies have to develop new products for four important reasons. Such development requires doing initial research and identifying the target market. This information becomes the basis for determining the marketing mix, which consists of four key strategy considerations—the "4 Ps" of product, price, place, and promotion.

Four Reasons to Develop New Products

A **new product** is defined as a product that either (1) is a significant improvement over existing products or (2) performs a new function for the consumer. New products (which may be new to the company, if not necessarily the marketplace) are the lifeblood of any company and of the free-market system.

To Stay Ahead of or Match the Competition

History is full of examples of companies that thought they were dominant in their fields and failed to recognize how important a competitor's development was.

This is evident with technology and how quickly a product can become obsolete. Take, for example, the advancements in smartphones. Every year companies continue to try to stay ahead or at least match the competition.

To Continue to Expand Revenues and Profits

Some small businesses may be content to have the same earnings every year. But other businesses need to grow to continue rewarding shareholders. And to do that, they need to introduce new products.

For example, a company that owns a quick service restaurant may want to open more stores so that it can build a franchise model and scale to become a regional or national brand.

To Fill Out a Product Line

Some companies may offer certain products and it makes sense for them to create new products that are a natural extension of what they offer to fill out a product line.

For example if a company made dog food, it would make sense for it to launch treats and canned food.

To Take Advantage of an Opportunity

For a period of time, there may be an opening in the market and companies may want to capitalize on a trend.

For example, there may be information that comes out about a new "super food" and companies may take advantage of the trend by creating products that feature that food or ingredient.

Decisions

Mark, did you get a chance to look at those concession stand sales reports I sent you?

Yes, I did, and it sure looks like we are selling a lot of soft drinks but not so much beer, and beer is where we make the most money.

Good eye! I think we need to expand our beer selection to give customers some options and this would bolster our _____.

A. product line

B. beer expenditures

C. investor expectations

Yes, and this will directly impact our _____.

A. marketing mix

B. revenues and profits

C. competition

Correct Answers: A; B

Understanding the 4 Ps

Once a firm has determined that it needs a new product, the next challenges are:

- To conduct research to determine opportunities and challenges
- To identify the target market
- To determine the strategies for the marketing mix

The Process of Building a Marketing Mix

A **marketing mix** consists of the four key strategy considerations called the 4 Ps: product, pricing, place, and promotion strategies. Specifically, the marketing mix involves:

1. Developing a product that will fill consumer wants
2. Pricing the product
3. Distributing the product to a place where consumers will buy it
4. Promoting the product

All these blended together constitute a marketing program.

Let's see how the marketing process works.

Conducting Research and Determining the Target Market

The marketing process begins with conducting a survey or research to determine whether there's a market for the product the company is considering producing. That research should help to establish the target market for the product.

The Product Strategy

A marketing program starts with designing and developing a product—a good, service, or idea intended to satisfy consumer wants and needs. The designers must consider shape, size, color, brand name, packaging, and product image.

In reaching these decisions, a company needs to consider such matters as how well the product differs from other products. It also may do concept testing and test marketing to get a sense of consumer likes and dislikes.

- **Concept testing** is marketing research designed to solicit initial consumer reaction to new product ideas. That is, you might go out among the population you've identified as your target population and ask them if they think your potential product is a good idea.
- **Test marketing** is the process of testing products among potential users. That is, you try out a sample of the potential product among the target population to see what they think of it.

The Pricing Strategy

Pricing is figuring out how much to charge for a product—the price, or exchange value, for a good or service. The price of a product can depend on whether you have competitors, whether you need to offer low prices to get customers in the door, and the like.

The Place Strategy

Placing, or distribution, is the process of moving goods or services from the seller to prospective buyers. For example, retailers have expanded their abilities to serve customers who want products delivered to them directly by enhancing their e-commerce sites.

The Promotion Strategy

Promotion consists of all the techniques companies use to motivate consumers to buy their products—techniques such as advertising, public relations, publicity, personal selling, and other kinds of sales.

Decisions

Mark, you've picked up this information really quickly. I know Jim will be excited, and I'm sure he'll want to meet with you to discuss your ideas about potential new products.

Okay, but I'm a little nervous.

My guess is that Jim will probably ask you certain questions, based on the products that we mentioned earlier—primarily ticket options. It'll be really helpful if you have some of your responses ready.

A little bit later, Jim approaches Mark to chat.

Hi Mark! Ginger said you have ideas for getting more ticket sales?

Yes, as I see it, the primary product of the Doods is ticket sales for baseball games, but customers do not feel the _____ relates to value for them.

    A. placement

    B. promotion

    C. price

    D. product

Interesting. So if our single ticket price was lowered by $2 or so on week night games, do you think this would help get more customers?

Possibly so, but some of the problem is many of the customers said they don't really even know when the home games are, so I think we need to couple this price drop with more _____.

A. placement

B. market research

C. promotion

D. price drops

You know, Mark, you are asking for a price drop and more expenditures at the same time. That is going to cost quite a bit, so are you sure we will make enough money to cover this?

I think we will because I have spent the last six weeks _____ this idea with customers, and a large percentage of them agreed this would be more valuable to them.

A. concept testing

B. placing

C. marketing

D. market mixing

Let's hope so! Everything is a bit of a gamble, but your research helps greatly!

Correct Answers: C; C; A

Market Research

By the end of this lesson, you will be able to:

- Differentiate among the steps of the marketing research process.
- Differentiate among forces in the external marketing environment that can affect marketing strategy.

The Power of Knowing Your Market

"Making Informed Marketing Decisions with Research."

Mark has proven himself to be a great intern. He is not only learning a great deal about marketing but also contributing to the team with his creativity. As a result, Jim and Ginger want to involve Mark in gathering feedback from customers through market research.

Mark, I really like the innovative ideas you are coming up with for us!

Yes, I think we can really utilize your talent and work ethic to help us assess some marketing data from last year as well as build our market research plans for this season.

Let's go over the role market research plays in marketing. Then we'll give you a chance to help us better understand our market.

I'll get you started!

In this lesson, we'll help Mark understand the Doods' market by learning more about market research and the marketing environment.

Understanding the Marketing Research Process

Marketing research, part of the process of determining the 4 P marketing mix, is a four-step process of gathering and analyzing data about problems relating to marketing products, aiming to provide accurate information to marketers. Besides the marketing mix, marketing strategy must take into account the external marketing environment, which consists of seven outside forces.

Marketing Research: Getting Accurate Information to Make Marketing Decisions

For a marketing program to be successful, it depends on something crucial: accurate information. Accurate information is the province of **marketing research**, the systematic gathering and analyzing of data about problems relating to the marketing of goods and services.

Among other things, marketing research can tell you what consumers think about your firm's products, how satisfied they are with them compared with competitors', the effectiveness of your ads, what the sales potential is of new products, and what price changes might do to sales.

The marketing research process consists of four basic steps.

Define the Problem: Clarify the Question to Be Answered

Marketing professionals start defining the problem by analyzing the following questions:

- What is the present problem?
- What are the opportunities?
- What information is needed?
- How should we collect and analyze data?

Collect Facts: Use Published Data or Interviews, Observation, Experimentation, and Focus Groups to Get Information

Marketing research draws upon two kinds of data—secondary and primary. Most market researchers start with secondary data because it's cheaper and easier, although it has some disadvantages.

Secondary data is information acquired and published by others. Examples: U.S. Census Bureau data, various government publications, newspapers, magazines, academic journals, Internet searches, and blogs are all examples of secondary data sources.

Primary data is data derived from original research, such as that which you might conduct yourself. Examples: Direct observation, interviews, surveys, questionnaires, customer comment cards, and concept testing are all different sources of primary data. Some other important sources:

- **Focus groups** are small groups of people who meet with a discussion leader and give their opinions about a product or other matters. For example, a car company may have a group of consumers test drive a new model car and then give there feedback on the driving experience and features of the automobile.

- **Databases** are integrated collections of data stored in computer systems. In big companies, databases can be huge—so-called data warehouses—and allow market researchers to perform data mining, do computer searches of the data to detect patterns and relationships, such as customer buying patterns.
- **Neuromarketing** is the study of how people's brains respond to advertising and other brand-related messages by scientifically monitoring brainwave activity, eye tracking, and skin response.

Analyze the Data: Use Statistical Tools to Determine the Facts

Once data has been gathered, marketing researchers need to consider whether it needs to be treated further to make it useful. It may need **editing**, or checking over to eliminate mistakes. It may require the application of **data analysis**, subjected to statistical tools to determine its significance.

Take Action: Implement the Best Solution

Finally, with all the data and analysis in hand, the decision makers must decide how to use it—to determine the best solution and how it should be implemented.

Decisions

Ginger, I have been giving our product line a lot of thought, and I am drawing a blank on how to market our Dog House product, let alone come up with new products to sell.

I know how you feel! I really struggled with trying to figure out what our customers would want at the game when I first started, so I ended up asking a bunch of people at the games to get their feedback.

Yes! That is _____, and that is probably what I should do.

    A. secondary data

    B. the marketing process

    C. market research

I found it to be a great help, but I really needed more time with these people to ask them even more questions about what they like and don't like. I should have _____.

    A. collected secondary data from this group

    B. formed a focus group

    C. started the marketing process

Now you're talking! That would have been a great way to get the information we need directly from our customers. Who would have guessed that I'd actually be applying the concept of _____ in action this summer? Wow!

A. primary research

B. secondary research

C. customer relationship processing

Correct Answers: C; B; A

Understanding the Marketing Environment

In addition to developing a marketing strategy that involves (1) identifying the target market and (2) determining the right marketing mix, you must also begin (3) dealing with the external environment—specifically the external **marketing environment**, the outside forces that can influence the success of marketing programs. These forces are (1) global, (2) economic, (3) sociocultural, (4) technological, (5) competitive, (6) political, and (7) legal and regulatory.

The Marketing Environment: Outside Factors That Influence Marketing Programs

To understand this environment, marketing managers working on marketing strategy need to do **environmental scanning**—looking at the wider world around them and identifying what factors can affect the marketing program.

Marketers usually can't control the external environment, but they need to understand how they are hindered or aided by it.

Global Forces

Global forces consist of influences brought about by all our global interconnections. For example, sites like Alibaba have increased access to foreign suppliers for individuals to be able to launch new businesses and source products in different markets.

Economic Forces

Economic forces—recessions, inflation, and the like—certainly affect consumers' buying power and willingness to buy.

For example, the Great Recession deeply impacted the housing market through foreclosures. Through the recovery process, interest rates remained low for a considerable amount of time to allow home buyers to lock in historically low interest rates.

Sociocultural Forces

Sociocultural forces include cultural changes reflecting customs, beliefs, and lifestyles of groups that differ in social class, ethnicity, age, and so on.

For example, companies may adjust their marketing efforts to become more diverse and inclusive to better reflect their customers.

Technological Forces

Technological forces consist of influences both highly visible that affect retailing, such as being able to quickly build online e-commerce sites to launch products and companies, and less visible that affect manufacturing and distribution such as automation, which change the nature of delivering goods and services.

Competitive Forces

Competitive forces consist of the actions of competing firms, industries, or countries. For example, as consumers begin consuming entertainment through devices, more companies are developing services and business models to compete for these consumers.

Political Forces

Political forces are influences that occur because of the decisions of politicians and public officials. Based on legislation that is enacted and policy decisions at the local, state, and federal level, companies may need to adapt to stay viable. Companies need to also look for new business opportunities as a result of political forces.

Legal and Regulatory Forces

Legal and regulatory forces consist of laws and government regulations designed to protect consumers and restrain anti-competitive business behavior. Companies must also stay aware to stay in compliance with laws.

Decisions

Mark has learned a great deal about marketing through his internship and is ready to help Jim and Ginger have a successful season marketing the Doods!

Ginger, I spent last night _____ of the Doods in order to narrow down what forces are impacting us the most right now, and I think it's the economy.

A. scanning the environment

B. researching the business

C. watching the game on television

D. planning marketing research

Really? How do you know?

Because I have tracked the ticket sales of the Doods over the last 20 years, and it seems to follow directly with the economy. When the economy is doing well, then the Doods sell more tickets regardless of how the team is doing.

Excellent analysis! Jim and I have been stuck on the idea that the city just goes in cycles and falls in and out of love with the Doods based on how they were playing that season. We thought ticket sales were driven by _____ forces.

A. sociocultural

B. political

C. economic

D. competitive

That's right, but maybe you are on to something, Mark! If this is true, and we are experiencing a strong surge in the economy, then we might want to try to _____.

A. raise ticket prices right now

B. lower ticket prices to accommodate the situation right now

C. scan the political environment for opportunities

D. cut back on the sale of beer right now

I think so! This really might turn out to be a winning situation for the Doods!

Correct Answers: A; A

Introduction to Marketing: Test

1. Once Ned and Brad realized they had a problem with their leaky windows, they asked friends and looked on the Internet to see what options they had to solve the problem. This represents which step of the consumer buying process?

   A. problem recognition

   B. information search

   C. evaluating alternatives

   D. purchase decision

   E. postpurchase evaluation

2. Luz Maria and Mohammed have different ideas about what color to paint the house. Luz Maria wants a bright blue like her childhood bedroom in Mexico, and Mohammed wants a steel gray like his mosque's prayer room. Which element of consumer buying behavior is most likely influencing their decisions?

   A. culture and subculture

   B. social class

   C. reference groups

   D. personal image

   E. situational matters

3. An upscale jewelry store was considering moving into a transitional neighborhood with millennials in new housing mixed with older homes and lower incomes. Which customer attribute is most likely to be an issue?

   A. Customers have access to the product.

   B. Customers have decision-making power to buy the product.

   C. Customers have money to afford the product.

   D. Customers are not already served by competitors.

   E. Customers have a particular need that the firm can serve.

4. _____ segmentation consists of categorizing consumers according to statistical characteristics of a population, such as gender, age, income, and so on.

   A. Demographic

   B. Geographic

   C. Psychographic

   D. Benefit

   E. User rate

5. Beach Shack tends to locate its stores in tourist areas in beach towns. Which type of marketing segmentation does Beach Shack use?

   A. demographic

   B. geographic

   C. psychographic

   D. benefit

   E. physical

6. Action Vacations promotes trips to risk-oriented individuals who enjoy physical activity, like mountain hiking, helicopter skiing, ocean sailing, and white-water rafting. Action Vacations' market is most likely segmented by _____ segmentation.

   A. demographic

   B. geographic

   C. psychographic

   D. social class

   E. user rate

7. A commercial laundry targets restaurants and hotels that require uniforms for their staff. This is _____ segmentation.

   A. niche

   B. geographic

   C. customer-based

   D. B2C

   E. product-use-based

8. Which of the four Ps involves distributing the product to a place where consumers will buy it?

   A. product

   B. price

   C. place

   D. promotion

   E. public relations

9. Connie's Chalupas has placed samples of its product in grocery stores in mostly Hispanic neighborhoods to see how customers react to them. This company is conducting

   A. test marketing.

   B. competitive comparison.

   C. one-on-one marketing.

   D. concept testing.

   E. advertising testing.

10. Efron is in the stage of marketing research in which he needs to determine how he should collect and analyze data. This is the _____ step.

    A. define the problem

    B. collect facts

    C. analyze the data

    D. take action

    E. access databases

11. The United Way has a team that is responsible for creating content targeted at potential customers and clients in the community. This team is most likely a(n) _____ team.

    A. human resources

    B. marketing

    C. administration

    D. information technology

    E. accounting

12. Heritage Crest Bakery started out with a sourdough bread recipe. Over the years, it has added other styles of bread like rye, wheat, white, and potato. Together, the Heritage Crest breads can best be described as a

    A. product mix.

    B. promotional line.

    C. purchase point.

    D. product line.

    E. price segment.

13. When Apple releases a new iPhone, it often releases a captivating advertising campaign to bring awareness to the product. This statement best demonstrates which factor that influences buying behavior?

    A. situational matters

    B. culture and subculture

    C. social class

    D. personal image

    E. reference groups

14. August buys a puppy and takes her to his parents' anniversary dinner. August's sister Luz absolutely loves the puppy, and August encourages her to buy another puppy from the litter. After the party, Luz goes online and buys a puppy of her own. Which of the factors that influence buying behavior does this most likely represent?

    A. culture and subculture

    B. one-to-one marketing

    C. psychographic influence

    D. social class

    E. reference groups

15. Max Clubber is a famous retired boxer and stays in great shape due to the Superflex Home Gym system. Superflex hires him to be its spokesperson knowing that many individuals will buy the gym system because they want to look like Max. Superflex believes that Max will most likely impact which factor that influences consumer buying behavior?

A. economics and pricing

B. niche promotion

C. personal image

D. reference groups

E. social class

16. Laguna Steelworks has divided its customer base into two groups—commercial and personal. It utilizes different pricing and promotion models for each group. Which concept best describes the process Laguna used to classify its customer bases?

A. market segmentation

B. niche marketing

C. reference groups

D. neuromarketing

E. one-to-one attributes

17. Juniper Concrete is growing, and its management team has decided to create a formal marketing strategy. How should the company begin?

A. by researching external marketing forces

B. by identifying its target market

C. by analyzing secondary data

D. by preparing a marketing mix summary

E. by enhancing its product line

18. Clarion Shampoo creates a new shampoo that is supposed to eliminate dandruff while also eliminating grey hair. It begins soliciting volunteers willing to have their hair professionally cleaned with the new shampoo. The volunteers are then asked for their feedback on the shampoo. This process can best be described as _____, a part of the _____ strategy step in the marketing process.

A. concept testing; promotion

B. test marketing; product

C. concept testing; target market

D. test marketing; research

E. product testing; pricing

19. Revival Mineral Water has hired a web development company to create a new storefront app for mobile devices. It hopes that the storefront app will make it easier for customers to purchase its water in the future. This scenario would most likely be part of the _____ strategy in the marketing process.

A. product

B. user-to-user

C. technology

D. place

E. promotion

20. The leadership team at Simplicity Uniforms recently hired a compliance officer who will be responsible for ensuring that the company is compliant with all relevant finance and accounting laws. Which external marketing force is most likely at play in this example?

A. political

B. global

C. legal and regulatory forces

D. ethical

E. culture and subculture

8 Accounting and Financial Statements

What To Expect

By the end of this lesson, you will be able to:

- Explain the purpose of accounting, as it relates to users of financial data and a company's success.

- Explain how a business's financial information is organized utilizing the six-step accounting process, in accordance with GAAP.

Chapter Topics

- **8-1** What Is Accounting?
- **8-2** Financial Statements: The Balance Sheet
- **8-3** Financial Statements: The Income Statement
- **8-4** Financial Statements: The Cash Flow Statement
- **8-5** Financial Ratios

Copyright © McGraw Hill Natee Meepian/Shutterstock

What Is Accounting?

Glitz n' Glamour: Naomi's Predicament

"Why Can't I Get Ahead?"

Naomi, a talented fashionista and small boutique owner, sighs heavily as she sinks into the chair across from her friend. Her friend, Luke, nods sympathetically. In the three years since she became an entrepreneur, Naomi's frustrations with her business, Glitz n' Glamour, have only grown.

In fact, it seems that every time they meet, she is struggling with the same mystery—she cannot understand why her seemingly "booming" business still isn't making a profit.

I just don't get it! Why am I not making any money? I work every day—even weekends!

Still? Wow. I mean, the store seems like business is booming! My wife said it was packed when she dropped in yesterday.

Yeah, things have really picked up in the last eight months, but when the bills come in, we always come up short. It's like all of those extra sales have had no impact at all. There must be something that I'm doing wrong.

Maybe it's marketing? Or, what about your financial records—are they accurate? I have a friend who is taking some business courses; would you like me to connect you?

Oh, would you? I'll take any help I can get.

Sure; why not? I'll make a call tonight. Let's meet back here tomorrow and I'll let you know what we discuss.

The next day, Naomi and Luke meet up to talk about his conversation with his friend.

Naomi, great news! My friend is happy to help you out. The best place to start is looking over your books with your accountant. You can set up a meeting, right? Or, if your accountant isn't available, I'm sure going through your books will be a good start. Naomi? Are you okay?

Whoa! Slow down! My books? My accountant? I don't have either of those. I mean, my business is really small, so I haven't really been managing it any differently than my personal spending. Is all of that really necessary?

Uh oh. It looks like Naomi is lacking key knowledge in the area of accounting. As a result, her business is underperforming, impacting her profits, and quite possibly jeopardizing the future success of Glitz n' Glamour.

In this lesson, we will work together to teach Naomi the fundamental accounting knowledge and skills she needs to implement appropriate accounting practices, build key financial statements, and analyze her business to make better (and more informed) business decisions and gain new insight on how to control her costs and increase her profits.

Accounting and Bookkeeping

Our first challenge is to help Naomi understand what accounting is, and why she should let us help her get her business on track using accounting functions.

Accounting measures, classifies, analyzes, and communicates financial information to people inside and outside a company.

Bookkeeping is one function of accounting, which includes recording a company's financial transactions.

Although many people (falsely) assume that all accountants are bookkeepers, accounting is more than just bookkeeping. Engaging in proper accounting functions can help business owners, employees, and outside parties—like suppliers or investors—make informed financial decisions.

Types and Functions of Accounting

Although it can seem daunting at first, accounting can be broken into two distinct types, with three different kinds of accounting professionals. Let's break it down.

Functions of Accounting

Managerial accounting is concerned with preparing accounting information and analyses for managers and other decision makers inside an organization.

Financial accounting is concerned with preparing accounting information and analyses primarily for people outside of the organization, such as stockholders, government agencies, creditors, lenders, suppliers, unions, customers, consumer groups, and so on.

Managerial Accounting	Financial Accounting
• Prepare accounting information and analyses for managers and decision makers.	• Prepare accounting information and analyses for people outside of the organization.
• Prepare and monitor department and company-wide budgets.	• Perform audits to ensure accuracy of the financial information.
• Analyze the costs of production and marketing.	• Prepare and file taxes and other documents for government agencies.
• Manage and control inventory and production costs.	

Managerial Accounting

Who uses managerial accounting?

Managers: use accounting info to make plans and guide the company to achieve goals and outcomes set by the business

Production managers: use sales forecasts to set production levels

Marketing managers: use accounting info to evaluate the impact of promotion strategies

Employees: use accounting info to evaluate the impact of promotion strategies

Financial Accounting

Who uses financial accounting?

Stockholders, investors: evaluate firm's financial health to see how well the firm is doing and whether it is profitable

Managers: plan, set goals, control

Employees: measure financial health

Lenders and suppliers: evaluate credit ratings

Government agencies: confirm taxes and regulatory compliance

Who Uses Accounting?

Types of Accountants

There are three types of accountants. **Private accountants** are internal accountants working for a single organization. On the other hand, **public accountants** provide accounting services to clients on a fee basis. Lastly, **not-for-profit accountants** work for governments and nonprofit organizations and perform the same services as for-profit accounts—except they're concerned primarily with efficiency, not profits.

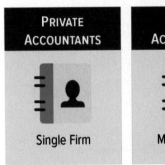  

PRIVATE ACCOUNTANTS	PUBLIC ACCOUNTANTS	NOT-FOR-PROFIT ACCOUNTANTS
Single Firm	Multiple Firms	Governments and Nonprofits

- Private accountants work for a single company or firm like Netflix.
- Public accountants work for many clients such as Glitz n' Glamour.
- Not-for-profit accountants specialize in nonprofit organizations such as the Red Cross.

Decisions

Hi Luke!

Hey Naomi! What's up?

Just overwhelmed, as usual.

Oh no, not again. Did you contact that _____ I told you about? You know, the accountant that is available to hire on a contract basis?

A. certified public accountant (CPA)

B. financial analyst

C. work-for-hire

D. private accountant

No, but I am going to this afternoon. Her name was Chitra, right? I'm hoping she can help, but what I really need is someone who will be able to look at my financials and tell me some options of what I need to do.

You're in luck, she specializes in _____, and she works with business owners to help them get their entire business under control from a numbers point of view.

A. financial accoutning

B. managerial accounting

C. tax accounting

D. CNA accoutning

Luke, you are totally getting my hopes up! I sure hope she can help me because I don't have the money to hire a(n) _____ to work here with me part-time, let alone full-time.

A. public accountant

B. in-house accountant

C. private accountant

D. broker

Yes, hiring on someone would cost quite a bit of money. I'm anxious to hear what you think of Chitra after your meeting today. Keep me posted!

Correct Answers: A; B; C

GAAP: The Trademark of a Reputable Accountant

Accounting relies on *standards*, known as **Generally Accepted Accounting Principles (GAAP)**, which ensure that financial statements are relevant, reliable, consistent, and comparable. When financial statements are consistent and comparable, stakeholders can compare them with earlier statements within the company and with statements from other companies.

RELEVANT — Information should help users understand the company's financial status and performance.

CONSISTENT — Information should always be based on the same assumptions and procedures. Any changes to this must be clearly explained.

RELIABLE — Information should be accurate, objective, and verifiable.

COMPARABLE — Information should allow users to compare data with other companies' data and with prior data from the company.

The Six-Step Accounting Process

To create *relevant*, *reliable*, *consistent*, and *comparable* financial statements, we must apply the **accounting process**, which involves six activities: collection, recording, classification, summarization, reporting, and analysis.

An adept accountant will:

1. Locate and sort records (collection).

2. Record daily transactions in journals (recording).

3. Organize journal entries in categories within a ledger (classification).

4. Test the accuracy of the ledger by running a trial balance (summarization).

5. Issue financial statements (reporting).

6. Assess the firm's financial condition via ratio analysis (analysis).

Collect: Find and Sort Records of Relevant Business Transactions

The accounting process begins by collecting the results of bookkeeping—that is, the records of all relevant business **transactions**: sales invoices, cash receipts, travel records, shipping documents, and so on. Today, many or most of these transactions exist as computerized data. The transactions are analyzed by the bookkeeper and sorted into meaningful categories according to various strategies, some of which involve ways of reducing tax obligations.

At Glitz n' Glamour, the business should be counting the revenue received from each sales transaction on a daily basis into an accounting system or spreadsheet. The company would also want to enter any data related to travel, shipping, or other transactions made to help run the business.

Record: Put Daily Transactions in Journals, Using Double-Entry Bookkeeping

The bookkeeper then records financial data from the original transaction documents in a journal, a record book, or part of a computer program containing the daily record of the firm's transactions, including a brief description of each.

At Glitz n' Glamour, the individual tasked with bookkeeping would want to ensure the transactions are accurately recorded into the firm's accounting system.

Double Entry Accounting System

The format for recording each journal entry is known as **double-entry bookkeeping** because each transaction is recorded in two different accounts to make sure each add up to the same amount, as a check on errors. Thus, if a bookkeeper enters $9.49 in one place, but mistakenly puts $9.94 in another, when the two accounts don't produce the same total it will be a tip-off that an error occurred.

With double-entry bookkeeping, notice that for each **debit**, there is an equal and opposite **credit**. Thus, the total of all debits must equal the total of all credits. If they don't, obviously an error has occurred. Recording each transaction as both a debit and a credit keeps the books in balance, as we'll discuss with the balance sheet.

Example: Singe-Entry Versus Double-Entry Bookkeeping

If you run a bicycle repair shop, a *single-entry bookkeeping transaction* to repair a tire would appear as follows:

Date	Service or Sale	Revenues	Expenses
February 6	Tire repair	$30.00	

A *double-entry bookkeeping transaction* would look like this:

Date	Service or Sale	Debit	Credit
February 6	Cash	$30.00	
	Revenue		$30.00

Classify: Put Journal Entries in Categories in a Ledger

Suppose you want to know what Naomi's **expenses** were for the past month. The **journal** will show these expenses scattered throughout, but not all lumped together. That is the purpose of the bookkeeper's transferring (usually on a monthly basis) journal entries to a **ledger**, a specialized record book or computer program that contains summaries of all journal transactions that are accumulated into specific categories. The ledger is divided into accounts, such as cash, inventories, and receivables.

At Glitz n' Glamour, the individual tasked with bookkeeping would want to ensure the transactions are accurately coded into the firms accounting system.

Summarize: Test the Accuracy of Ledger Data by Running a Trial Balance

At the end of every accounting period (every three months, for example), the bookkeeper does a check for accuracy. This is known as running a **trial balance**, making a summary of all the data in the ledgers to see if the figures are accurate, or balanced. Balanced means both columns in the double-entry format have similar totals—they balance each other.

At Glitz n' Glamour, the individual tasked with bookkeeping creates the trial balance making sure that each column in the double-entry format have similar totals.

Report: Issue Financial Statements Such as the Balance Sheet, Income Statement, and Statement of Cash Flows

Once the bookkeeper has the correct figures, he or she (or the accountant) can use that summarized data to issue three reports, or financial statements—the balance sheet, the income statement, and the statement of cash flows. Most companies prepare computer-generated financial statements every month, three months (quarterly), or six months (semiannually). Financial reports may also be tied to two other matters—the organization's fiscal year and the release of its annual report.

Naomi can use this information to run reports and share with key stakeholders such as managers, employees, suppliers, banks, accountants, or investors.

The Fiscal Year

Financial reports are required of all publicly traded companies at the end of the firm's **fiscal year**, the 12-month period designated for annual financial reporting purposes. This period may coincide with the end of:

- The calendar year, January 1 to December 31.
- The U.S. government's fiscal year, October 1 to September 30; for firms with government contracts, financial reports may appear sometime after September 30.
- A particular industry's natural cycle. In agriculture, for example, it is September 1 to August 31 (when the harvest is over).

The Annual Report

After the fiscal year-end, a firm issues an **annual report**, showing its financial condition and outlook for the future. This report is utilized by managers and executives to evaluate the health of the business as well as to plan for the next fiscal year. This information is also used by shareholders and potential investors to evaluate the organization's financial performance.

Analyze: Assess The Company's Financial Condition, Using Ratio Analysis

With the financial statements in hand, the accountant can then make an assessment of the company's financial condition.

Naomi can now analyze Glitz n' Glamour using verified data and validated accounting practices to better understand the performance of her business as well as the company's financial condition.

Decisions

Help Naomi align her accounting process. Choose the step in the process that best aligns with the statement.

1. Glitz n' Glamour should be counting the revenue received from each sales transaction each day into an accounting system or spreadsheet. The company should also enter any data related to shipping or other expenses made to help run the business.

   A. Summarize

   B. Analyze

   C. Record

   D. Collect

   E. Report

   F. Classify

2. The individual tasked with bookkeeping should ensure the transactions are accurately recorded and coded into the firms accounting system.

   A. Summarize

   B. Correct.

   C. Record

   D. Collect

   E. Classify

   F. Report

   G. Analyze

3. The individual responsible for bookkeeping would transfer journal entries into a ledger that shows the different account categories.

   A. Report

   B. Collect

   C. Summarize

   D. Analyze

   E. Record

   F. Classify

4. Naomi can use this information to run reports and share with key stakeholders such as managers, employees, suppliers, banks, accountants, or investors.

   A. Analyze

   B. Summarize

   C. Collect

   D. Classify

   E. Record

   F. Report

5. With the financial statements in hand, the accountant can then make an assessment of the company's financial condition. Naomi can now analyze Glitz n' Glamour using verified data and validated accounting practices to better understand the performance of her business as well as the company's financial condition.

   A. Collect

   B. Report

   C. Summarize

   D. Analyze

   E. Classify

   F. Record

Correct Answers: 1. D; 2. C; 3. F; 4. F; 5. D

Financial Statements: The Balance Sheet

By the end of this lesson, you will be able to:

- Using provided data, construct an accurate, well-organized balance sheet.

Naomi Studies the Numbers

"The Data Is in Disarray!"

Naomi has hired Chitra and is learning that her seemingly successful business isn't as healthy as it appears. She knows she needs some help understanding her financial statements and figuring out what to do.

Wow, I just looked at these financial reports. It's like reading a foreign language. The one thing I can tell is we have a lot less profit than I realized, and I am not sure how that happened. I know we have great products, awesome people, and we are implementing great processes. I want to use this information to grow our business. Do you think you can help me better understand these numbers and what they mean so I can better lead the company forward?

Definitely! Let's take a look at each of the financial statements. We will walk through them and then we'll look at some financial ratios to analyze the business.

Naomi seems very engaged and excited to learn more about her company's performance so she can better lead her company to growth and profitability. In this lesson, we will work together to teach her about one type of financial statement that is central to understanding her business: the balance sheet.

The Balance Sheet

Measuring the Health of a Business

Have you ever gone into the doctor for an annual check-up?

Healthy businesses use data to make informed decisions that will keep them healthy. In businesses, we utilize **financial statements** as metrics to analyze the health of the business. One of the primary statements used to measure a company's vitals is the **balance sheet**, which examines the overall health of the business.

As we begin to learn how to analyze the performance of a business, it is important to understand the key elements that make up the balance sheet.

The Accounting Equation

For a business to be successful it is mission critical for accountants, owners, and managers to understand the balance sheet. The **accounting equation** ensures that the balance sheet does exactly that—it balances. If applied correctly, total assets (things of value owned by a business) should equal total liabilities (what the business owes) plus owners' equity. Accountants employ the accounting equation to determine what a firm is worth.

The accounting equation is:

Reviewing a Balance Sheet

The balance sheet reports a firm's financial condition at a given time by showing its **assets**, **liabilities**, and **owners' equity**. It is called a balance sheet because it shows a balance between a firm's (a) assets and (b) liabilities plus owners' equity.

Although Naomi's accountant has prepared a balance sheet for Glitz n' Glamour, Naomi isn't sure how to read it. Let's use it to walk her through the basics and break down each section. Starting with the balance sheet in its totality.

You'll see it is laid out starting with the company's assets, which are the items the business has that are of value. Then you'll see the company's liabilities, what they owe to others, and lastly you'll see the company's owners' equity, which is reflective of both the owners' investments into the business, any **stock** sold to investors, and any earnings (profits) retained by the company.

The Balance Sheet

Glitz n' Glamour

Balance Sheet

	FY-2018	FY-2019
Current Assets		
Cash	$ 9,000.00	$ 15,500.00
Accounts Receivable	53,000.00	45,000.00
Inventory	80,000.00	76,000.00
Prepaid Expenses	9,500.00	8,900.00
Total Current Assets	**151,500.00**	**145,400.00**
Fixed Assets		
Land	100,000.00	100,000.00
Building	180,000.00	180,000.00
Less: Accumulated Depreciation	(2,000.00)	(4,000.00)
Equipment	47,000.00	50,000.00
Less: Accumulated Depreciation	(8,000.00)	(10,000.00)
Furniture and Fixtures	36,000.00	45,000.00
Less: Accumulated Depreciation	(6,000.00)	(7,000.00)
Total Fixed Assets	**347,000.00**	**354,000.00**
Intangible Assets		
Goodwill	23,000.00	19,600.00
Total Assets	**521,500.00**	**519,000.00**
Current Liabilities		
Accounts Payable	40,000.00	45,000.00
Current Portion Notes Payable	40,000.00	40,000.00
Total Current Liabilities	**80,000.00**	**85,000.00**
Long-term Liabilities		
Notes Payable	120,000.00	100,000.00
Mortgage Payable	280,000.00	270,000.00
Total Long-term Liabilities	**400,000.00**	**370,000.00**
Stockholders' Equity		
Common Stock	37,000.00	37,000.00
Retained Earnings	4,500.00	27,000.00
Total Stockholders' Equity	**41,500.00**	**64,000.00**
Total Liabilities and Stockholders' Equity	**521,500.00**	**519,000.00**

Let's dissect the balance sheet based on its component parts.

Copyright © McGraw Hill

Assets: What Things of Value Do We Own?

A balance sheet always begins with the items the firm owns. This includes buildings, land, supplies, inventories, cash, money owed to the firm, patents, and trademarks.

The assets are then broken into current, fixed, and intangible.

Current Assets: Items That Can Be Converted to Cash within One Year

Current assets are defined as items that can be converted into cash within one year. This includes not only cash itself (currency and coin), but also marketable securities, accounts receivable, and merchandise inventory.

The essential characteristic of current assets is their **liquidity**. Current assets are easily converted into cash, whereas assets such as land and buildings are not. Besides cash, two common items found on most balance sheets include accounts receivable and inventory.

- **Accounts receivable** is the total amount owed to a firm from customers who have purchased goods or services on credit. Accounts receivable is often referred to as A/R.
- **Inventory** on the balance sheet refers to the value of the products or merchandise that is being held for resale to customers.

Additionally, some businesses may also show prepaid expenses and marketable securities as part of their current assets.

- **Marketable securities** are stocks, bonds, government securities, and money market certificates, which can be easily converted to cash.
- **Prepaid expenses** are expenditures that are paid for in one accounting period, even though assets will not be consumed until a later time. An example is insurance.

For Glitz n' Glamour we see that Naomi's business has current assets that include cash, accounts receivable, and inventory. Naomi has prepaid some of her expenses as well. These represent the current assets of the company.

Current Assets on the Balance Sheet

Glitz n' Glamour

Balance **Sheet Breakout**

	FY-2018	FY-2019
Current Assets		
Cash	$ 9,000	$ 15,500
Accounts Receivable	53,000	45,000
Inventory	80,000	76,000
Prepaid Expenses	9,500	8,900
Total Current Assets	**151,500**	**145,400**

Fixed Assets: Items Held for a Longer Time

Often called *property, plant, and equipment*, **fixed assets** are items that are held for a long time and are relatively permanent, such as land, buildings and improvements, equipment and vehicles, and furniture and fixtures. Fixed assets are expected to be used for several years.

Accumulated depreciation is the reduction in value of assets to reflect their wearing down or obsolescence over time.

For Glitz n' Glamour you'll see that Naomi's accountant has accounted for land, building, equipment, furniture, and fixtures, and then reduced the value by applying the accumulated depreciation.

Fixed Assets on the Balance Sheet

Glitz n' Glamour
Balance Sheet Breakout

	FY-2018		FY-2019	
Fixed Assets				
Land		100,000		100,000
Building	180,000		180,000	
Less: Accumulated Depreciation	(2,000)	178,000	(4,000)	176,000
Equipment	47,000		50,000	
Less: Accumulated Depreciation	(8,000)	39,000	(10,000)	40,000
Furniture and Fixtures	36,000		45,000	
Less: Accumulated Depreciation	(6,000)	30,000	(7,000)	38,000
Total Fixed Assets		**347,000**		**354,000**

Intangible Assets: Valuable Assets That Aren't Physical Objects

Intangible assets are assets that are not physical objects but are nonetheless valuable, such as patents, trademarks, and goodwill. **Goodwill** is an amount paid for a business beyond the value of its other assets, based on its reputation, customer list, loyal employees, and similar intangibles.

Naomi believes the Glitz n' Glamour brand is worth the amount noted on her balance sheet based on its reputation and the customer list she created over the years.

Intangible Assets on the Balance Sheet

Glitz n' Glamour
Balance Sheet Breakout

	FY-2018	FY-2019
Intangible Assets		
Goodwill	23,000	19,600

Understanding Liabilities: What Are Our Debts to Outsiders?

A **liability** is a debt owed by a firm to an outside individual or organization. Examples: Vendors may deliver supplies but not insist on immediate payment, allowing the firms 30 or 60 days to pay their bills. Banks may loan farmers money to enable them to operate, but want to be paid after the crop has been harvested and sold. Employees who have provided labor but not yet been paid also represent a debt to the firm.

Liabilities are of two types: current and long term.

Current Liabilities: Payments Due within One Year or Less

Current liabilities are obligations in which payments are due within one year or less. The most common current liabilities are accounts payable and notes payable.

- **Accounts payable** is money owed to others that the firm has not yet paid. If the company has not yet paid its electricity bill this month, that debt belongs in accounts payable. Accounts payable is commonly referred to as A/P.

- **Notes payable** is money owed on a loan based on a promise (either short term or long term) the firm made. If you arranged a bank loan, for example, you would be obligated to pay it back by a prearranged date.

Glitz n' Glamour currently has debts that it owes to vendors that we can see on there A/P. The company is also paying back some loans, which we can see through their notes payable.

Current Liabilities on the Balance Sheet

Glitz n' Glamour

Balance Sheet Breakout

	FY-2018	FY-2019
Current Liabilities		
Accounts Payable	40,000	45,000
Current Portion Notes Payable	40,000	40,000
Total Current Liabilities	**80,000**	**85,000**

Long-Term Liabilities: Payments Due in One Year or More

Long-term liabilities are obligations in which payments are due in one year or more, such as a long-term loan from a bank or insurance company.

- Two common long-term liabilities are **notes payable** and **bonds payable**, long-term liabilities that represent money lent to the firm that must be paid off.

- In some cases, a business may also own property, and as a result, have a **mortgage** it must repay. Because those payments are structured over a long period of time, they are categorized as long-term liabilities.

Glitz n' Glamour has a long-term loan they are paying back. In addition, the business owns a building, which is why it has a mortgage listed under the long-term liabilities section.

Long-Term Liabilities on the Balance Sheet

Glitz n' Glamour

Balance Sheet Breakout

	FY-2018	FY-2019
Long-Term Liabilities		
Notes Payable	120,000	100,000
Mortgage Payable	280,000	270,000
Total Long-Term Liabilities	**400,000**	**370,000**

Owners' Equity: "What Is Our Value If We Were to Sell Our Assets and Pay Off Our Debts?"

Owners' equity, or stockholders' equity, represents the value of a firm if its assets were sold and its debts paid. Owners' equity is considered important because it is used to indicate a company's financial strength and stability. Before making loans to a company, for example, lenders want to know the amount of owners' equity in it.

Owners' equity consists of (1) common stock and (2) retained earnings.

- **Common stock** refers to ownership in a business. As it pertains to the balance sheet, common stock accounts for the amount of stock that has been allocated to owners of the company.

- **Retained earnings** are net profits minus **dividend** payments made to stockholders; that is, they are earnings retained by a firm for its own use—for buying more land and buildings, say, or acquiring other companies.

At Glitz n' Glamour, Naomi made the business decision to issue common stock to some investors, meaning she allowed individuals to invest money in her company, and as result they received equity through stock in the company. The value of the investment is shown on the balance sheet as common stock. She has also been keeping some of the annual profit, which appears as retained earnings for Glitz n' Glamour.

Owners' Equity on the Balance Sheet

Glitz n' Glamour

Balance Sheet Breakout

	FY-2018	FY-2019
Owners' Equity		
Common Stock	37,000	37,000
Retained Earnings	4,500	27,000
Total Owners' Equity	**41,500**	**64,000**

Decisions

Chitra, I sure am glad I hired you on as my CPA. I am lost when it comes to all this financial information.

No problem, and believe it or not, you will be making sense of this stuff in no time. It's probably best if we start by trying to figure out your net worth by looking at what you have and what you owe on the _____.

A. asset statement

B. balance sheet

C. income statement

D. statement of cash flows

Net worth? I'm sure it's negative by now!

Don't be too sure about that! We can find out pretty quickly if you're wrong. All we need to do is look at how your assets balance out against your liabilities. This is called the _____.

A. asset paradox

B. Pythagorean theorem

C. fundamental accounting equation

D. balance sheet equation

Alright, so if we assess what I owe, are we looking only at the _____? You know, the stuff I owe to people in the long term?

A. short-term liabilities

B. owners' equity

C. long-term liabilities

D. total liabilities

No, we will look at all your liabilities, and then we will compare that to your asset value. Once we do this, we will know your _____, and that will give us a good idea of where you stand currently.

A. liquidity

B. notes payable

C. retained earnings

D. owners' equity

Yes, I see what you are talking about now. At least this will give me a firm footing of how Glitz n' Glamour is doing right now! It's better to know than not to know. Let's see where we stand!

Correct Answers: B; C; C; D

Lesson 8-3
Financial Statements: The Income Statement

By the end of this lesson, you will be able to:

- Using provided data, construct an accurate, well-organized income statement.

The Bottom Line: Profit and Loss

"Are We Making Money?"

Naomi is excited to learn more about financial statements and is anxious to better understand the income statement, so she meets with Chitra once more.

I just ran a report out of our software from last year's numbers: cost of goods sold, gross profit, gross sales, net profit, and net sales. I know there is a difference, and if I can get a hang of what's on this report, I can help our business grow and thrive! Do you think you can walk me through the income statement to help me better understand our numbers?

I know these terms seem a bit abstract, but once we go through them I think you'll be able to better understand how this statement is a reflection of all the hard work you and your team do, and it will give you an opportunity to see where you may want to make some adjustment to your business strategy.

Naomi is excited to continue her growth as a business owner. In this lesson, we'll analyze whether a business is making money by learning about the income statement.

The Income Statement

The **income statement**, once known as the profit-and-loss statement, shows a firm's revenues and expenses for a particular time period and the resulting profit or loss. The income statement itself has four principal parts: (1) sales revenue, (2) cost of goods sold, (3) operating expenses, all of which lead to the bottom line of (4) net income.

Glitz n' Glamour

Income Statement FY 2019

Sales		871,000
Less: Sales Returns and Allowances		(11,000)
Net Sales		860,000
Less: Cost of Goods Sold		(516,000)
Gross Profit		344,000
Less: Operating Expenses		
Salaries and Wages	187,000	
Advertising	42,500	
Insurance	28,000	
Property Taxes	17,700	
Utilities	15,000	
Interest	14,500	
Depreciation/Amortization	8,400	
Supplies	6,200	
Total Operating Expenses		(319,300)
Income before Taxes		24,700
Less: Income Tax Expense		(2,200)
Net Income		22,500

Gross Profit: Net Sales and Our Cost of Goods

Organizations first must account for their overall revenue, and then they must take into account any returns and allowances, then they must account for what it costs to acquire, make, or provide merchandise. As a result, a company can determine their gross profits.

This portion of the income statement is comprised of the following:

- **Sales revenues** are the funds received from the sales of goods and services during a certain period. The figure of interest to us is arrived at by taking gross sales and subtracting sales returns and allowances, to arrive at net sales.

- **Gross sales** are the funds received from all sales of the firm's products.

- **Sales returns** are products that customers return to the company for a refund.

- **Allowances** are partial refunds to customers for damaged products they choose to keep, not return.

- **Net sales** refers to the money resulting after sales returns and allowances are subtracted from gross sales.

- **Cost of goods sold** is commonly referred to as COGS and represents the cost of producing a firm's merchandise for sale during a certain period. For a company like Naomi's, this may include purchasing garments from manufacturers and designers.

For Glitz n' Glamour, Naomi's company was able to generate $871,000 in sales, she then deducts $11,000 for returns and allowances, which left her with net sales of $860,000. Then the company must subtract out the cost of goods sold, which leaves the company with $344,000. This amount refers to the **gross profit**, or gross margin, which is the amount remaining after the cost of goods sold is subtracted from the net sales.

Gross Profit on the Income Statement

Glitz n' Glamour

Income Statement FY 2019 Breakout

Sales	871,000
Less: Sales Returns and Allowances	(11,000)
Net Sales	860,000
Less: Cost of Goods Sold	(516,000)
Gross Profit	344,000

Operating Expenses: "What Were Our Selling and Administrative Expenses?"

Although a business may have a strong gross profit, the firm must still account for the expenses associated with the business. We refer to these as **operating expenses**, which are selling and administrative expenses incurred by the company.

- **Selling expenses** are all the expenses incurred in marketing the firm's products, such as salespeople's salaries, advertising, and supplies.

- **Administrative expenses** are costs incurred for the general operation of the business, such as salaries, supplies, depreciation, insurance, rent, and utilities.

For Glitz n' Glamour, the company has total operating expenses of $319,300. Its selling expenses are related to salaries and wages as well as advertising. The company's administrative expenses may also include salaries and wages as the company may include wages for all employees in one line item. It also includes insurance, property taxes, interest, utilities, depreciation/amortization, and supplies.

Operating Expenses on the Income Statement

Glitz n' Glamour

Income Statement FY 2019 Breakout

Less: Operating Expenses	
Salaries and Wages	187,000
Advertising	42,500
Insurance	28,000
Property Taxes	17,700
Utilities	15,000
Interest	14,500
Depreciation/Amortization	8,400
Supplies	6,200
Total Operating Expenses	(319,300)

Now that we know the companies gross profit and operating expenses we can determine the companies profit before and after taxes.

Net Income—The Bottom Line: "What After-Tax Profit or Loss Did We End Up With?"

Net income, the firm's profit or loss after paying income taxes, is determined by subtracting expenses from revenues. Net income is an important measure of company success or failure.

In the case of Glitz n' Glamour, Naomi's business made $24,700, which is the amount the government uses to calculate what the business owes in taxes. Therefore, after Glitz n' Glamour pays $2,200 in taxes, the company made $22,500. Because this is the last line of the income statement and tells whether or not a company made or lost money, it is often called the bottom line.

Net Income on the Income Statement

Glitz n' Glamour

Income **Statement FY 2019 Breakout**

Income before Taxes	24,700
Less: Income Tax Expense	(2,200)
Net Income	22,500

Decisions

Chitra, I hate to take out my frustrations on you each time we meet, but I just don't know what in the world is going on with my business! I am selling so much inventory, but I really don't know why I am not making much money in the end.

That's alright, Naomi, I have many clients who do all sorts of things in my office: they cry, yell, laugh hysterically, and even just stare at the wall. Sometimes numbers overwhelm people, but when you mention selling lots of product and not having as much money as you thought you'd have, we need to start by looking at the _____.

   A. balance sheet

   B. sales forecast

   C. income statement

   D. inventory turnover statement

Well I had $871,000 in sales revenue, so where did it all go?

In order to get to the bottom line, we need to check out where your money is going. Your net income before taxes is calculated by _____.

A. subtracting gross profit from sales revenue

B. subtracting net income before taxes from gross profit

C. adding expenses to net income before taxes

D. subtracting expenses from gross profit

Yes, and I am sitting at $24,700. This seems way too low. What is happening?

Your _____ is/are way too high.

A. expenses

B. net income after taxes

C. sales revenue

D. gross profit

I see it now, and I really wondered about this. I need to start cutting back, right?

Well, that is probably true. The two places you are spending money before taxes would be _____ and _____.

A. expenses; net income before taxes

B. cost of goods sold; expenses

C. expenses; gross profit

D. sales revenue; expenses

Yes, and I need to get those under control. See, I am feeling empowered already!

Correct Answers: C; D; A; B

Financial Statements: The Cash Flow Statement

By the end of this lesson, you will be able to:

- Using provided data, construct an accurate, well-organized cash flow statement.

The Cash Flow Statement: How Money Came and Went

"Where Is the Cash Flowing?"

Naomi is gaining a better understanding of her financial statements, she is curious about what she can learn about a company's operations by viewing a statement of cash flows. She follows up with Chitra for more information.

Okay, so one statement tells me the big picture of the business, another tells me how I am doing in relation to sales and expenses; I wish there was a way to dial in how money was coming and going from the business.

We do have a financial statement that helps us do just that.

You've got to be kidding me!

Hey, I wouldn't joke when it comes to your cash! The statement is called the cash flow statement, and it tells us how money is coming into the business and where it is going. Let me show you!

Naomi can hardly contain her excitement! With this newfound knowledge, she is gaining confidence in her ability to better run Glitz n' Glamour. In this lesson, you will learn how to find the cash coming in and out of a business.

The Cash Flow Statement

The **cash flow statement**, or statement of cash flows, reports over a period of time, first, the firm's cash receipts and, second, disbursement related to the firm's (1) operating, (2) investing, and (3) financing activities, which leads to the bottom line of (4) the cash balance.

Cash Flow Statement

Glitz n' Glamour

Cash Flow Statement FY 2019

Cash from Operating Activities		
Cash Received from Sales	868,000	
Cash Paid for Inventory	(507,000)	
Cash Paid for Operating Expenses	(312,500)	
Net Cash Provided by Operating Activities		**48,500**
Cash from Investing Activities		
Purchase of Equipment	(3000)	
Purchase of Furniture and Fixtures	(9,000)	
Net Cash Used by Investing Activities		**(12,000)**
Cash from Financing Activities		
Payment of Notes Payable	(20,000)	
Payment of Mortgage Payable	(10,000)	
Net Cash Used by Financing Activities		**(30,000)**
Net Increase in Cash		6,500
Cash Balance FY-2018		9,000
Cash Balance FY-2019		15,500

Operating Activities: "What Were the Incomes and Costs of Running Our Business?"

Cash flows from operating activities reflect income from sales and other income and payments for salaries, interest, taxes, and so forth. These are the ordinary costs of running a business.

For Glitz n' Glamour we can see the cash coming from sales and going out via purchasing inventory and paying operating expenses.

Glitz n' Glamour

Statement of Cash Flows FY 2019 Breakout

Cash from Operating Activities

Cash Received from Sales	868,000
Cash Paid for Inventory	(507,000)
Cash Paid for Operating Expenses	(312,500)
Net Cash Provided by Operating Activities	**48,500**

Investing Activities: "How Much Did We Earn from Our Investments?"

Cash flows from investing activities reflect the cash received from selling long-term assets, cash spent on buying equipment, and other investment activities.

Glitz n' Glamour did not earn any money from investing. Although they did make some investments in equipment, furniture, and fixtures.

Glitz n' Glamour

Statement of Cash Flows FY 2019 Breakout

Cash from Investing Activities

Purchase of Equipment	(3,000)
Purchase of Furniture and Fixtures	(9,000)
Net Cash Used by Investing Activities	**(12,000)**

Financing Activities: "How Well Did We Do from Our Loans to Others, Payment of Debt, and Our Stock Transactions?"

Cash flows from financing activities reflect the inflows and outflows of borrowed funds and long-term debt, sales of new stock, and payment of dividends.

Glitz n' Glamour is continuing to pay their loan via the notes payable and the building they own through the mortgage.

Glitz n' Glamour

Statement of Cash Flows FY 2019 Breakout

Cash from Financing Activities

Payment of Notes Payable	(20,000)
Payment of Mortgage Payable	(10,000)
Net Cash Used by Financing Activities	**(30,000)**

Cash Balance: "How Much Money Is Available at the End of the Year?"

Cash balance is the balance in the firm's cash account at the end of the year. Analyzing and understanding cash flow is vital to the success of any firm because many failed businesses blame their financial distress on inadequate cash flow.

Over the year Naomi's business has seen a cash increase of $6,500, and for the latest fiscal year, Glitz n' Glamour has a cash balance of $15,500.

Glitz n' Glamour
Statement of Cash Flows FY 2019 Breakout

Net Increase in Cash	6,500
Cash Balance FY-2018	9,000
Cash Balance FY-2019	15,500

Decisions

Chitra, is there a statement that would explain how much money I actually have right now?

Yes, it's the statement of cash flows, and it consists of _____.

A. operating cash, financing activities, expenses, and your cash balance

B. financing activities, sales revenues, expenses, net income after taxes, and your bottom line

C. sales revenues, expenses, and your cash balance

D. operating cash, investing cash, financing activity, and your cash balance.

Great, because I need to know how much money I can spend this month, and with all this money up in the air, I am hoping my checks don't bounce at the bank! Haha!

Yes, we can see these numbers because we can create a cash flow statement _____.

    A. from the net income after tax numbers from the income statement

    B. for any time period that we want

    C. only monthly

    D. only annually

If I'm looking at this correctly, I have more money in the end this year than I did last year, and this is called a _____.

    A. profit

    B. bottom line

    C. net increase in cash

    D. net income in cash

That's right, so keep it up, and next year might even be better!

Correct Answers: D; B; C

Lesson 8-5
Financial Ratios

By the end of this lesson, you will be able to:

- Interpret financial ratios in relation to organizational performance.

Using Financial Data to Analyze the Business

"What Do We Do with the Data?"

Naomi, elated with financial statements in hand, started to ponder how her business compares to others in her industry. She also wondered if there were any goals, standards, or benchmarks she should be comparing her business against. These thoughts had her hungry to learn more about accounting.

Having these financial statements is really helpful in understanding the business. I guess I wish there was a way to determine how well we are doing.

Naomi, we absolutely have a way to accomplish this goal.

Well, I know we have the accounting equation, profit and loss, and cash balance, but I'd like to start to analyze what we can do to make the business perform better.

I can help you with that. Now that we have the financial statements, we can conduct financial analysis using different ratios. These numbers can tell you how the business is doing and give you a chance to set some goals.

Naomi is ready to gain a deeper understanding of these numbers and how they can help her set new goals for the future of the business.

In this lesson, we will work together to teach Naomi how she can utilize the data from her financial statements to analyze her business's performance by using ratio

Copyright © McGraw Hill

analysis. Once Naomi can benchmark her firm's performance and become more aware of how her company operates, she will be more informed and empowered to make business decisions for the future.

Introduction to Accounting Ratios

Accountants don't just prepare financial statements. They also analyze the financial data to provide the firm's managers and investors with a better understanding of financial performance. One way of doing so is through ratio analysis. (Two other ways are horizontal analysis and vertical analysis, which can be used to compare financial statement numbers and ratios over a number of years. Expect to learn more about these analysis types in later studies.)

Ratio analysis uses one of a number of financial ratios—such as liquidity, efficiency, leverage, and profitability—to evaluate variables in a financial statement. Ratio analysis can be used to analyze a firm's performance (1) compared to its stated objectives and (2) compared to the performance of similar firms.

Ratio analysis evaluates the variables within a financial statement. Four types of financial ratios are:

1. **Liquidity ratios**, which determine how well a firm can pay its liabilities as they come due

2. **Activity ratios**, which determine how well the firm manages its assets to generate revenue

3. **Debt to owners' equity ratios**, which determine how much the firm relies on borrowing to finance its operations

4. **Profitability ratios**, which determine how high the firm's profits are in relation to its sales, assets, or owners' equity

Understanding Liquidity Ratios

We discuss four types of financial ratios in this lesson starting with the liquidity ratios.

Liquidity Ratios: Current Ratio and Acid-Test Ratio

Liquidity ratios measure a firm's ability to meet its short-term obligations when they become due. They are of interest to anyone who wants to know whether a firm is able to pay its short-term debts on time.

Two important liquidity ratios are:

- The **current ratio** consists of current assets divided by current liabilities. A goal for most businesses is to have 2.0 or higher ratio. The reason this is the benchmark is because the company has a two to one ratio of assets to liabilities, meaning it could more than likely pay back its current debts.

- The **acid-test ratio**, or quick ratio, consists of cash + marketable securities + receivables, all divided by current liabilities. The standard for this ratio is 1.0 or higher. This benchmark looks at a company's most liquid assets compared to its current debt. Therefore, a company which has a ratio of $1.00 of assets to $1.00 of liabilities has a strong likelihood of being able to service their current debts.

Current Ratio Equation Applied at Glitz n' Glamour

For Glitz n' Glamour, the balance sheet for fiscal year 2018 indicates that current assets are $145,400 and current liabilities are $85,000. When the assets are divided by the liabilities it produces a ratio of 1.71. This means the company has $1.71 in assets for every $1.00 in liabilities. Although this indicates there are enough current assets to manage the current liabilities, most banks and investors feel more secure lending and investing in a company that has a current ratio of 2.0 ($2.00 of assets for every $1.00 of liabilities) or higher.

$$current\ ratio = \frac{current\ assets}{current\ liabilities} = \frac{\$145,400}{\$85,000} = 1.71$$

Acid-Test Ratio Equation Applied at Glitz n' Glamour

Glitz n' Glamour's balance sheet for fiscal year 2018 shows $15,500 in cash, $0.00 in marketable securities, and $45,000 in accounts receivables, totaling $60,500. The current liabilities are $85,000.

$$acid\text{-}test\ ratio = \frac{cash + marketable\ securities + receivables}{current\ liabilities} = \frac{\$15,500 + \$0.00 + \$45,000}{\$85,000}$$

With a ratio of 0.71, Glitz n' Glamour is below the conventional acid-test ratio of 1.0. Because the result is less than 1.0, Naomi might have to boost her cash by borrowing from a high-cost lender, obtaining additional cash from investors, reducing dividend payments to stockholders, or trying to sell inventory.

Decisions

Hi, Chitra!

Naomi! How is Glitz n' Glamour going lately?

It's picking up this season, and I even thought about trying to buy a new inventory tagging system so I can keep track of my inventory in real-time. Problem is, I decided to try and take out a short-term loan of $7,500 from the bank to buy the tagging system, and the loan officer kept asking for my financial ratios. I didn't know what to tell him.

Yes, financial ratios. That's music to my ears! Well, almost!

I found it to be more like nails on a chalkboard.

Haha! All the information you need to get these financial ratios is already at your fingertips in your financial statements. I bet the loan officer wanted your current ratio, right? It compares _____.

A. total assets with total liabilities

B. current assets with total liabilities

C. current liabilities with acid assets

D. current assets with current liabilities

Yes, he did, and I asked why, and he said it would give him _____.

A. a better idea if Glitz n' Glamour could turn its inventory into cash quickly

B. a better idea if Glitz n' Glamour could have cash left over after the loan is made

C. a better idea if Glitz n' Glamour could service its current debts

D. a better idea if Glitz n' Glamour could pay back its current debts

Indeed, that is true. Did he also ask about the _____ ratio? It indicates if the company is able to service its immediate debts, thereby giving the bank an indication of how likely you would be in making your loan payments each month.

- **A.** ending cash
- **B.** debt
- **C.** acid-test
- **D.** current

Yes, he did, but I looked a bit like a deer in the headlights by then, so I gracefully bowed out of his office until I could meet with you. I guess I didn't realize these ratios were just figures derived from information I already had. Well, I guess I'm learning day by day.

Correct Answers: D; C

Understanding Activity Ratios

Activity or efficiency ratios are used to evaluate how well management uses a firm's assets to generate revenue. That is, they express how well a company can turn its assets (such as inventory) into cash to pay its short-term debts.

One of the primary ratios a company uses in determining its efficiency is the inventory turnover ratio, which measures the number of times a company sells its inventory in a year's time. The more frequently a firm can sell its inventory, the greater its revenue.

Inventory Turnover Ratio

The **inventory turnover ratio** consists of cost of goods sold in one year divided by the average value of the inventory.

Inventory turnover ratios vary by industry and by company, with Nike, for example, turning over its inventory about 4.5 times a year and Starbucks 14.7 times a year. A high ratio may indicate efficiency. A low ratio may indicate too much obsolete inventory or a need to sharpen the buying strategy. What is considered a "good" number of turns varies between industries.

Inventory Turnover Ratio Applied at Glitz n' Glamour

Glitz n' Glamour's income statement shows costs of goods sold was $516,000. Although for simplicity's sake we did not show the average inventory on that statement, it is determined by adding the inventory value at the end of fiscal year 2018 to the inventory value at the end of the previous year (fiscal year 2017) and dividing by 2, which is $78,000.

$$inventory\ turnover\ ratio = \frac{cost\ of\ goods\ sold}{average\ inventory} = \frac{\$516,500}{\$78,000} = 6.62$$

Glitz n' Glamour's inventory turnover ratio is somewhat low. It may have too much obsolete inventory or a buying strategy that needs to be sharpened.

Decisions

Hey Naomi! I just was in the neighborhood, and I thought I'd pop in to say hello!

Luke! So glad you stopped in! Check out these we just got in!

Sweet! These shirts are wicked cool!

Yes, they are fab! I sure hope they sell better than the ones over in that corner of the shop. Those even have a bit of dust on them! Dust, man! Hard to believe I'm actually dusting my inventory!

No kidding! That's not a good sign. Your _____ must be pretty low.

- **A.** sales to no-sales ratio
- **B.** asset sales ratio
- **C.** sales margins
- **D.** inventory turnover

You know about that? Wow, why have I been spending all this money on my accountant! Ha!

No, not really, but I guess I got lucky with my wording! Seriously, I do recall learning about it, but how does it work again?

It _____ in order to find out how frequently I'm selling off my current inventory of products.

A. analyzes the inventory turnover divided by the industry average turnover

B. analyzes the cost of goods sold in one year divided by the average value of the inventory

C. analyzes the cost of goods sold in one year divided by sales revenue

Interesting. So, how do you know if you are on track then?

Most companies compare their figures to _____.

A. the best company in their industry

B. the firm's figures for the previous year

C. industry averages

D. the worst company in their industry

So how is yours then?

It's a bit low, and as you can tell from the dust, I need to get crackin' on selling those clothes!

Correct Answers: D; B; C

Understanding Debt to Owners' Equity Ratios

The **debt to owners' equity ratio** is a measure of the extent to which a company uses debt, such as bank loans, to finance its operations. It is found by dividing total liabilities by owners' equity. If a firm takes on too much debt, it may have problems repaying borrowed funds or paying dividends to stockholders.

Debt to Owners' Equity Ratio Applied at Glitz n' Glamour

Glitz n' Glamour's balance sheet shows that total liabilities were $455,000 and total owners' equity was $64,000.

$$debt\ to\ owners'\ equity\ ratio = \frac{total\ liabilities}{owners'\ equity} = \frac{\$455,000}{\$64,000} = 711\%$$

With a ratio of 711%, this means that Glitz n' Glamour has borrowed $711 for every $100 the owners have provided. Clearly, Glitz n' Glamour has a high debt to equity ratio. However, it is important to compare their debt ratio to other firms in the their industry. With a a debt ratio over 100%, it may be more difficult for the company to borrow money from lenders. For some lenders and investors, a 100% ratio is acceptable; however, more conservative investors and lenders like to see this ratio around 70% or lower. Glitz n' Glamour far exceeds the preferred ratio, and the owner should look further into company's debt.

Decisions

Hi Naomi! I got your message this morning on my voicemail, and I was close by so I decided to just drop by and chat.

Thanks for coming by, Chitra! I had some questions about my debt ratio. The loan officer at the bank needs this ratio before considering my loan request, but I didn't know what to tell him. Where do I find this?

Sure, no problem. The debt to equity ratio is calculated by _____.

  A. dividing current liabilities to owners' equity

  B. multiplying owners' equity by total liabilities

  C. dividing total liabilities by owners' equity

  D. dividing total equity by total liabilities

Okay, but what is that really showing me?

Good question. The debt to equity ratio is most commonly used to _____.

  A. show what extent a business uses debt to finance its operations

  B. show how much debt the business has on its balance sheet

  C. show how much the business is worth through its equity

  D. show how much profit a business has earned

That makes sense now. The calculation is pretty straight forward, and I think Glitz n' Glamour needs to re-think taking on any new debt until we can get that ratio down.

True. Taking on debt is always a big decision, so think hard about it, but you also need to think hard if you can live without that real-time inventory tagging system. That system really might free up some of your time to devote to other things.

Yeah, like trying to pick some better shirts that will sell fast!

Correct Answers: C; A

Profitability ratios are used to measure how well profits are doing in relation to the firm's sales, assets, or owners' equity. Three important profitability ratios are return on sales (profit margin), return on assets, and return on owners' equity.

Glitz n' Glamour may know what its net income is after taxes—$22,500, according to the income statement. However, to determine how well the firm is using its resources, Naomi will want to put this result into each of the three ratios to get a better understanding of her companies performance.

Return on Sales

The **return on sales**, or profit margin, is net income divided by sales. This information helps the company understand how much profit is being generated by every dollar of sales.

For Glitz n' Glamour this means taking the $22,500 net income from the income statement and dividing by the net sales of $860,000 from the income statement.

$$\text{return on sales} = \frac{\text{net income}}{\text{net sales}} = \frac{\$22,500}{\$860,000} = 2.61\%$$

This means for every $100 in sales, the firm had a profit of $2.61. Between 4% and 5% is considered a reasonable return; so in its return on sales, Glitz n' Glamour needs to identify some ways to increase this percentage.

Return on Assets

Return on assets is net income divided by total assets. This information helps the company understand how well they are using their assets to generate profits.

For Glitz n' glamour this equates to $22,500 in net income from the income statement, and $519,000 by adding up the company's assets for fiscal year 2018 from the balance sheet.

$$\text{return on assets} = \frac{\text{net income}}{\text{total assets}} = \frac{\$22,500}{\$519,000} = 4.33\%$$

A return of $4.33 on every $100 invested in assets is quite a low return, which suggests Glitz n' Glamour has an opportunity to improve how they utilize their assets to generate profits for the company.

Return on Owners' Equity

Return on owners' equity, also called return on investment (ROI), is net income divided by owners' equity. This information helps a company understand how much profit the company is returning to shareholders based on their invested capital.

Glitz n' Glamour generates $35.15 of profit for every $100 invested in the business.

$$return\ on\ owners'\ equity = \frac{net\ income}{owners'\ equity} = \frac{\$22{,}500}{\$64{,}000} = 35.15\%$$

Because the average for business in general is 12% to 15%, Glitz n' Glamour is delivering a good return to its owners (investors or stockholders).

Decisions

Hi, Chitra! Thanks for seeing me on such short notice.

No problem at all, Naomi. What did you want to talk about?

It seems like it's coming back to the same problem I faced before. I seem to be selling lots of merchandise, but I just don't seem to be making as much money in the end as I thought.

This sounds like you are talking about _____, this is also known as gross margin.

    A. return on sales

    B. return on assets

    C. retrun on profit

    D. return on equity

I guess? What does this really mean though?

If you divide your net income, which you think is too low, by your net sales, which you think is actually quite high, then you will arrive your return on sales. This tells you _____.

A. how much money you are making overall

B. how much profit is being generated by each dollar of sales

C. how many sales you are achieving for each dollar of profit you earn

D. how much profit is being generated by each dollar of assets you own

Okay, but why is this number important? Don't I already know how much money I'm making?

Because it starts to show you if you are actually profiting from all of your sales. If not, then you know that either _____ or _____.

A. your expenses are too low; prices are not high enough

B. your expenses are too high; prices are too high

C. your expenses are too low; prices are too high

D. your expenses are too high; prices are not high enough

Really? You know that might really help me narrow down on what I should actually do about this problem!

Yes! See, this is fairly straight forward, and these financial ratios can help paint a picture of the health of your business.

Indeed! Let's get painting, haha!

Correct Answers: A; B; D

Accounting and Financial Statements: Test

1. Delores is a financial accountant. One of her roles is to

   A. prepare accounting information and analyses for managers and decision makers.

   B. prepare and monitor department and company-wide budgets.

   C. analyze the costs of production and marketing.

   D. manage and control inventory and production costs.

   E. perform audits to ensure accuracy of the financial information.

2. Lester, Lester & Lester, a law firm, has an accountant on staff to manage its financial information. This accountant is a(n) _____ accountant.

   A. private

   B. public

   C. organization

   D. not-for-profit

   E. community

3. Dr. Badger's Pet Store is applying for a loan from the bank. The company has liabilities of $670,000 and owners' equity of $250,000. What is the debt to owners' equity ratio for Dr. Badger's Pet Store?

   A. 4.20 percent

   B. 3.11 percent

   C. 2.68 percent

   D. 0.37 percent

   E. 1.10 percent

4. Pedro's job is to keep track of all of the company's financial transactions and record them. Pedro is

   A. a bookkeeper.

   B. a financial manager.

   C. a department head.

   D. an investor.

   E. a board member.

5. On the balance sheet, insurance would be listed a(n)

   A. marketable security.

   B. fixed liability.

   C. one-time expense.

   D. prepaid expense.

   E. fixed expense.

6. Nakia has a small accounting company with three employees. She buys each person a new computer every three years. The reduction in value of Nakia's older computers would be listed on a balance sheet as

   A. asset decay.

   B. accumulated depreciation.

   C. asset decline.

   D. inventory deterioration.

   E. equipment downgrade.

7. Akito has not yet paid the rent on his office for the month. How would this debt be labeled on a balance sheet?

   A. notes payable

   B. fixed liability

   C. accounts payable

   D. long-term liability

   E. common liability

8. A mechanic took out a mortgage from a bank to buy the garage he and his employees work out of. How would this be listed on a balance sheet?

   A. notes payable

   B. fixed liability

   C. accounts payable

   D. long-term liability

   E. common liability

9. Yelena just completed her income statement. She included her company's sales revenue, operating expenses, and net income. Which principal part of an income statement did Yelena forget to include?

   A. profit

   B. cost of goods sold

   C. taxes

   D. liabilities

   E. payroll expenses

10. In a cash flow statement, cash flows from investing activities would include

    A. cash received from sales.

    B. payment of notes payable.

    C. payment of mortgage payable.

    D. purchase of equipment.

    E. cash paid for inventory.

11. Ratio analysis can be used to analyze a firm's performance compared to

    A. its previous year's performance.

    B. its objectives.

    C. the industry as a whole.

    D. its liquidity.

    E. its profitability.

12. A low inventory turnover ratio may indicate

    A. higher revenue.

    B. having to replenish inventory often.

    C. low customer satisfaction.

    D. having too much obsolete inventory.

    E. efficiency in selling inventory.

13. Tree Down Landscaping recently took out a mortgage for its new vehicle storage facility. When it prepares its balance sheet, the mortgage will be classified as

    A. a fixed asset.

    B. owner's equity.

    C. a short-term liability.

    D. an intangible asset.

    E. a long-term liability.

14. A(n) _____ is a specialized record book or computer program that contains summaries of all journal transactions that are accumulated into specific categories.

    A. bulletin

    B. ledger

    C. balance sheet

    D. journal

    E. transaction log

15. Second Harvest Tractors sold 10,000 shares of new stock last year. How would this be classified on a cash flow statement?

    A. financing activities

    B. shareholder activities

    C. operating activities

    D. investing activities

    E. fixed activities

16. Tamarack Camping Company has a common stock balance of $50,000 and retained earnings of $20,000. It has notes payable of $100,000, current notes payable of $25,000, mortgage payable of $200,000, and accounts payable of $50,000. Using this information, calculate its debt to owners' equity ratio.

A. 53.57%

B. 10.71%

C. 42.86%

D. 60%

E. 75%

17. Alabaster Enterprises has net income of $35,000, total assets of $300,000, common stock of $50,000, and retained earnings of $25,000. Calculate its return on investment.

A. 50.00%

B. 57.50%

C. 46.00%

D. 62.50%

E. 50.00%

18. Paresh called his investors to let them know that the funds received from all sales of the firm's products reached $1 million, not counting returns or allowances. Paresh was referring to his D.

A. cost of goods sold.

B. gross profit.

C. current assets.

D. gross sales.

E. net sales.

19. Zenon is an accountant for the United Way, a charitable organization. Zenon is a(n) _____ accountant.

A. private

B. public

C. organization

D. not-for-profit

E. community

20. According to the Generally Accepted Accounting Principles (GAAP), financial statements must be relevant, consistent, reliable, and

A. timely.

B. subjective.

C. comparable.

D. understandable.

E. flexible

Glossary

A

360-degree assessment Employees are appraised not only by their managers but also by their coworkers, subordinates, and sometimes customers or clients

absolute advantage Exists when one country has a monopoly on producing a product more cheaply or efficiently than any other country can

accelerator Accelerators are programs that help entrepreneurs bring their products into the marketplace through providing support and resources designed to help the business launch and scale operations.

accessory equipment Smaller, more mobile equipment

accountability Managers must report and justify their work results to managers above them

accounting The process of measuring, classifying, analyzing, and communicating financial information

accounting equation Assets = liabilities + owners' equity

accounting process the process of collecting, recording classifying, summarizing, reporting, and analyzing financial data

accounting process Six activities that result in converting information about individual transactions into financial statements that can then be analyzed

accounts payable Money owed to others that the firm has not yet paid

accounts receivable The total amount owed to a firm from customers who have purchased goods or services on credit

accumulated depreciation The reduction in value of assets to reflect their wearing down or obsolescence over time

acid-test ratio (Cash + marketable securities + receivables) ÷ current liabilities (also known as *quick ratio*)

acquisition Occurs when one company buys another one

Active Corps of Executives (ACE) A Small Business Association mentoring program composed of executives who are still active in the business world but have volunteered their time and talents

activity ratios Used to evaluate how well management uses a firm's assets to generate revenue (also known as *efficiency ratios*)

actual close the salesperson concludes the presentation by asking the prospect to purchase the product

actual close The salesperson concludes the presentation by asking the prospect to purchase the product

administrative expenses Costs incurred for the general operation of the business

advertising Paid nonpersonal communication by an identified sponsor (person or organization) using various media to inform an audience about a product

advertising media The variety of communication devices for carrying a seller's message to prospective buyers

advocacy advertising Concerned with supporting a particular opinion about an issue

affirmative action Aims to achieve equality of opportunity within an organization

agency shop Workplace in which workers must pay the equivalent of union dues, although they are not required to join the union

agents Specialists who bring buyers and sellers together and help negotiate a transaction (also known as *brokers*)

agents Tend to maintain long-term relationships with the people they represent

allowances Partial refunds to customers for damaged products they choose to keep, not return

analytic transformation The process in which resources are broken down to create finished products

angel investor Individuals who invest their own money in a private company, typically a start-up

annual report A year-end report that shows a firm's financial condition and outlook for the future

antitrust law A set of laws designed to keep markets competitive by deterring big businesses from driving out small competitors

Appellate courts Appellate courts: courts that review cases appealed from lower courts, considering questions of law but not questions of fact

application (DEI) The action of putting DEI into operation

appreciation (DEI) Recognition and enjoyment of the good qualities of DEI

apprenticeship Training program in which a new employee works with an experienced employee to master a particular craft

arbitration The process in which a neutral third party listens to both parties and makes a decision that the parties have agreed will be binding on them

arbitration The process in which a neutral third party, an arbitrator, listens to both parties in a dispute and makes a decision that the parties have agreed will be binding on them

Asia-Pacific Economic Cooperation (APEC) Common market of 21 Pacific Rim countries whose purpose is to improve economic and political ties

ask Highest selling price asked

assembly line Consists of a series of steps for assembling a product, each step using the same interchangeable parts and each being performed repetitively by the same worker

assets Anything of value that is owned by a firm

at-will employment The employer is free to dismiss any employee for any reason at all—or no reason—and the employee is equally free to quit work (also known as *employment at will*)

auction site a digital retail site that lists from individuals or firms that can be purchased through an auction bidding process or directly through a "purchase now" feature.

authority The legitimacy an organization confers on managers in their power to make decisions, give orders, and utilize resources

autocratic leaders Make decisions without consulting others

automation Using machines as much as possible rather than human labor to perform production tasks

B

B corporation Legally requires that the company adhere to socially beneficial practices, such as helping communities, employees, consumers, and the environment (also known as benefit corporation)

balance of trade The value of a country's exports compared to the value of its imports over a particular period of time

balance sheet Statement of a firm's financial condition at a given time showing its assets, liabilities, and owners' equity

bankruptcy The legal means of relief for debtors unable to pay their debts

bargain hunting digital purchasing behavior that involves coupon or auction sites. Bargain hunting is often combined with browsing and may or may not lead to a purchase.

barter To trade goods or services without the exchange of money

barter The trading of goods and/or services for other goods and/or services

base pay Consists of the basic wage or salary workers are paid for doing their jobs

benchmarking A process by which a company compares its performance with that of high-performing organizations

benefit segmentation Consists of categorizing people according to the benefits, or attributes, that people seek in a product

benefits Nonwage or nonsalary forms of compensation paid for by the organization for its employees

bid Highest price a buyer (bidder) is willing to pay

bill of materials Essentially a list of materials that go into the finished product

blue-chip stocks Preferred or common stocks of big, reputable companies, which also usually pay regular dividends

bond rating measures the quality and safety of a bond, indicating the likelihood that the debt issuer will be able to meet scheduled repayments, which dictates the interest rate paid.

bonds Contracts between issuer and buyer in which the purchase price represents a loan by the buyer and for which the issuing firm pays the buyer interest

bonds Long-term IOUs issued by governments and corporations, contracts on which the issuer pays the buyer interest at regular intervals

Bonds contracts between issuer and buyer in which the purchase price represents a loan by the buyer and for which the issuing firm pays the buyer interest

Bonds long-term IOUs issued by governments and corporations, contracts on which the issuer pays the buyer interest at regular intervals.

bonds payable Long-term liabilities that represent money lent to the firm that must be paid off

bonuses Cash awards given to employees who achieve particular performance objectives

Bonuses are cash awards given to employees

who achieve particular performance objectives.

book value a company subtracts its liabilities from its assets, and the resulting figure, the shareholders' equity, is then divided by the number of shares available of the stock.

book value A company subtracts its liabilities from its assets, and the resulting figure, the shareholders' equity, is then divided by the number of shares available of the stock

bookkeeping Recording a company's financial transactions

bootstrapping a process of funding a business by using personal funds rather than seeking debt or equity investment.

bots a software application that runs automated tasks over the Internet.

bounce rate the percentage of visitors who enter a website and then quickly depart, or bounce, rather than continuing to view other pages within the same site.

brain drain The emigration of highly skilled labor to other countries in order to better their economic condition

Brain drain the emigration of highly skilled labor to other countries in order to better their economic condition

brainstorming A process wherein individuals or members of a group generate multiple ideas and alternatives

brand A unique name, symbol, or design that identifies an organization and its product or service

brand advertising Consists of presentations that promote specific brands to ultimate consumers (also known as *product advertising*)

brand awareness Consumers recognize the product

brand equity The marketing and financial value derived from the combination of factors that people associate with a certain brand name

brand insistence Consumers insist on the product; they will accept no substitutes

brand loyalty Commitment to a particular brand—the degree to which consumers are satisfied with a product and will buy it again

brand manager Person responsible for the key elements of the marketing mix—product, price, place, and promotion—for one brand or one product line (also known as *product manager*)

brand marks The parts of a brand that cannot be expressed verbally, such as graphics and symbols

brand names The parts of a brand that can be expressed verbally, such as by words, letters, or numbers

brand preference Consumers habitually buy the product if it is easily available, but will try alternatives if they can't find it

break-even analysis A way to identify how much revenue is needed to cover the total costs of developing and selling a product

break-even point The point at which sales revenues equal costs; that is, the point at which there is no profit but also no loss

brokerage firms Companies that buy and sell stocks and bonds for individuals and offer high-interest-rate combination checking and savings accounts

Brokerage firms companies that buy and sell stocks and bonds for individuals and offer high-interest-rate combination checking and savings accounts.

brokers Usually hired on a temporary basis; relationship with the buyer or the seller ends once the transaction is completed

browsing digital purchasing behavior wherein the consumer is not really looking to make a purchase.

budget A detailed financial plan showing estimated revenues and expenses for a particular future period, usually one year

bundling The practice of pricing two or more products together as a unit

business Any activity that seeks to make a profit by satisfying needs through selling goods or services and generating revenue; a for-profit organization

business cycle The periodic but irregular pattern of ups and downs in total economic production

business environment The arena of forces (economic, technological, competitive, global, and social) that encourage or discourage the development of business

business market Consists of those business individuals and organizations that want business goods and

services that will help them produce or supply their own business goods and services (also known as *business-to-business market*)

business model The needs the firm will meet, the operations of the business, the company's components and functions, and its expected revenues and expenses

business plan A document that outlines a proposed firm's goals, the methods for achieving them, and the standards for measuring success

business services Services used in operations

business-to-business market Consists of those business individuals and organizations that want business goods and services that will help them produce or supply their own business goods and services (also known as *business market*)

business-to-consumer (B2C) refers to selling products and services directly to the consumer of the products or services

buying club site a digital retail site that allows consumers to buy in bulk

buzz marketing Using high-profile entertainment, social media, or news to get people to talk about their product

C

C corporation A state-chartered entity that pays taxes and is legally distinct from its owner

callable bonds Bonds in which the issuer may call

them in and pay them off at a predetermined price before the maturity date

Callable bonds bonds in which the issuer may call them in and pay them off at a predetermined price before the maturity date.

canned presentation uses a fixed, memorized selling approach to present the product

canned presentation Uses a fixed, memorized selling approach to present the product

capital budgets Used to predict purchases of long-term assets

capital expenditures Major investments in tangible or intangible assets

capital gain The return made by selling a security for a price that is higher than the price the investor paid for it

capital items Large, long-lasting equipment

capitalism An economic system in which the production and distribution of goods and services are controlled by private individuals rather than by the government (also known as *free-market economy*)

Carroll's Global Corporate Social Responsibility Pyramid Archie Carroll's guide for thinking about the day-to-day practical and moral matters that businesses encounter; the pyramid suggests that an organization's obligations in the global economy are to be a good global corporate citizen, to be ethical, to obey the law, and to be profitable

cash balance Balance in the firm's cash account at the end of the year

cash budgets Used to predict cash shortages or surpluses during the year

Cash Budgets: used to predict cash shortages or surpluses during the year.

cash flow forecasts A prediction about how money will come into and go out of a firm in the near future

cash flow statement Reports over a period of time, first, the firm's cash receipts and, second, disbursement related to the firm's (1) operating, (2) investing, and (3) financing activities, which leads to the bottom line of (4) the cash balance

cash-and-carry wholesaler A limited-function wholesaler that sells mainly to small retailers, who come to the wholesaler, pay cash for a product, and carry it out ("cash and carry")

Cash-and-carry wholesaler A limited-function wholesaler that sells mainly to small retailers, who come to the wholesaler, pay cash for a product, and carry it out ("cash and carry").

catalog marketing Consists of mailing customers catalogs, from which they may choose merchandise to be ordered via mail, telephone, or online (also known as *mail-order marketing*)

cause marketing A commercial activity in which a business forms a partnership with a charity or nonprofit to support a worthy cause, product, or service.

cause-related marketing A commercial activity in which a business forms a partnership with a charity or nonprofit to support a worthy cause, product, or service; also known as *cause marketing*

central-planning economies Economic systems in which the government owns most businesses and regulates the amounts, types, and prices of goods and services (also known as *command economies*)

centralized authority Important decisions are made by higher-level managers

certificate of deposit Pays interest upon the certificate's maturity date

chatter Another form of consumer feedback that occurs when a consumer shares, forwards, or "retweets" a marketing message. For marketers, the level of chatter represents consumer feedback.

checking account Allows you to deposit money in a bank account and then write checks on that account

checking account allows you to deposit money in a bank account and then write checks on that account

click path a sequence of hyperlink clicks that a website visitor follows on a given site, recorded and reviewed in the order the consumer viewed each page after clicking on the hyperlink.

closed shop An employer may hire only workers for a job who are already in a union

co-branding Two noncompeting products link their brand names together for a single product

code of ethics A written set of ethical standards to help guide an organization's actions

Cognitive diversity Cognitive diversity utilizes the different experiences and perspectives of individuals to address particular situation, challenge, opportunity, or problem.

cold-call sales prospecting technique Consists of calling on prospects with whom you have had no previous contact and to whom you do not have any kind of introduction

collateral Asset that is pledged to secure the loan

collective bargaining Consists of negotiations between management and employees in disputes over compensation, benefits, working conditions, and job security

collective bargaining The process by which labor and management representatives meet to negotiate pay, benefits, and other work terms

command economy Economic system in which the government owns most businesses and regulates the amounts, types, and prices of goods and services (also known as *central-planning economy*)

commercial bank A federal- or state-chartered profit-seeking financial institution that accepts deposits from individuals and businesses and uses part of them to make personal, residential, and business loans

commercial finance companies Organizations willing to make short-term loans to borrowers who can offer collateral

commercial paper Unsecured, short-term promissory notes over $100,000 issued by large banks and corporations

commercialization The full-scale production and marketing of the product

commodities trading Trading in raw materials and agricultural products used to produce other goods

commodity exchange A security exchange in which futures contracts are bought and sold

common market Group of nations within a geographical region that have agreed to remove trade barriers with one another (also known as *economic community* or *trading bloc*)

common stock Stockholders are able to vote on major company decisions, but they get (1) last claim on the company's dividends and (2) last claim on any remaining assets if the company goes out of business and its assets are sold

communism An economic system in which the government owns all property and everyone works for the government

Community Development Financial Institution (CDFI) A Community Development Financial Institution (CDFI) is a private financial institution who provide investing as well as personal and business lending opportunities to underserved communities within the United States.

comparative advantage Economic principle stating that a country sells to other countries those products and services it produces most cheaply or efficiently; the country buys from other countries those goods or services that it does not produce most cheaply or efficiently

compensation and benefits Laws and administration around worker's hours, pay, and benefits

competitive advantage An organization's ability to produce goods or services more effectively than its competitors

competitive advertising Promotes a product by comparing it more favorably to rival products (also known as *comparative advertising*)

competitive pricing The strategy in which price is determined in relation to rivals, factoring in other considerations such as market dominance, number of competitors, and customer loyalty

competitor People or organizations that are rivals for a company's customers or resources

compliance-based ethics code Ethical code that attempts to prevent criminal misconduct by increasing control and by punishing violators

component parts Finished or nearly finished products for making principal product

compressed workweek An employee works a full-time job in less than five days of standard 8- or 9-hour shifts

computer-aided design (CAD) Programs that are used to design products, structures, civil engineering drawings, and maps

computer-aided manufacturing (CAM) The use of computers in the manufacturing process

computer-integrated manufacturing (CIM) Systems in which computer-aided design is united with computer-aided manufacturing

concept testing Marketing research designed to solicit initial consumer reaction to new product ideas

conceptual skills The ability to think analytically, to visualize an organization as a whole, and understand how the parts work together

consideration Promising to do a desired act or refrain from doing an act you are legally entitled to do in return for something of value, such as money

consumer buying process The five steps by which consumers make decisions when considering whether to buy a product

consumer feedback different ways that customers can report their satisfaction or dissatisfaction with a firm's products.

consumer market Consists of all those individuals or households that want goods or services for their personal use

consumer price index (CPI) An index that encapsulates the monthly costs of a "market basket" of about 400 representative consumer goods and services that allow data analysts to measure the rate of inflation or deflation

consumer review a direct assessment of a product (good, service, or idea) that is expressed through social media for others to see and consider.

consumer sovereignty The idea that consumers influence the marketplace through their decisions of which products they choose to buy or not to buy

consumer-protection laws Laws concerned with protecting buyers' rights

containerization Products are packed into 20- or 40-foot-long (by about 8-foot square) containers at the point of origin and retrieved from the containers at the point of destination

contingency planning The creation of alternative hypothetical courses of action that a company can use if its original plans don't prove workable

continuity The timing of the ads, how often they appear or how heavily they are concentrated within a time period

continuous innovation Modest improvements to an existing product to distinguish it from competitors; they require little consumer behavior change

continuous processes A production process in which goods or services are turned out in a long production run on an ongoing basis over time

control process A four-step process: (1) establish standards; (2) monitor performance; (3) compare performance against standards; and (4) take corrective action, if needed

control standard The desired performance level for a given goal

controlling Monitoring performance, comparing it with goals, and taking corrective action as needed

convenience goods and services Inexpensive products that people buy frequently and with little effort

conversion rate the percentage of users who take a desired action, such as making a purchase.

convertible bonds convertible bonds are bonds that can be converted into the issuing corporation's common stock.

convertible bonds Bonds that can be converted into the issuing corporation's common stock

convertible bonds are bonds that can be converted into the issuing corporation's common stock.

cookies data files stored on websites that can generate a profile or other data about consumers.

Cooperative Cooperative: a corporation owned by its user members, who have pooled their resources for their mutual benefit

Corporate bonds issued by businesses as a source of long-term funding, consist of secured and unsecured bonds.

corporate citizenship a concern for taking actions that will benefit society as well as the organization

corporate culture The shared beliefs and values that develop within an organization and guide the behavior of its members (also known as *organizational culture*)

Corporate policy A company's stated positions on political and social issues

corporate social responsibility (CSR) A concern for taking actions that will benefit society as well as the organization

corporation A company or group of people authorized to act as a single entity (legally a person) and recognized as such in law.

cost of capital The rate of return a firm must earn to cover the cost of generating funds in the marketplace

cost of goods sold The cost of producing a firm's merchandise for sale during a certain period

cost per thousand (CPM) The cost a particular medium charges to reach 1,000 people with an ad

cost-based pricing The strategy in which the cost of producing or buying the product—plus making a profit—is the primary basis for setting price

Cost-based pricing The strategy in which the cost of producing or buying the product—plus making a profit—is the primary basis for setting price.

countertrading Bartering goods for goods (or services)

creative selling The selling process in which salespeople determine customer needs, then explain their product's benefits to try to persuade buyers to buy the product

credit An entry recording a sum received

credit union depositor-owned, nonprofit, financial cooperatives that offer a range of banking services to their members

critical path The sequence of tasks that takes the longest time to complete

cross-functional self-managed teams Groups of workers with different skills who are given the authority to manage themselves

crowdfunding The practice of funding a project or venture by raising many small amounts of money from a large number of people, typically via the Internet

Crowdfunding Crowdfunding involves funding a project or venture by raising money from a large number of people, typically through an online site.

cultural norms The ethics, values, attitudes, and behaviors that are deemed to be normal or typical in a given culture

culture The shared set of beliefs, values, knowledge, and patterns of behavior common to a group of people

culture shock The feelings of discomfort and disorientation associated with being in an unfamiliar culture

currency Government-issued coins and paper money

currency exchange rate The rate at which one country's currency can be exchanged for the currency of another country

current assets Items that can be converted into cash within one year

current liabilities Obligations in which payments are due within one year or less

current ratio Current assets ÷ current liabilities

customer loyalty program A customer loyalty program is designed to recognize and reward loyal repeat customers with rewards, coupons, discounts, or other benefits.

customer relationship management (CRM) Emphasizes finding out everything possible about customers and then using that information to satisfy and even exceed their expectations in order to build customer loyalty over the long term

customer satisfaction The concept of offering a product to please buyers by meeting their expectations

customers People or companies that pay to use an organization's goods or services

D

dashboard a central location where all social media activity can be easily monitored.

data analysis Subjected to statistical tools to determine its significance

databases Integrated collections of data stored in computer systems

day's range Highest and lowest price for the stock during the day

debit The recording or entry of debt in an account

debt to owner's equity ratio Measures of the extent to which a company uses debt, such as bank loans, to finance its operations

debt to owners' equity ratio A measure of the extent to which a company uses debt, such as bank loans, to finance its operations; total liabilities ÷ owners' equity

decentralized authority Decisions are made by middle-level and supervisory-level managers

decision A choice made from among available alternatives

decision making Process of identifying and choosing alternative courses of action

decline stage The period in which the product falls out of favor, and the organization eventually withdraws it from the marketplace

deficit An excess of spending over revenue

Deficit an excess of spending over revenue

deflation A general decline in the prices of most goods and services

Delegation The process of assigning work to subordinates.

demand Economic concept that expresses buyers'

willingness and ability to purchase goods and services at different prices

Demand curve diagram that illustrates the quantity demanded of a good at various prices

demand deposit A commercial bank's or other financial institution's checking account, from which you may make withdrawals at any time

democratic political system A political system that relies on free elections and representative assemblies

demographic segmentation Consists of categorizing consumers according to statistical characteristics of a population, such as gender, age, income, education, social class, ethnicity, and so on

demographics Measurable characteristics such as gender, age, race, and family composition

demotion When an employee's current responsibilities and pay are taken away

departmentalization The dividing up of an organization into smaller units, or departments, to facilitate management

depression A particularly severe and long-lasting recession, accompanied by falling prices (deflation)

devaluation Occurs when the value of a nation's currency is lowered relative to the value of other countries' currencies

developed countries Countries with a high level of economic development and a generally high average

income level among their citizens

developing countries Countries with low economic development and low average incomes

digital mall a digital retail site where a variety of sellers stock their goods.

digital marketing online marketing that can deliver content immediately to consumers through digital channels, devices, and platforms.

digital marketplace a digital retail side made up of small, independent sellers.

direct channel A producer sells directly to consumers, using mail order, telemarketing, the Internet, and TV ads

direct mail marketing Consists of mail promotions—letters, brochures, and pamphlets—sent through the postal service to customers

direct selling Face-to-face selling directly to customers in their homes or where they work

direct-action advertising Attempts to stimulate an immediate, or relatively immediate, purchase of a product through such devices as one-day sales, one-time promotions, or announcements of a special event

Direct-action advertising attempts to stimulate an immediate, or relatively immediate, purchase of a product through such devices as one-day sales, one-time promotions, or

announcements of a special event.

discipline Punishing an employee, often for a poor performance appraisal, usually by suspending or demoting that employee

discontinuous innovation The product is totally new, radically changing how people live

discount brokers Execute the buy and sell orders indicated by clients but don't offer advice and tax planning

discount rate The interest rate at which the Federal Reserve makes short-term loans to member banks

discounting Assigning regular prices to products, but then resorting to frequent price-cutting strategies, such as special sales, to undercut the prices of competitors

discretionary order An order in which the customer trusts the broker's professional experience and judgment and leave it to him or her to decide the right time and price for buying or selling a security

discrimination When people are hired or promoted—or denied hiring or promotion—for reasons not relevant to the job

distribution center Provides storage of product for the short periods of time for collection and distribution elsewhere

distribution channel A system for conveying goods or services from producers to customers

distribution mix The combination of distribution

channels a company uses to get its products to customers

distribution strategy An overall plan for moving products from producer to customer

distributor A person or organization (such as a dealer or retailer) that helps sell goods and services to customers

diversification Choosing securities in such a way that a loss in one investment won't have a devastating impact on your total portfolio

diversity Diversity typically refers to the similarities and differences among individuals including dimensions of personality and identity, as well as perspective and experience.

dividend and yield Annual dividend as a percentage of the price per share

dividends Part of a company's profits that are distributed to stockholders

Division of labor Different parts of a task are done by different people.

divisional structure Employees are grouped by purpose: customer groups, geographic regions, work processes, products, or industries

door-to-door selling Salespeople call directly on people at their homes or workplaces

double-entry bookkeeping The process of recording a transaction in two different accounts in order for the books to balance as a check on errors

Dow Jones Industrial Average (DJIA) Also known as "*the Dow,*" a general measure of the movement of U.S. stock prices, and an index of the average of prices of the stocks of 30 large corporations

drop shipper A limited-function wholesaler who owns (has title to) the products, but does not have physical custody of them; the drop shipper takes orders and has the producer ship the product directly to the customer

dumping Occurs when a foreign company sells its products abroad for less—even less than the cost of manufacture—than the price of the domestic product

dynamically continuous innovation Marked changes to an existing product that require a moderate amount of consumer learning or behavior change

E

e-business Using the Internet to facilitate every aspect of running a business

e-cash Money held, exchanged, and represented in electronic form and transacted over the Internet

e-commerce The buying and selling of products or services over computer networks

earned media when a business or company receives recognition or acknowledgment organically

economic community A group of nations within a geographical region that have agreed to remove trade barriers with one another (also known as *common market* or *trading bloc*)

economic responsibility Seeking to be profitable as a means to create a strong economic foundation

economics The study of the production, distribution, and consumption of scarce goods and services

economies of scale The savings realized from buying materials or manufacturing products in large quantities

editing Refers to checking over to eliminate mistakes

effective To achieve results; to realize the firm's goals by making the right decisions and executing them successfully

efficient To use people, money, raw materials, and other resources wisely and cost-effectively

electronic commerce The buying and selling of products or services over computer networks

electronic funds transfer systems (EFTSs) Computerized systems that move funds from one institution to another over electronic links

email marketing a cost-effective form of digital marketing used to retain, nurture, or attracting customers

embargo A complete ban on the import or export of certain products

Emotional Intelligence the capacity to be aware of, control, and express one's emotions, and to handle interpersonal relationship with empathy

employee benefits The benefits to which employees are entitled

employee buyout A firm's employees borrow money against their own assets, such as their houses or their pension funds, to purchase the firm from its present owners; the employees then become the new owners of the firm

employee non-compete contract The employee non-compete contract is a legally binding arrangement between an employee and their employer

employment at will The employer is free to dismiss any employee for any reason at all—or no reason—and the employee is equally free to quit work (also known as *at-will employment*)

employment tests Consist of any procedure used in the employment selection decision process

empowerment Employees share management responsibilities, including decision making

endless-chain sales prospecting technique Consists of asking each sales prospect to provide the salesperson with some names of other prospects who might be interested in the product

enterprise resource planning (ERP) A computer-based system that collects and provides information about a company's entire enterprise, including identifying customer needs, receipt of orders,

distribution of finished goods, and receipt of payment

enterprise zone A specific geographic area in which government tries to attract business investment by offering lower taxes and other government support

entrepreneur A person who sees a new opportunity for a product or service and who risks time and money to start a business with the goal of making a profit

entrepreneurial team A group of people with different kinds of expertise who form a team to create a new product

entrepreneurs Business owners who see a new opportunity for a product or service and start a firm

entrepreneurship The process of taking risks to try to create a new business

environmental scanning Involves looking at the wider world to identify what matters can affect the marketing program

Equal Employment Opportunity (EEO) Commission Enforces antidiscrimination and other employment-related laws

equilibrium price Determined by the point at which quantity demanded and quantity supplied intersect (also known as *market price*)

equity Equity refers to fair treatment in access, opportunity, and advancement for all individuals.

equity theory Focuses on employee perceptions as to how fairly they think they are

being treated compared to others

Equity theory Focuses on employee perceptions as to how fairly they think they are being treated compared to others.

ethical responsibility Taking host-country and global standards into consideration when making business decisions

ethics Principles of right and wrong that influence behavior

ethics officer Company executive whose job is to integrate the organization's ethics and values initiatives, compliance activities, and business conduct practices into the company's decision-making processes

European Union (EU) The European common market, consisting of 28 trading partners in Europe

everyday low pricing (EDLP) A strategy of continuously setting prices lower than those of competitors and then not doing any other price-cutting tactics such as special sales, rebates, and cents-off coupons

exchange-traded fund (ETF) A collection of stocks that is traded on an exchange that can be traded *throughout* the trading day

excise tax Taxes based on the value of services or property other than real estate, such as airline tickets, gasoline, and firearms; beer, liquor, and cigarettes (sin taxes); and yachts, expensive cars, and fur coats (luxury taxes)

expectancy theory Proposes that people are motivated by (1) how strongly they want something, and (2) how likely they think they are to get it

expenses Costs incurred as part of a company's operating activities

exporting Producing goods domestically and selling them outside the country

expropriation Occurs when a government seizes a domestic or foreign company's assets

external recruiting What companies do in trying to attract job applicants from outside the organization

extrinsic motivator The external payoff, such as money or recognition, a person receives from others for performing a particular task

F

facility layout The physical arrangement of equipment, offices, rooms, people, and other resources within an organization for producing goods or services

facility location The process of selecting a location for company operations

factoring accounts receivable A firm sells its accounts receivable at a discount to a financial institution

factors of production The resources used to create wealth

family brands The same brand name is given to all or most of a company's products

favorable balance of trade Exists when the value of a country's total exports exceeds the value of its total imports

fear-appeal advertising Attempts to stimulate the purchase of a product by motivating consumers through fear of loss or harm

federal budget deficit Occurs when the federal government spends more than it collects in tax revenues

Federal Deposit Insurance Corporation (FDIC) An independent agency of the U.S. government that insures bank deposits up to $250,000

Federal Reserve System Called *the Fed*; the central bank of the United States and controls the U.S. money supply

Finance the business function of obtaining funds for a company and managing them to accomplish the company's objectives

finance companies Nondeposit companies that make short-term loans at higher interest rates to individuals or businesses that don't meet the credit requirements of regular banks

financial accounting Preparing accounting information and analyses primarily for people outside of the organization

financial budgets Concentrate on the company's financial goals and the resources needed to achieve them

financial control Process by which a company periodically compares its actual revenues and expenses with those predicted in its budget

financial leverage the technique of using borrowed funds to increase a firm's rate of return

financial leverage The technique of using borrowed funds to increase a firm's rate of return

financial management The job of acquiring funds for a firm and managing them to accomplish the firm's objectives

financial managers The people responsible for planning and controlling the acquisition and uses of funds

financial plan A document that lays out a firm's strategy for reaching its financial goals

Financial plan a firm's strategy for reaching its financial goals

financial statements A summary of all transactions occurring during a particular time period; there are three types of financial statements: balance sheets, income statements, and statements of cash flows

fiscal policy The U.S. government's attempts to stabilize the economy by (1) raising or lowering taxes, or (2) borrowing and spending money

fiscal year The 12-month period designated by a company for annual financial reporting purposes

fixed assets Items that are held for a long time and are relatively permanent

fixed costs Those expenses that don't change, no matter how many products are sold; examples might include rent, insurance, utilities, and property taxes

fixed-position layout Materials, equipment, and labor are transported to one location

flexible manufacturing system (FMS) A facility that can be modified quickly to manufacture different products

flexible time Consists of flexible working hours, or any schedule that gives an employee some choices in working hours (also known as *flextime*)

Flextime Consists of flexible working hours, or any schedule that gives an employee some choices in working hours (also known as *flexible time*)

focus group Small group of people who meet with a discussion leader and give their opinions about a product or other matters

for-profit organization An organization formed to make money, or profits, by selling goods and services

forced ranking performance review systems Systems in which all employees within a business unit are ranked against one another, and grades are distributed along some sort of bell curve; top grade earners are then rewarded with bonuses and promotions, and low grade earners are warned or dismissed

forecasting Predicting revenues, costs, and expenses for a certain period of time

Foreign Corrupt Practices Act U.S. law that makes it illegal for employees of U.S. companies to make "questionable" or "dubious" contributions to political decision makers in foreign nations

foreign licensing A company gives a foreign company permission, in return for a fee, to make or distribute the licensing company's product or service

foreign subsidiary A company in a foreign country that is totally owned and controlled by the parent company

form utility The value that people add in converting resources—natural resources, capital, human resources, entrepreneurship, and knowledge—into finished products

formal appraisals Appraisals that are conducted at scheduled times of the year and are based on pre-established performance measures

franchise An arrangement in which a business owner allows others the right to use its name and sell its goods or services within a specific geographical area

franchisee The buyer of the franchise

franchising A company allows a foreign company to pay it a fee and a share of the profit in return for using a brand name and a package of materials and services

franchisor The business owner that gives others the rights to sell its products or services

free trade The movement of goods and services among nations without political or economic restrictions

free-market economy An economic system in which the production and distribution of goods and services are controlled by private individuals rather than by the government (also known as *capitalism*)

free-rein leaders Set objectives, and employees are relatively free to choose how to achieve them.

Freelancer A freelancer is an individual who is self-employed, and utilizes their knowledge, skills, and abilities, to perform a tasks, services or functions for a customer.

frequency The average number of times each member of the audience is exposed to an ad

front-line managers Make daily operating decisions, directing the daily tasks of individual contributors and nonmanagerial personnel

full-service brokers Offer a wide range of investment-related services, not only execution of trades but also investment research, advice, and tax planning (also known as *traditional brokers*)

full-service merchant wholesalers An independently owned firm that takes title to—that is, becomes owner of—the manufacturer's products and performs all sales and distribution, as well as provides credit and other services

functional structure People performing similar activities or occupational specialties are put together in formal groups

futures contract Making an agreement with a seller or broker to buy a specific amount of a commodity at a certain price on a certain date

G

gainsharing The distribution of savings or "gains" to groups of employees that reduced costs and increased measurable productivity

Gantt chart A kind of time schedule—a specialized bar chart that shows the relationship between the kind of work tasks planned and their scheduled completion dates

Gantt Chart A kind of time schedule—a specialized bar chart that shows the relationship between the kind of work tasks planned and their scheduled completion dates.

general obligation bonds Used by tax-levying government agencies to pay for public projects that will not generate revenue, such as road repairs

general partnership Two or more partners are responsible for the business, and they share profits, liabilities (debt), and management responsibilities

Generally Accepted Accounting Principles (GAAP) A set of accounting standards used in the preparation of financial statements to ensure that they are relevant, reliable, consistent, and comparable

geographic segmentation Categorizes customers according to geographic location

geotargeting Geotargeting allows marketers to specify the location where specific ads and content will be seen by a customer based on geographic location.

geotracking use of a consumer's geographic location to determine what goods will come up in a search and at what price.

global climate change an increase in the average temperature of Earth's atmosphere.

Global Compact A voluntary agreement established in 2000 by the United Nations that promotes human rights, good labor practices, environmental protection, and anticorruption standards for businesses

global economy The increasing interaction of the world's economies as a single market instead of many national markets

global outsourcing Using suppliers outside the United States to provide labor, goods, or services (also known as *offshoring*)

Global warming an increase in the average temperature of Earth's atmosphere.

globalization Refers to the movement of the world economy toward becoming a more interdependent system

globalization The increasing connectivity and interdependence of the world's economies, societies, and cultures because of advances in communication, technology, trade, international investment, currency movement, and migration

goal A broad, long-range target that an organization wishes to attain

goal-setting theory Proposes that employees can be motivated by goals that are specific and challenging but achievable

going public Occurs when a privately owned company becomes a publicly owned company by issuing stock for sale to the public

good A tangible product (one that you can touch)

goodwill An amount paid for a business beyond the value of its other assets, based on its reputation, customer list, loyal employees, and similar intangibles

Government bonds bonds sold by the U.S. Treasury, consist of treasury notes and treasury bonds

government regulators Government agencies that establish rules and regulations under which organizations must operate

grievance is a complaint by an employee that management has violated the terms of the labor-management agreement.

grievance is a complaint by an employee that management has violated the terms of the labor-management agreement.

grievance A complaint by an employee that management has violated the terms of the labor-management agreement

gross domestic product (GDP) The total value of all the goods and services that a country produces within its borders in one year

gross domestic product (GDP) The total value of all the goods and services that a country produces within its borders in one year

gross profit The amount remaining after the cost of goods sold is subtracted from the net sales

gross sales The funds received from all sales of the firm's products

growth stage The most profitable stage, this is the period in which customer demand increases, the product's sales grow, and later competitors may enter the market

growth stocks stocks issued by small, innovative new companies in hot industries

growth stocks Stocks issued by small, innovative new companies in hot industries

guerrilla marketing Consists of innovative, low-cost marketing schemes that try to get customers' attention in unusual ways

H

Hawthorne Effect The name given to a Harvard research group's conclusion that employees work harder if they receive added attention—if employees think managers care about their welfare and that supervisors pay special attention to them

Hero In the business sense, a person whose accomplishments embody the values of the organization.

Hierarchy of Authority An arrangement for making sure that work specialization produces the right result—that the right people do the right things at the right time.

host country The country in which a company is doing business

Hostile Environment Harassment Offensive or Intimidating Workplace.

hostile takeover Situation in which an outsider (a *corporate raider*) buys enough shares in a company to be able to take control of it against the will of the corporation's top management and directors

house-party selling A host has friends and acquaintances in for a "party" with refreshments, in return for a gift from a sponsor, who typically gives a sales presentation

human capital The productive potential of employee experience, knowledge, and actions

Human capital the productive potential of employee experience, knowledge, and actions.

Human relations movement Proposed that better human relations could increase worker productivity.

human resource (HR) management Consists of the activities managers perform to obtain and maintain an effective workforce to assist organizations in achieving goals

human skills The ability to work well in cooperation with other people to get things done

hybrid structure One in which an organization uses functional and divisional structures in different parts of the same organization

hybrid work environment A hybrid work environment typically involves an employee working a certain percentage of time in a physical office space and a certain amount of time working off-site.

I

idea generation Coming up with new product ideas, ideally by collecting ideas from as many sources as possible

ideate Ideate is used in business to reference the process of forming an idea

import quota A trade barrier that limits the quantity of a product that can be imported

importing Buying goods outside the country and reselling them domestically

inbound marketing a form of digital marketing that utilizes such tools as blogs, webinars, or follow-up emails to entice customers to a product or service offer without forcing an interaction or a purchase.

incentive A commission, bonus, profit-sharing plan, or stock option that induces employees to be more productive and attract and retain top performers

inclusion Inclusion describes the extent to which each person feels welcomed, respected, supported, and valued by a group, team, or company.

income statement Once known as the *profit-and-loss statement*, this financial statement shows a firm's revenues and expenses for a particular time period and the resulting profit or loss

income tax Taxes paid on earnings received by individuals and businesses

Income tax taxes paid on earnings received by individuals and businesses

Income tax taxes paid on earnings received by individuals and businesses

incubator A facility that offers small businesses low-cost offices with basic services

indenture terms Terms of the lending agreement

individual brands Different brand names are given to different company products

Individual Contributor Some employees are considered individual contributors. They do not have any people management responsibilities but may oversee or be accountable for managing projects, programs, or processes.

industrial goods Products used to produce other products

inflation A general increase in the prices of most goods and services

inflation A general increase in the cost of most goods and services as a result of increased prices

infomercials Extended TV commercials ranging from 2 (short form) to 28.5 (long form) minutes that are devoted exclusively to promoting a product in considerable detail

informal appraisals Appraisals that are conducted at unscheduled times and consist of less rigorous indications of employee performance

informational advertising Provides consumers with straightforward knowledge about the features of the product offered, such as basic components and price

infrastructure The set of physical facilities (including telecommunications, roads, and airports) that form the basis for a country's level of economic development

initial public offering (IPO) The first time a corporation's stock is offered for sale

innovation A product that customers perceive as being newer or better than existing products

installations Large capital purchases

institutional advertising Consists of presentations that promote a favorable image for an organization

institutional investors Large and powerful organizations such as pension funds and insurance companies, which invest their own or others' funds

insurance companies Nondeposit companies that accept payments from policyholders

Insurance companies nondeposit companies that accept payments from policyholder.

intangible assets Assets that are not physical objects but are nonetheless valuable, such as patents, trademarks, and goodwill.

integrated marketing communication (IMC) Combines all four promotional tools to execute a comprehensive, unified promotional strategy

integrity-based ethics code Ethical code that seeks to foster responsible employee conduct by creating an environment that supports ethically desirable behavior

intentional tort A willful act resulting in injury

interest groups Groups whose members try to influence businesses and governments on specific issues

interest rate The price paid for the use of money over a certain period of time

intermediaries The people or firms that move products between producer and customers

intermittent processes A production process in which finished goods or services are turned out in a series of short production runs and the machines are changed frequently to make different products

intermodal shipping Shipping that combines use of several different modes of transportation

internal recruiting What companies do when they make employees already working for the organization aware of job openings

International Monetary Fund (IMF) International organization designed to assist in smoothing the flow of money among nations; operates as a last-resort lender that makes short-term loans to countries suffering from an unfavorable balance of payments

intrapreneur Someone who works inside an existing organization who sees an opportunity for a product or service and mobilizes the organization's resources to turn the opportunity into a reality

intrinsic motivator The internal satisfaction, such as a feeling of accomplishment, a person receives from performing the particular task itself

introduction stage The stage in the product life cycle in which a new product is introduced into the marketplace

inventory The name given to goods kept in stock to be used for the production process or for sales to customers

inventory The name given to goods kept in stock to be used for the production process or for sales to customers

inventory control The system for determining the right quantity of resources and keeping track of their location and use

Inventory Control The system for determining the right quantity of resources and keeping track of their location and use

inventory turnover ratio Cost of goods sold in one year ÷ average value of inventory

investment bankers Companies that engage in buying and reselling new securities

investment-grade bonds Bonds that are relatively safe, with a low probability of default; they have a bond rating of BBB or above

Investment-grade bonds bonds that are relatively safe, with a low probability of default; they have a bond rating of BBB or above.

invisible hand Adam Smith's term for the market forces that convert individuals' drive for prosperity into the goods and services that provide economic and social benefits to all

Invisible hand Adam Smith's term for the market forces that convert individuals' drive for prosperity into the goods and services that provide economic and social benefits to all

ISO 9000 series Quality-assurance procedures companies must install—in purchasing, manufacturing, inventory, shipping, and other areas—that can be audited by "registrars," or independent quality-assurance experts

J

job analysis Determine the basic elements of a job, using observation and analysis

job description Outlines what the holders of the job do and how and why they do it

Job enlargement Consists of increasing the number of tasks in a job to improve employee satisfaction, motivation, and quality of production.

Job enrichment Consists of creating a job with motivating factors such as recognition, responsibility, achievement, stimulating work, and advancement.

job postings Putting information about job vacancies on company websites, break-room bulletin boards, and newsletters

job rotation Consists of rotating employees through different assignments in different departments to give them a broader picture of the organization

job routine What is required in the job for which a person was hired, how the work will be evaluated, and who the immediate coworkers and managers are

job sharing Two people divide one full-time job

job sharing two people divide one full-time job. Working at Working at home with telecommunicat ions between office and home is called

Job simplification Reducing the number of tasks a worker performs.

job specification Describes the minimum qualifications people must have to perform the job successfully

joint venture A U.S. firm shares the risk and rewards of starting a new enterprise with a foreign company in a foreign country (also known as *strategic alliance*)

journal A record book or part of a computer program containing the daily record of the firm's transactions

judiciary The branch of government that oversees the court system

just-in-time (JIT) inventory control Only minimal supplies are kept on the organization's premises and others are delivered by the suppliers on an as-needed basis

K

knockoff brands Illegal imitations of brand-name products

knowledge workers People who work primarily with information or who develop and use knowledge in the workplace

L

labor unions Organizations of employees formed to protect and advance their members' interests by bargaining with management over job-related issues

laws Rules of conduct or action formally recognized as binding or enforced by a controlling authority

leading Motivating, directing, and otherwise influencing people to work hard to achieve the organization's goals

lean manufacturing The production of products by eliminating unnecessary steps and using the fewest resources, while continually striving for improvement

ledger A specialized record book or computer program that contains summaries of all journal transactions classified into specific categories

legal responsibility Obeying the laws of host countries as well as international law

less-developed countries Countries with low economic development and low average incomes

leveraged buyout (LBO) Occurs when one firm borrows money to buy another firm; the purchaser uses the assets of the company being acquired as security for the loan being used to finance the purchase

liabilities Debts owed by a firm to an outside individual or organization

limit order Telling a broker to buy a particular security only if it is less than a certain price or to sell it only if it is above a certain price

limited liability company (LLC) Combines the tax benefits of a sole proprietorship or partnership—one level of tax—with the limited liability of a corporation

limited liability partnership (LLP) Each partner's liability—and risk of losing personal assets—is limited to just his or her own acts and omissions and those of his or her directly reporting employees

limited partnership One or more general partners plus other, limited partners who contribute an investment but do not have any management responsibility or liability

limited-function merchant wholesaler An independently owned firm that takes title to—becomes owner of—the manufacturer's products but performs only selected services, such as storage only

line managers Involved directly in an organization's goals, have authority to make decisions, and usually have people reporting to them

line of credit How much a bank is willing to lend the borrower during a specified period of time

liquidity The essential feature of current assets, as they are easily converted into cash

liquidity ratios Measure a firm's ability to meet its short-term obligations when they become due

load funds Commission is charged for each purchase

Load funds a commission is charged for each purchase.

logistics Planning and implementing the details of moving raw materials, finished goods, and related information along the supply chain, from origin to points of consumption to meet customer requirements

long-term forecasts Predictions for the next 1, 5, or 10 years

long-term liabilities obligations in which payments are due in one year or more

long-term liabilities Obligations in which payments are due in one year or more, such as for a long-term loan from a bank or insurance company

loss Occurs when business expenses exceed revenues

loss leaders Products priced at or below cost to attract customers

M

M1 The narrowest definition of the money supply, money that can be accessed quickly and easily

M1 the narrowest definition of the money supply, is defined as money that can be accessed quickly and easily

M2 (1) Money that can be accessed quickly and easily (that is, M1) *and* (2) money that takes more time to access

M2 (1) money that can be accessed quickly and easily (that is, M1) AND (2) money that takes more time to access

macroeconomics The study of large economic units, such as the operations of a nation's economy and the effect on it of government policies and allocation of resources

management Planning, leading, organizing, and controlling the activities of an enterprise according to certain policies to achieve certain objectives

management The pursuit of organizational goals

effectively and efficiently through (1) planning, (2) organization, (3) leading, and (4) controlling the organization's resources

Management by Objectives (MBO) A four-stage process in which a manager and employee jointly set objectives for the employee, manager develops an action plan for achieving the objective, manager and employee periodically review the employee's performance, and manager makes a performance appraisal and rewards employee according to results

managerial accounting Preparing accounting information and analyses for managers and other decision makers inside an organization

manufacturer-owned wholesaler A wholesale business that is owned and operated by a product's manufacturer

Manufacturer's branch office An office that is owned and managed by a manufacturer that not only has offices for sales representatives, but also carries an inventory from which the staff can fill orders.

manufacturer's brands An individual company creates a product or service and brands the product or service using the company name; also called *national* or *producer brands*, or even *global brands* when extended worldwide

Manufacturer's sales office An office that is owned and managed by a manufacturer and

that has offices for sales representatives who sell products that are delivered at a later time.

Market Opportunity A market opportunity is an analysis of the potential need or want of a particular product or service.

market order Telling a broker to buy or sell a particular security at the best available price

market price Determined by the point at which quantity demanded and quantity supplied intersect (also known as *equilibrium price*)

market segmentation Divides a market into groups whose members have similar characteristics or wants and needs

market share The percentage of the market of total sales for a particular product or good

market value market value is the price at which a stock is currently selling

market value The price at which a stock is currently selling

marketable securities Stocks, bonds, government securities, and money market certificates, which can be easily converted to cash

marketing The activity, set of institutions, and processes for creating, communicating, delivering, and exchanging offerings that have value for customers, clients, partners, and society at large

marketing concept Focuses on customer satisfaction, service, and profitability

marketing environment Consists of the outside forces that can influence the success of marketing programs. These forces are (1) global, (2) economic, (3) sociocultural, (4) technological, (5) competitive, (6) political, and (7) legal and regulatory

marketing mix Consists of the four key strategy considerations called the 4 Ps: product, pricing, place, and promotion strategies. Specifically, the marketing mix involves (1) developing a product that will fill consumer wants, (2) pricing the product, (3) distributing the product to a place where consumers will buy it, and (4) promoting the product

marketing research The systematic gathering and analyzing of data about problems relating to the marketing of goods and services

marketing strategy A plan for (1) identifying the target market among market segments, (2) creating the right marketing mix to reach that target market, and (3) dealing with important forces in the external marketing environment

Maslow's Hierarchy of Needs theory Proposes that people are motivated by five levels of needs, ranging from low to high: (1) physiological, (2) safety, (3) social, (4) esteem, and (5) self-actualization

Mass customization Using mass production techniques to produce customized goods or services

mass production The production of uniform goods in great quantities

master budgets Used to pull together the other budgets into an overall plan of action

master limited partnership (MLP) The partnership acts like a corporation, selling stock on a stock exchange, but it is taxed like a partnership, paying a lower rate than the corporate income tax

materials handling The physical handling of goods to and from and within warehouses

materials requirement planning (MRP) A computer-based method of delivering the right amounts of supplies to the right place at the right time for the production of goods

matrix structure One which combines, in grid form, the functional chain of command and the divisional chain of command—usually product—so that there is a vertical command structure and a horizontal command structure

maturity date the issuing organization is legally required to repay the bond's principal in full to the bondholder.

maturity stage The period in which the product starts to fall out of favor and sales and profits start to level off

mechanization The use of machines to do the work formerly performed by people

media planning The process of choosing the exact kinds of media to be used for an advertising campaign

mediation The process in which a neutral third party listens to both sides in a dispute, makes suggestions, and encourages them to agree on a solution without the need for a court trial

mediation The process in which a neutral third party, a mediator, listens to both sides in a dispute, makes suggestions, and encourages them to agree on a solution

Mediation is the process in which a neutral third party, a mediator, listens to both sides in a dispute, makes suggestions, and encourages them to agree on a solution.

medium of exchange Characteristic of money that makes economic transactions easier and eliminates the need to barter

mentor An experienced person who coaches and guides lesser-experienced people by helping them understand an industry or organization's culture and structure

mentoring The process by which an experienced employee, the mentor, supervises, teaches, and provides guidance for a less-experienced employee, the mentee or protégé

Mentoring describe s the process in which an experienced employee, the mentor, supervises, teaches, and provides guidance for a lessexperienced employee, the mentee or protégé

Mercosur The largest common market in Latin America, with 13 member countries at different levels of

participation (full, associate, observer)

merger Occurs when two firms join to form a new firm

microeconomics The study of small economic units, the operations of particular groups of people, businesses, organizations, and markets

Microloan a small sum of money lent at low interest to a new business

micropreneur A person who takes the risk of starting and managing a business that remains small (often home-based)

middle managers Implement the policies and plans of the top managers above them and supervise and coordinate the activities of the supervisory managers below them

mission statement A statement of the organization's fundamental purposes

mixed economy A blended economic system in which some resources are allocated by the free market and some resources are allocated by the government, resulting in a somewhat better balance between freedom and economic equality

mobile marketing a set of practices that enables organizations to communicate and engage with their audience in an interactive and relevant manner through and with any mobile device or network.

mobile payment A transaction completed through a portable electronic device via an application.

modular structure One in which a firm assembles pieces, or modules, of a product provided by outside contractors

monetary policy The U.S. government's attempts to manage the money supply and interest rates in order to influence economic activity

money Any medium of value that is generally accepted as payment for goods and services

money market accounts Offer interest rates competitive with those of brokerage firms but they require higher minimum balances and limit check writing

Money market accounts offer interest rates competitive with those of brokerage but they require higher minimum balances and limit check writing.

money market instruments Short-term IOUs, debt securities that mature within one year, which are issued by governments, large corporations, and financial institutions

Money market instruments short-term IOUs, debt securities that mature within one year, which are issued by governments, large corporations, and financial institutions.

money supply the amount of money the Federal Reserve System makes available for people to buy goods and services.

money supply The amount of money the Federal Reserve System makes available for people to buy goods and services

monopolistic competition A type of free market that has many sellers who sell similar products, but the sellers have found ways to distinguish among their products, or buyers perceive the products as being different

monopoly A type of free market in which there is only one seller and no competition

mortgage A loan in which property or real estate is used as collateral

motivation The psychological processes that induce people to pursue goals

multilevel marketing Independent businesspeople, or distributors, sell products both on their own and by recruiting, motivating, supplying, and training others to sell those products, with the distributors' compensation being based on both their personal sales and the group's sales

multinational corporations Organizations with multinational management and ownership that manufacture and market products in many different countries

Municipal bonds bonds issued by state and local governments and agencies, consist of revenue bonds and general obligation bonds.

mutual fund A fund operated by an investment company that brings together money from many people and invests it in an array of diversified stocks, bonds, or other securities

mutual savings bank For-profit financial institutions similar to savings and loans, except that they are owned by their depositors rather than by shareholders

Mutual savings bank for-profit financial institutions similar to savings and loans, except that they are owned by their depositors rather than by shareholders.

N

narrow span of control Limited number of people reporting to a manager

NASDAQ Composite Index Tracks not only domestic but also foreign common stocks traded on the NASDAQ exchange

National Credit Union Administration (NCUA) An independent agency that provides up to $250,000 insurance coverage per individual per credit union

national debt The amount of money the government owes because federal spending has exceeded federal revenue

National Labor Relations Board Enforces procedures allowing employees to vote to have a union and the rules for collective bargaining

necessity entrepreneur An entrepreneur who suddenly must earn a living and is simply trying to replace lost income

need-satisfaction presentation consists of determining customer needs and then tailoring your presentation to address those needs

need-satisfaction presentation Consists of determining customer needs and then tailoring your presentation to address those needs

negligence An unintentional act that results in injury

net income The firm's profit or loss after paying income taxes; net income = revenue − expenses

net period Length of time for which the supplier extends credit

net sales The money resulting after sales returns and allowances are subtracted from gross sales

neuromarketing The study of how people's brains respond to advertising and other brand-related messages by scientifically monitoring brainwave activity, eye tracking, and skin response

new product A product that either (1) is a significant improvement over existing products or (2) performs a new function for the consumer

niche marketing Consists of dividing market segments even further, to microsegments for which sales may be profitable

no-load funds There is no sales charge but the investment company may charge a management fee

No-load funds there is no sales charge but the investment company may charge a management fee.

non-disclosure agreement A non-disclosure agreement binds the individuals from disclosing proprietary information owned by one of the parties.

nonbanks Financial institutions—insurance companies, pension funds, finance companies, and brokerage firms—that offer many of the same services as banks provide

nonprofit organization An organization that exists to earn enough profit to cover its expenses and further its goals

nonstore retailers sell merchandise in ways other than through retail stores

nonverbal communication Messages sent outside of the written or spoken word, such as what constitutes permissible interpersonal space

North American Free Trade Agreement (NAFTA) Agreement that established a common market consisting of the 450 million people of the United States, Canada, and Mexico

not-for-profit accountants Those who work for governments and nonprofit organizations, perform the same services as for-profit accountants—except they are concerned with efficiency, not profits

notes payable Money owed on a loan based on a promise (either short term or long term) the firm made

NOW account Pays interest and allows you to write an unlimited number of checks, but you have to maintain a minimum monthly balance

O

objective A specific, short-term target designed to

achieve the organization's goals

objective appraisals Appraisals that are based on facts and often based on numbers related to employees

off-the-job training Consists of classroom programs, videotapes, workbooks, online distance learning programs, and similar training tools

oligopoly A type of free market that has a few sellers offering similar but not identical products to many small buyers

on-the-job training Takes place in the workplace while employees are working at job-related tasks

onboarding Process that is designed to help a newcomer fit smoothly into the job and the organization

one-time shopping digital purchasing behavior that may combine product-focused shopping, browsing, researching, and bargain hunting all at the same time. Consumers are shopping for a gift or using a gift card and will not return to the shop once the purchase is made.

one-to-one marketing Consists of reducing market segmentation to the smallest part—individual customers

online retailing Nonstore retailing of products directly to consumers using the Internet

Online retailing Nonstore retailing of products directly to consumers using the Internet.

open shop Workers may choose to join or not join a union

open-market operations The Federal Reserve controls the money supply by buying and selling U.S. Treasury securities, or government bonds, to the public

operating budgets Used to predict sales and production goals and the costs required to meet them

operating expenses Selling and administrative expenses

operational planning Determining how to accomplish specific tasks with existing resources within the next one-week to one-year period

operations Any process that takes basic resources and converts them into finished products—inputs into outputs (also known as *production*)

operations management The management of the process of transforming materials, labor, and other resources into goods and/or services

opportunities Favorable circumstances that present possibilities for progress beyond existing goals

opportunity entrepreneur An ambitious entrepreneur who starts a business to pursue an opportunity (and large profits)

order processing Consists of receiving customer orders and seeing that they are handled correctly and that the product is delivered

organization A group of people who work together to accomplish a specific purpose

organization's mission and operations The purpose,

products, operations, and history of an organization

organizational chart A box-and-lines illustration of the formal lines of authority and the official positions or work specializations

organizational culture The shared beliefs and values that develop within an organization and guide the behavior of its members (also known as *corporate culture*)

organizing Arranging tasks, people, and other resources to accomplish the work

outsourcing Using suppliers outside the company to provide goods and services (also known as *contract manufacturing*)

owned media the marketing channels that a company develops

owners Those who can claim the organization as their legal property

owners' equity Represents the value of a firm if its assets were sold and its debts paid (also known as *stockholders' equity*)

P

packaging The covering or wrapping around a product that protects and promotes the product

packaging Covering or wrapping that protects and promotes a product

paid display advertising Includes everything from banner ads to YouTube video advertising. These ads generate awareness as well as (hopefully) drive traffic to a website.

paid media all the online marketing channels that the business pays for

paid search online advertising in which a company pays to be a sponsored result of a customer's Web search.

paid stories ads that appear as content designed to look like stories to the viewer.

paid stories ads that appear as content designed to look like stories to the viewer.

par value the face value of a share of stock, an arbitrary figure set by the issuing corporation's board of directors agment

par value The face value of a share of stock, an arbitrary figure set by the issuing corporation's board of directors

Paris agreement The Paris Agreement is a bridge between today's policies and climate-neutrality before the end of the century. Source: https://ec.europa.eu/clima/policies/international/negotiations/paris_en

part-time work Any work done on a schedule less than the standard 40-hour workweek

participation to take a meaningful and active role in organizational activities

participative leaders Delegate authority and involve employees in their decisions.

partnership A business owned and operated by two or more persons as a voluntary legal association

pay for performance bases pay on the employee's work results.

pay for performance Bases pay on the employee's work results

peak The point at which an economic expansion starts to lose steam

peer-to-peer lending The process of obtaining financing from other individuals instead of a traditional financial institution like a bank or credit union.

penetration pricing Setting a low price to attract many customers and deter competition; designed to generate customers' interest and stimulate them to try out new products

pension funds Nondeposit institutions that provide retirement benefits to workers and their families

perfect competition A type of free market that has many small sellers who sell interchangeable products to many informed buyers, and no seller is large enough to dictate the price of the product

performance appraisal Consists of a manager's assessing an employee's performance and providing feedback (also known as *performance review*)

performance review Consists of a manager's assessing an employee's performance and providing feedback (also known as *performance appraisal*)

personal selling In-person, face-to-face communication

and promotion to influence customers to buy goods and services

personal selling Face-to-face communication and promotion to influence customers to buy goods and services

persuasive advertising Tries to develop a desire among consumers for the product

PERT chart A diagram for determining the best sequencing of tasks

philanthropic responsibilities Acting as a good global corporate citizen, contributing resources to the community, and seeking to improve the quality of life for individuals as defined by the host country's expectations

philanthropy Charitable donations to benefit humankind

physical distribution All of the activities required to move products from the manufacturer to the final buyer

piece rate Employees are paid according to how much output they produce

Pitch Deck A summary of the company, future vision, market opportunity and business plan delivered via a presentation software consisting of typically between 10–20 slides.

placing The process of moving goods or services from the seller to prospective buyers (also known as *distribution*)

planning Setting goals and deciding how to achieve them

pledging accounts receivable A firm uses its accounts receivable as collateral, or security, to obtain a short-term loan

portfolio The collection of securities representing a person's investments

preferred stock Stockholders are not able to vote on major company decisions, but they get (1) preferred, or first, claim on the company's dividends and (2) first claim on any remaining assets if the firm goes bankrupt and its assets are sold

prepaid expense An expenditure paid for during an accounting period, but the asset will not be consumed until a later time

press release A brief statement written in the form of a news story or a video program that is released to the mass media to try to get favorable publicity for a firm or its products (also known as a *news release* or *publicity release*)

price skimming Setting a high price to make a large profit; it can work when there is little competition

price/earnings ratio Price of stock divided by firm's per-share earnings

pricing Figuring out how much to charge for a product

pricing objectives Goals that product producers⬜as well as retailers and wholesalers⬜hope to achieve in pricing products for sale

primary data Data derived from original research, such as that which you might conduct yourself

primary securities market The financial market in which new security issues are first sold to investors

principle of motion economy Every job can be broken down into a series of elementary motions

Principle of motion economy Every job can be broken down into a series of elementary motions.

Principle of motion economy Every job can be broken down into a series of elementary motions.

private accountants In-house accountants that work for a single organization; sometimes called corporate accountants

private placements Selling stock to only a small group of large investors

private-label brands Brands attached to products distributed by one store or a chain

problems Difficulties that impede the achievement of goals

process layout Similar work is grouped by function

process materials Materials for making principal product that are not readily identifiable in that product

producer price index (PPI) A measure of prices at the wholesale level (wholesale goods are those purchased in large quantities for resale)

product A good (tangible) or service (intangible) that can satisfy customer needs

product analysis Doing cost estimates to calculate the product's possible profitability

product development The production of a prototype of the product, a preliminary version, so the company can see what the product will look like

product differentiation The attempt to design a product in a way that will make it be perceived differently enough from competitors' products that it will attract consumers

product layout Equipment and tasks are arranged into an assembly line—a sequence of steps for producing a single product in one location

Product Layout Equipment and tasks are arranged into an assembly line—a sequence of steps for producing a single product to one location.

product life cycle A model that graphs the four stages that a product or service goes through during the "life" of its marketability: (1) introduction, (2) growth, (3) maturity, (4) decline

product line A collection of products designed for a similar market, or a collection of products that are physically similar

product mix The combination of all product lines that a company offers

product placement in which sellers of a product pay to have that product prominently placed in a TV show or film so that many people will see it.[iii]

[iii] E. Porter, "Would You Buy a New Car from Eva Longoria?" *New York Times*, July 10, 2008, p. A22; S. Clifford, "Product Placements Acquire a Life of Their Own on Shows," *New York Times*,

July 14, 2008, pp. C1, C4; and S. Clifford, "A Product's Place Is on the Set," *New York Times*, July 22, 2008, pp. C1, C6.

product screening Elimination of product ideas that are not feasible

product-focused shopping digital purchasing behavior that involves replacing an existing product or purchasing a product that has been pre-chosen.

production Any process that takes basic resources and converts them into finished products—inputs into outputs (also known as *operations*)

production management The management of the process of transforming materials, labor, and other resources into goods

productivity The amount of output produced for each unit of input

Productivity The amount of output per input

profit Revenue minus expenses; the amount of money a business makes after paying for all its costs

profit sharing Sharing a percentage of the company's profits with employees

profitability ratios Used to measure how well profits are doing in relation to the firm's sales, assets, or owners' equity

promissory note A written contract prepared by the buyer who agrees to pay the seller a certain amount by a certain time

promotion Moving the employee to a higher management job within the company

promotion Consists of all the techniques companies use to motivate consumers to buy their products

promotion mix The combination of tools that a company uses to promote a product, selecting from among four promotional tools: (1) advertising, (2) public relations, (3) personal selling, and (4) sales promotion

property Anything of value for which a person or firm has right of ownership

property tax Taxes paid on real estate owned by individuals and businesses, as well as on certain kinds of personal property

proportional relationship Two quantities are in a proportional relationship if they have a constant ratio, or if the graph of the quantities on a coordinate plane is a straight line through the origin.

prospecting The process of identifying potential customers, who are called *prospects*

prototype A preliminary version of a product

psychographic segmentation Consists of categorizing people according to lifestyle, values, and psychological characteristics

psychological pricing The technique of pricing products or services in odd, rather than even, amounts to make products seem less expensive

Psychological safety An environment where people believe candor is welcome

public accountants Professionals who provide accounting services to clients on a fee basis

public offerings Selling stock to the general public in securities market

public relations (PR) Unpaid, nonpersonal communication that is concerned with creating and maintaining a favorable image of the firm, its products, and its actions with the mass media, consumers, and the public at large

public service advertising Consists of presentations, usually sponsored by nonprofit organizations, that are concerned with the welfare of the community in general; such ads are often presented by the media free of charge

publicity Unpaid coverage by the mass media about a firm or its products

publicly traded company A publicly-traded company is a company that issues stock that is traded on the open market typically through a stock exchange.

pull promotional strategy Aimed directly at consumers, to get them to demand the product from retailers

purchasing The activity of finding the best resources for the best price from the best suppliers to produce the best goods and services

push promotional strategy is aimed at wholesalers and retailers, to encourage them to market the product to consumers.

push promotional strategy Aimed at wholesalers and retailers, to encourage them to market the product to consumers

Q

quadratic equation an equation containing a single variable of degree 2. Its general form is $ax^2 + bx + c = 0$, where x is the variable and a, b, and c are constants ($a \neq 0$).

qualifying Determining if the prospect has the authority to buy and the ability to pay

quality Refers to the total ability of a product or service to meet customer needs

quality assurance The process of minimizing errors by managing each stage of production

quality of life The level of a society's general well-being as measured by several key factors, including health care, educational opportunities, and environmental health; also called *human development*

R

rack jobber A limited-function wholesaler who furnishes products and display racks or shelves in retail stores and shares profits with retailers

ratio analysis Uses one of a number of financial ratios—such as liquidity, efficiency, leverage, and profitability—to evaluate variables in a financial statement

raw materials Basic materials for making principal product

reach The number of people within a given population that an ad will reach at least once

recession Two or more consecutive quarters of decline in gross domestic product (GDP)

recruiting The process by which companies find and attract qualified applicants for open jobs

referral sales prospecting technique Consists of asking satisfied customers to provide names of potential customers and to contact them on behalf of the salesperson

reinforcement theory Suggests that behavior with positive consequences tends to be repeated, whereas behavior with negative consequences tends not to be repeated

reliability Expresses how well a test measures the same thing consistently

reminder advertising Tries to remind consumers of the existence of a product

remote work environment A work environment in which employees do not work at a physical site such as an office, but work from an alternative space often a home office.

representation The action of speaking or acting on behalf of someone, or the state of being represented.

researching digital purchasing behavior wherein the consumer is purchasing a product for the first time. Unlike browsing, which has no expected outcome, research is more deliberate and will likely result in a purchase either online or offline.

reserve requirement The percentage of total checking and savings deposits that a bank must keep as cash in its vault or in a non-interest-bearing deposit at its regional Federal Reserve bank

resource development The study of how to develop the resources for creating and best utilizing goods and services

responsibility The obligation to perform the tasks assigned to you

retailers Intermediaries who sell products to the final customer

retained earnings The portion of the company profits that the owners choose to reinvest in the company

return on assets Net income ÷ total assets; this information helps the company understand how well they are using their assets to generate profits

return on owners' equity Net income ÷ owners' equity (also known as *return on investment (ROI)*)

return on sales Net income ÷ sales (also known as *profit margin*)

revenue The total amount of money that the selling of goods or services produces during a defined period of time (for example, one year)

revenue bonds Used to pay for public projects that will generate revenue, such as toll bridges

revolving credit agreement The bank guarantees the loan and is obligated to loan funds up to the credit limit

Revolving credit agreement the bank guarantees the loan and is obligated to

risk The possibility that the owner(s) of a business may invest time and money in an enterprise that fails (that is, does not make a profit)

risk-return trade-off Financial managers continually try to balance the firm's investment risk with the expected return from its investments

Rites and rituals The activities and ceremonies, planned and unplanned, that celebrate important occasions and accomplishments in the organization's life.

robotics The use of programmable machines

robots Programmable machines used to manipulate materials and tools to perform a variety of tasks

S

S corporation Has no more than 100 owners (shareholders), but, like a partnership, the owners are taxed only at the personal level, not the corporate level

sales commission Salespeople are paid a percentage of the earnings the company made from their sales

sales promotion Short-term marketing incentives to stimulate dealer interest and consumer buying

sales returns Products that customers return to the company for a refund

sales revenue The funds received from the sales of

goods and services during a certain period

sales support Consists not of selling products but of facilitating the sale by providing supportive services

Sales support consists not of selling products but of facilitating the sale by providing supportive services

sales tax Taxes collected by retail merchants on merchandise they sell

Sarbanes–Oxley Act U.S. law, enacted in 2002, that established protections for whistleblowers, recordkeeping requirements for public companies, and penalties for noncompliance

savings account A bank account that pays low interest and doesn't allow check writing

savings and loan associations (S&Ls) Financial institutions that accept deposits and were originally intended to make loans primarily for home mortgages

Savings Association Insurance Fund (SAIF) Insures depositors with accounts in savings and loan associations up to $250,000 per depositor per bank

scheduling The act of determining time periods for each task in the production process

Scientific Management Emphasized the scientific study of work methods to improve the productivity of individual workers.

Score A Small Business Association mentoring

program consisting of retired executives who volunteer as consultants to advise small-business people

SCORE A Small Business Association mentoring program consisting of retired executives who volunteer as consultants to advise small business people

search engine optimization (SEO) the process of driving traffic to a company's website from "free" or "organic" search results using search engines.

secondary data Information acquired and published by others

secondary securities market The financial market in which existing stocks and bonds are bought and sold by investors

secured bonds Backed by pledges of assets (collateral) to the bondholders

secured loan The borrower pledges some sort of asset, such as personal property, that is forfeited if the loan is not repaid

securities Financial instruments such as stocks and bonds

selection process Screens job applicants to hire the best candidate

self-assessment Employees rank their own performance to become involved in the evaluation process and to make them more receptive to feedback

self-sufficiency A country's ability to produce all of the products and services it needs or that its people want; no country is self-sufficient

selling The exchange of goods or services for an agreed sum of money

selling expenses Expenses incurred in marketing the firm's products

Selling Expenses Selling Expenses are all the expenses incurred in marketing the firm's products, such as salespeople's salaries, advertising, and supplies.

sentiment analysis a measurement that indicates whether people are reacting favorably or unfavorably to products or marketing efforts.

serial bonds Bonds that mature at different dates

Serial bonds bonds that mature at different dates.

Serial bonds bonds that mature at different dates.

Servant leader leadership philosophy and set of practices in which a leader strives to serve others by enriching the lives of individuals building better organizations, and ultimately creating a more just and caring world.

service An intangible product; usually a task that is performed for the purchaser

Service Corps of Retired Executives (SCORE) A Small Business Association mentoring program consisting of retired executives who volunteer as consultants to advise small businesspeople

Service Level agreements Service Level agreements often called SLAs are contracts with customers that identify what the customer will receive, when the customer

will receive it, the level of quality, and the cost.

sexual harassment Consists of unwanted sexual attention that creates an adverse work environment

shadowing An employee being trained on the job learns skills by watching more experienced employees perform their jobs

shareholders Those who own stock in a company

shopping goods and services Expensive products that people buy after comparing for value, price, quality, and style

short-term forecasts Predictions for the next year or less

Side Hustle A side hustle is a project or business that an individual works on outside of their regular employment.

sinking-fund bonds Bonds in which the issuer makes annual deposits to a bank to accumulate funds for paying off the bonds on maturity

Sinking-fund bonds bonds in which the issuer makes annual deposits to a bank to accumulate funds for paying off the bonds on maturity.

Six Sigma A rigorous statistical analysis process that reduces defects in manufacturing and service-related processes

Skunkworks Skunkworks: a team whose members are separated from an organization's normal operation and asked to produce a new, innovative project

small business In the United States, a business that (a) is

independently owned and operated, (b) is not dominant in its field of operation, and meets certain criteria set by the Small Business Administration for (c) number of employees and (d) annual sales revenue

Small Business Administration (SBA) The principal U.S. government agency charged with aiding small businesses by providing help in financing, management training, and support in securing government contracts

social audit A systematic assessment of a company's performance in implementing socially responsible programs, often based on predefined goals

social entrepreneurship An innovative, social value–creating activity that can occur within or across the for-profit and nonprofit sectors

social media influencers consumers who have a large following and credibility within a certain market segment.

social media marketing one of the most popular forms of digital marketing that utilizes online social networks and applications as a method to communicate mass and personalized messages about brands and products.

social media marketing campaign a coordinated marketing effort to advance marketing goals using one or more social media platforms.

social media platform a website-based media channel used to facilitate communication and connection.

socialism An economic system in which the government owns some major industries, but individuals own smaller businesses; the government redistributes much of the wealth or surplus of high incomes through social programs

sole proprietorship A business owned, and typically managed, by one person

solopreneur Business owners who work and operate their business alone

solvency Being able to pay debts when they become due

Span of control The number of people reporting to a particular manager.

special-interest group A group whose members try to influence businesses and governments on specific issues

specialty goods and services Very expensive products that buyers seldom purchase or that have unique characteristics that require people to make a special effort to obtain them

speculative-grade bonds High-risk bonds with a greater probability of default

Speculative-grade bonds high-risk bonds with a greater probability of default

sponsorship Firms that often sponsor YouTube or Instagram celebrities who in turn endorse the firms' products. These so-called online influencers are often compensated in multiple ways for their endorsements.

staff personnel Have advisory duties; they provide advice, recommendations, and research to line managers

staffing The recruitment, hiring, motivating, and retention of valuable employees

stakeholders Those who have any sort of stake or interest in a business

Standard & Poor's 500 (S&P 500) An index of stock prices for 500 major corporations in a range of industries

standard of living A component of a society's quality of life, defined by how many goods and services people can buy with the money they have

standard of value It can be used as a common standard to measure the values of goods and services

standardization The use of uniform parts that could be easily interchanged with similar parts

statistical process control A statistical technique that uses periodic random samples from production runs to see if quality is being maintained within a standard range of acceptability

stock Shares of ownership in a company

stock certificate A paper certificate listing the shareholder's name, name of the issuing company, number of shares you hold, and type of stock being issued

stock market indicators Indexes of stock market prices of groups of stocks that are related in some way

stock options Key employees are given the right to buy stock at a future date for a discounted price

stock split a company divides its existing shares into multiple shares.

stock split A company divides its existing shares into multiple shares

stockholders Those who own stock in a company

storage warehouses Warehouses that provide storage of products for long periods of time

store of wealth People can save it until they need to make new purchases

Stories A narrative based on true events, which is repeated—and sometimes embellished upon—to emphasize a particular value.

strategic partnership A strategic partnership is a relationship between individuals or organizations typically formed by an agreement or contract. The depth and breadth of the partnership may vary based on the parties' goals and any subsequent legal documents that outline the agreement.

strategic partnership agreement a strategic partnership agreement is an agreement between at least two parties that outlines how the parties will work with and benefit each other

strategic planning Determining the organization's long-term goals for the next one to five years with the resources they anticipate having

Strategy An organizational strategy is the sum of the actions a company intends to take to achieve long-term goals.

Structure Organizational structure defines how activities such as task allocation, coordination and supervision are directed toward the achievement of organizational aims

structured interview An interview wherein the interviewer asks each applicant the same identical, fixed questions and rates their responses according to some standard measure

subjective appraisals Appraisals that represent a manager's perceptions of a subordinate's traits or behaviors

supplier A person or organization that supplies raw materials, services, equipment, labor, energy, and other products to other organizations

supplies Goods to help make, but not become part of, principal product

supply Economic concept that expresses sellers' willingness and ability to provide goods and services at different prices

supply chain The sequence of suppliers that contribute to creating and delivering a product, from raw materials to production to final buyers

supply chain management Companies produce goods and services by integrating many facilities, functions, and processes, from suppliers to customers

supply chain management the strategy of planning and coordinating the movement of materials and products along the supply chain, from raw materials to final buyers

Supply curve diagram that illustrates the quantity supplied of a good at various prices

Supreme courts Supreme courts: courts that hear cases from appellate courts; the U.S. Supreme Court also hears cases appealed from state supreme courts

suspend Temporarily removed from the job (with or without pay)

sustainability Economic development that meets the needs of the present without compromising the ability of future generations to meet their own needs

swag Swag refers to free promotional marketing items.

sweatshop A shop, factory, or farm in which employees work long hours for low wages—or no wages, in the case of prison labor, slave labor, and some child labor—usually under environmentally, physically, or mentally abusive conditions

SWOT analysis A description of the strengths (S), weaknesses (W), opportunities (O), and threats (T) affecting the organization

Symbol An object, act, quality, or event that conveys meaning to others.

synthetic transformation The process in which resources are combined to create finished products

T

tactical planning Determining what contributions their work units can make with their existing resources during the next six months to two years

target costing The strategy in which a company starts with the price it wants to charge, figures out the profit margin it wants, then determines what the costs must be to produce the product to meet the desired price and profit goals (also known as *demand-based pricing*)

target market strategy Consists of marketing directly to such segments—the target market

target return on investment Making a profit, a specified yield on the investment

tariff A trade barrier in the form of a tax levied on imports

taxes Levies by the government to raise money to pay for government services

team A small group of people with complementary skills who are committed to common performance goals and approach to realizing them for which they hold themselves mutually accountable

technical skills Job-specific knowledge needed to perform well in a specialized field

technology Machines that help a company get a job done, including computers, data storage, delivery vans, and vending machines

Technology Any machine or process that gives an

organization a competitive advantage in changing materials used to produce a finished product.

telecommuting Working at home with telecommunications between office and home

telemarketing Consists of using the telephone to sell products directly to customers

term-loan agreement A promissory note indicating specific installments, such as monthly or yearly, for repayment

terms of trade The conditions the supplier (seller) gives the buyer when offering short-term credit

test marketing The introduction of a new product in a limited form to selected geographical markets to test consumers' reactions

Theory X Assumes workers to be irresponsible, resistant to change, lacking in ambition, hating work, and preferring to be led rather than to lead

Theory Y Makes the positive assumption that workers are capable of accepting responsibility, self-direction, and self-control and of being imaginative and creative

Theory Y Makes the positive assumption that workers are capable of acceptingresponsibility, self-direction, and self-control and of being imaginative and creative.

Theory Z A motivational approach that emphasizes involving employees at all levels, giving them long-term job security, allowing collective decision making,

emphasizing slow evaluation and promotion procedures, and treating workers like family

time deposits Bank funds that can't be withdrawn without notice or transferred by check

time to market The length of time it takes from a product being conceived until it is available for sale

top managers Make long-term decisions about the overall direction of the organization and establish the objectives, strategies, and policies for it

tort A civil wrongful act that results in injury to people or property

total product offering All the factors that potential buyers evaluate in a product when considering whether to buy it

total quality management (TQM) A comprehensive approach dedicated to continuous quality improvement, training, and customer satisfaction

totalitarian political system A political system ruled by a dictator, a single political party, or a special-membership group, such as a handful of ruling families or a military junta

trade association An organization consisting of individuals and companies in a specific business or industry organized to promote common interests

trade credit short-term financing by which a firm buys a product, then receives a bill from the supplier, then pays it later.

trade credit Short-term financing by which a firm buys a product, then receives a bill from the supplier, then pays it later

trade deficit Exists when the value of a country's total imports exceeds the value of its total exports

trade promotion Business-to-business sales promotion

trade protectionism The use of government regulations to protect domestic industries from foreign competition

trade show A gathering of manufacturers in the same industry who display their products to their distributors and dealers

trade surplus Exists when the value of a country's total exports exceeds the value of its total imports

trademarks Brand names and brand marks, and even slogans, that have been given exclusive legal protection

trading bloc A group of nations within a geographical region that have agreed to remove trade barriers with one another (also known as *common market* or *economic community*)

training and development Steps taken by the organization to increase employee performance and productivity

transaction A business deal that involves the buying, selling, or exchanging of something, usually goods or services

transaction loan Credit extended by a bank for a specific purpose

transactional leadership Focuses on creating a smooth-running organization, motivating employees to meet performance goals

transfer Movement of an employee sideways within the company to a different job with *similar responsibility*

transformational leadership Focuses on inspiring long-term vision, creativity, and exceptional performance in employees

Transformational leadership inspiring long-term vision, creativity, and exceptional performance in employees

treasury bills (T-bills) Short-term obligations of the U.S. Treasury with a maturity period of one year or less (typically three months)

treasury bonds Sold in denominations of $1,000 and $5,000; mature in 25 years or more

treasury notes Sold in minimum denominations of $100; mature in 10 years or less from the date of issue

trial balance In bookkeeping, making a summary of all the data in the ledgers to see if the figures are accurate or balanced

trial close is a question or statement that tests the prospect's willingness to buy.

trial close A question or statement that tests the prospect's willingness to buy

Trial courts Trial courts: general courts that hear criminal or civil cases not specifically assigned to other courts (for example,

special courts that hear probate, taxes, bankruptcy, or international trade cases)

trough The lowest point of the business cycle

two-factor theory A theory proposed by Frederick Herzberg that proposed that work dissatisfaction and satisfaction arise from two different factors—work satisfaction from higher-level needs called motivating factors, and work dissatisfaction from lower-level needs called hygiene factors

U

underwriting Activity of buying new issues of stocks or bonds from issuing corporations and reselling them to the public

unemployment rate The level of joblessness among people actively seeking work

unfavorable balance of trade Exists when the value of a country's total imports exceeds the value of its total exports

Uniform Commercial Code (UCC) A set of U.S. laws designed to provide uniformity in sales and other commercial law and to describe the rights of buyers and sellers

union shop Workers are not required to be union members when hired for a job, but they must join the union within a specified period of time

United States-Mexico-Canada Agreement (USMCA) A trade agreement among

the United States, Mexico, and Canada; it replaced the North American Free Trade Agreement (NAFTA).

universal product codes (UPCs) Bar codes printed on the package that can be read by bar code scanners

unsecured bonds Bonds for which no assets are pledged as collateral; backed only by the issuing company's reputation (also known as debenture bonds)

unsecured loan The borrower does not pledge any assets as collateral

unsought goods and services Those that people have little interest in, are unaware of, or didn't think they needed until an event triggers the need

unstructured interview An interview wherein the interviewer simply asks applicants probing questions in a conversational way

user-rate segmentation Consists of categorizing people according to volume or frequency of usage

Utility, want-satisfying ability Making products more useful or accessible to consumers.

V

validity The test measures what it claims to measure and is free of bias

value The customer's perception that a certain product offers a better relationship between costs and benefits than competitors' products do

value-added tax (VAT) (goods and services tax) A consumption tax, long used in Europe, that is levied at each stage of production based on the "value added" to the product at that stage

values The relatively permanent and deeply held underlying beliefs and attitudes that help determine people's behavior

variable costs Those expenses that change according to the number of products produced; examples might include cost of materials and labor

vendor A person or organization that supplies raw materials, services, equipment, labor, energy, and other products to other organizations

venture capital Funds acquired from wealthy individuals and institutions that are invested in promising start-ups or emerging companies in return for their giving up some ownership

venture capitalists Generally companies, not individuals, that invest in new enterprises in return for part ownership of them

vestibule training Off-the-job training in a simulated environment

video marketing Marketing to consumers on television, either through special cable TV channels or through certain programs on regular TV channels

viral campaign promotional messages spread quickly by social media users forwarding promotional messages

throughout their social networks.

viral marketing Companies produce content and, through various channels, the information spreads by being shared and reposted

virtual organization Consists of a company with a central core that is connected by computer network, usually the Internet, to outside independent firms, which help the core firm achieve its purpose

vision Long-term goal of what the organization wants to become

vulnerability The emotion that we experience during times of uncertainty, risk, and emotional exposure

W

warehousing The element of physical distribution that is concerned with storage of goods

welfare state A country in which the government offers citizens economic security by providing for them when they are unemployed, ill, or elderly and, in some countries, providing subsidized college educations and child care

whistleblower An employee who reports organizational misconduct to the government or the public; such conduct may include corruption, fraud, overcharging, waste, or health and safety problems

wholesalers Middlemen who sell products (1) to other businesses for resale to ultimate customers or (2) to

institutions and businesses for use in their operations

wide span of control Many people are reporting to the manager

Wilshire 5000 Index an index of that covers around 6,500 stocks traded on the New York Stock Exchange and the American Stock Exchange, and actively traded stocks on the NASDAQ; also known as "the total stock market"

word-of-mouth marketing A promotional technique in which people tell others about products they've purchased or firms they've used

work from home Some employers provide employees the opportunity to work from a home office rather than coming into a physical office space.

work rules Procedures and matters of law

Working at home Working at home with telecommunications between office and home is called telecommuting.

World Bank International organization that provides low-interest loans to developing nations for improving health, education, transportation, and telecommunications

World Trade Organization (WTO) International trade organization, consisting of 164 member countries, that is designed to monitor and enforce trade agreements

Y

yield Calculated by dividing dividend or income by the market price

Annotations

14. https://taxfoundation.org/us-has-more-individually-owned-businesses-corporations; http://www.businessnewsdaily.com/8163-choose-legal-business-structure.html.

12. https://www.statista.com/statistics/193290/unemployment-rate-in-the-usa-since-1990/

10. A. Maslow, "A Theory of Human Motivation," Psychological Review, July 1943, pp. 370–396.

11. https://www.sba.gov/blogs/how-estimate-cost-starting-business-scratch

3. For standard dimensions of ocean containers, see www.foreign-trade.com/reference/ocean.cfm.

Zumbrun, J. (2020, Jul 01). USMCA takes effect but north american trade tensions remain; nafta's replacement, a trump administration priority, kicks in after years of negotiation even as certain matters have emerged to complicate its rollout. Wall Street Journal (Online)

1. Adapted from Canadian Association of Logistics Management, www.calm.org/calm/AboutCALM/AboutCALM.html, February 23, 1998 (accessed July 7, 2011).

9. National Federation of Independent Business, "Small Business Facts."

15. M. Amon and T. Panchal, "BP Puts Tab for Gulf Disaster at $62 Billion," The Wall Street Journal, July 14, 2016, https://www.wsj.com/articles/bp-estimates-remaining-material-deepwater-liabilities-1468517684.

1. D. R. Baker, "Hyping 'Free Gas' to Fuel Sales," San Francisco Chronicle, June 22, 2008, pp. C1, C4.

2. A. Martin and R. Lieber, "Alternative to Banks, Now Playing Offense," New York Times, June 12, 2010, pp. B1, B5.

5. K. Spors, "Do Start-Ups Really Need Formal Business Plans?" The Wall Street Journal, January 9, 2007.

https://ethisphere.com/2018-worlds-most-ethical-companies/

1. http://www.humanesociety.org/issues/pet_overpopulation/facts/pet_ownership_statistics.html

9. K. Spors, "Do Start-Ups Really Need Formal Business Plans?" The Wall Street Journal, January 9, 2007.

11. http://www.businessinsider.com/pwc-ranking-of-biggest-economies-ppp-2050-2017-2/#2-india-44128-trillion-31.

4. Interactive Advertising Bureau, "The Native Advertising Playbook," Interactive Advertising Bureau, December 4, 2013, https://www.iab.com/wp-content/uploads/2015/06/IAB-Native-Advertising-Playbook2.pdf.

13. http://www.nj.gov/dca/affiliates/uez/publications/pdf/NJUEZ_Locations.pdf

8. R. Tannenbaum and W. H. Schmidt, "How to Choose a Leadership Pattern," Harvard Business Review, May 1, 1973, pp. 162–164.

17. "2018 World's Most Ethical Companies," Ethisphere.com, February 12, 2018, https://ethisphere.com/2018-worlds-most-ethical-companies/.

10. M. R. Barrick, M. K. Mount, and T. A. Judge, "Personality and Performance at the Beginning of the New Millennium: What Do We Know and Where Do We Go Next?" Personality and Performance, March/June 2001, pp. 9–30; and S. N. Kaplan, M. M. Klebanov, and M. Sorensen, "Which CEO Characteristics and Abilities Matter?" NBR Working Paper, No. 14195, Issued June 2008, National Bureau of Economic Research. See also D. Brooks, "In Praise of Dullness," New York Times, May 19, 2009, p. A23.

14. S. Tobak, "Top 10 CEOs in Prison: Why'd They Do It?" CBS News Moneywatch, June 14, 2010, http://www.cbsnews.com/news/top-10-ceos-in-prison-whyd-they-do-it/.

11. R. Kark, B. Shamir, and C. Chen, "The Two Faces of Transformational Leadership: Empowerment and Dependency," Journal of Applied Psychology, April 2003, pp. 246–255. Parts of this section are adapted from Kinicki and Williams, Management, 2009, pp. 455–56.

3. https://www.usatoday.com/story/money/business/small-business-central/2017/05/21/what-percentage-of-businesses-fail-in-their-first-year/101260716/

1. P. F. Drucker, Innovation and Entrepreneurship (New York: Harper & Row, 1986), pp. 27–28.

15. http://realbusiness.co.uk/current-affairs/2014/12/19/5-historic-trade-embargoes-and-their-economic-impact/2/.

11. C. Song, "Stock Market Reaction to Corporate Crime: Evidence from South Korea," Journal of Business Ethics, Vol, 143, No. 2., pp. 323–51; https://www.sixsigmaonline.org/six-sigma-training-certification-information/the-consequence-of-unethical-business-behavior/.

6. R. L. Katz, "Skills of an Effective Administrator," Harvard Business Review, September–October 1974, p. 94. This section also adapted from Kinicki and Williams, Management, 2009, pp. 4, 27–28.

9. "The Consequence of Unethical Business Behavior," Six Sigma Online, https://www.sixsigmaonline.org/six-sigma-training-certification-information/the-consequence-of-unethical-business-behavior/.

4. https://data.worldbank.org/indicator/SL.AGR.EMPL.ZS?locations=US

3. K. Blumenthal, "The Holdup at Online Banks," Wall Street Journal, October 22, 2008, p. D3.

6. https://www.sba.gov/managing-business/running-business/energy-efficiency/sustainable-business-practices/small-business-trends

5. National Federation of Independent Business, "Small Business Facts."

5. National Federation of Independent Business, "Small Business Facts."

13. http://www.businessinsider.com/cost-of-fast-food-franchise-2014-11.

7. https://www.sba.gov/blogs/how-estimate-cost-starting-business-scratch

14. J. Stacy Adams, "Toward an Understanding of Inequity," Journal of Abnormal and Social Psychology, November 1963, pp. 422–436; and J. Stacy Adams, "Injustice in Social Exchange," in L. Berkowitz, ed., Advances in Experimental Social Psychology, 2nd ed. (New York: Academic Press, 1965), pp. 267–300.

16. https://www.statista.com/statistics/190313/estimated-number-of-us-franchise-establishments-since-2007/.

3. Adapted from Robbins and Coulter, Management, 2007, p. 185; and Kinicki and Williams, Management, 2009, pp. 141–42.

4. Box Tops For Education, http://www.boxtops4education.com/about/history.

11. https://www.bls.gov/spotlight/2012/recession/pdf/recession_bls_spotlight.pdf

7. https://www.cia.gov/library/publications/the-world-factbook/fields/2128.html?countryName=Korea,%20North&countryCode=kn&regionCode=eas&#kn2

7. Adapted from A. Kinicki and B. K. Williams, Management: A Practical Introduction, 4th ed. (New York: McGraw-Hill/Irwin, 2009), p. 407.

1. Global Entrepreneurship Monitor, 2002 study by London Business School and Babson College, reported in J. Bailey, "Desire—More Than Need—Builds a Business," Wall Street Journal, May 21, 2002, p. B4.

http://fortune.com/2015/12/02/zuckerberg-charity/

4. http://money.cnn.com/2016/03/29/news/economy/us-manufacturing-jobs/index.html.

1. Adapted from S. C. Certo and S. T. Certo, Modern Management: Concepts and Skills, 11th ed. (Upper Saddle River, NJ: Prentice Hall, 2009), p. 185; S. P. Robbins and M. Coulter, Management, 9th ed. (Upper Saddle River, NJ: Pearson , 2007), p. 157; and A. Kinicki and B. K. Williams, Management: A Practical Introduction, 4th ed. (New York: McGraw-Hill/Irwin, 2009), pp. 205–208.

   http://www.cbsnews.com/news/top-10-ceos-in-prison-whyd-they-do-it/

2. N. T. Sheehan and G. Vaidyanathan, "The Path to Growth," Wall Street Journal, March 3–4, 2007, p. R8.

   https://www.acfe.com/rttn2016/docs/2016-report-to-the-nations.pdf

19. American Red Cross, http://www.redcross.org/about-us/our-work/international-services/international-disasters-and-crises.

2. https://minerals.usgs.gov/minerals/pubs/commodity/gemstones/mcs-2015-gemst.pdf

8. E. Newman, "Effects of Unethical Behaviour on Business," Yonyx, November 19, 2015, http://corp.yonyx.com/customer-service/effects-of-unethical-behaviour-on-business/.

2. http://money.cnn.com/2016/04/18/pf/taxes/how-are-tax-dollars-spent/index.html

8. D. Arthur, "The Importance of Body Language," HRFocus, June 1995, pp. 22–23; and N. M. Grant, "The Silent Should Build Bridges, Not Barriers," HRFocus, April 1995, p. 16.

1. J. Collins, "How the Mighty Fall," BusinessWeek, May 24, 2009, pp. 26–38.

   http://corp.yonyx.com/customer-service/effects-of-unethical-behaviour-on-business/

5. J. Pfeffer, The Human Equation: Building Profits by Putting People First (Cambridge, MA: Harvard Business School Press, 1996).

1. https://www.ama.org/AboutAMA/Pages/Definition-of-Marketing.aspx

   xiv B. F. Skinner, Walden Two (New York: Macmillan, 1948); Science and Human Behavior (New York: Macmillan, 1953); and Contingencies of Reinforcement (New York: Appleton-Century-Crofts, 1969).

7. Adapted from A. Kinicki and B. K. Williams, Management: A Practical Introduction, 4th ed. (New York: McGraw-Hill/Irwin, 2009), p. 407.

6. http://www.cnsnews.com/news/article/terence-p-jeffrey/usa-has-run-annual-trade-deficits-41-straight-years.

5. Adapted from Kinicki and Williams, Management, 2009, pp. 255–261.

9. C. Crossen, "Early Industry Expert Soon Realized a Staff Has Its Own Efficiency," Wall Street Journal, November 6, 2006, p. B1.

8. https://www.sba.gov/business-guide/plan/market-research-competitive-analysis.

1. http://fortune.com/2016/12/28/mergers-and-acquisitions-donald-trump/

8. http://www.worldometers.info/world-population/china-population/

12. D. M. Long and S. Rao, "The Wealth Effects of Unethical Business Behavior," Journal of Economics and Finance, Summer 1995, pp. 65–73.

7. Matthew Ingram, "Mark Zuckerberg Is Giving Away His Money, but with a Twist," Fortune.com, December 2, 2015, http://fortune.com/2015/12/02/zuckerberg-charity/.

4. A. Martin and R. Lieber, "Alternative to Banks, Now Playing Offense," New York Times, June 12, 2010, pp. B1, B5.

2. http://www.businessinsider.com/pwc-ranking-of-biggest-economies-ppp-2050-2017-2/#2-india-44128-trillion-31

4. https://www.statista.com/statistics/264985/ad-spend-of-selected-beverage-brands-in-the-us/

1. http://www.consumerreports.org/cro/news/2015/03/cost-of-organic-food/index.htm

6. Park Howell, "10 Sustainable Brands That Turned Green Marketing Campaigns Into Movements," businessofstory.com, https://businessofstory.com/10-sustainable-brands-that-turned-green-marketing-campaigns-into-movements/#comments; http://www.newsweek.com/green-2016/top-green-companies-us-2016.

14. Adapted from Robbins and Coulter, Management, pp. 529–533; and Kinicki and Williams, Management: A Practical Introduction, McGraw-Hill Companies, Incorporated, 2009, pp. 508–510.

9. K. Spors, "Do Start-Ups Really Need Formal Business Plans?"

12. D. McGregor, The Human Side of Enterprise (New York: McGraw-Hill, 1960).

3. http://www.cnbc.com/2016/05/17/its-a-disgrace-this-is-how-much-more-ceos-make-than-workers.html

10. Definition adapted from InvestorWords,www.investorwords.com/629/business_model.html.

2. J. Emerson, "The Nature of Returns: A Social Capital Markets Inquiry into Elements of Investment and the Blended Value Proposition," Social Enterprise Series No. 17 (Boston: Harvard Business School Press, 2000), p. 36.

D. M. Long and S. Rao, "The Wealth Effects of Unethical Business Behavior," Journal of Economics and Finance, Summer 1995, pp. 65–73.

3. Amy Schade, "Designing for 5 Types of E-Commerce Shoppers," Nielsen Norman Group, March 2, 2014, https://www.nngroup.com/articles/ecommerce-shoppers/.

6. Zach Brooke, "Five Tourism Campaigns That Backfired," American Marketing Association, April 7, 2016, https://www.ama.org/publications/eNewsletters/Marketing-News-Weekly/Pages/tourism-ad-marketing-fails-backfire.aspx.

4. https://www.sba.gov/business-guide/plan/market-research-competitive-analysis.

10. https://www.sba.gov/managing-business/running-business/energy-efficiency/sustainable-business-practices/small-business-trends

http://oilprice.com/Energy/Energy-General/Most-Of-BPs-208-Billion-Deepwater-Horizon-Fine-Is-Tax-Deductible.html

13. Report to the Nations on Occupational Fraud and Abuse: 2016 Global Fraud Study, ACFE, https://www.acfe.com/rttn2016/docs/2016-report-to-the-nations.pdf.

https://www.sixsigmaonline.org/six-sigma-training-certification-information/the-consequence-of-unethical-business-behavior/

14. http://www.nbcnews.com/id/3540959/ns/business-world_business/t/us-imposes-quotas-china-textiles/#.WVQ8dBPyul4.

1. Global Entrepreneurship Monitor, 2002 study by London Business School and Babson College, reported in J. Bailey, "Desire—More Than Need—Builds a Business," Wall Street Journal, May 21, 2002, p. B4.

12. https://taxfoundation.org/us-has-more-individually-owned-businesses-corporations; http://www.businessnewsdaily.com/8163-choose-legal-business-structure.html.

13. https://dataweb.usitc.gov/scripts/tariff_current.asp.

5. http://atlas.media.mit.edu/en/profile/country/deu.

12. Adapted from Kinicki and Williams, Management, 2009, pp. 506–510.

2. http://www.americanpetproducts.org/press_industrytrends.asp

This definition of sustainability was developed in 1987 by the World Commission on Environment and Development.

2. Based on Collins, "How the Mighty Fall," 2009.

1. M. Boyle, "Performance Reviews: Perilous Curves Ahead," Fortune, May 15, 2001, www.fortune.com/fortune/subs/print/0,15935,374010,00.html (accessed April 19, 2010); C. M. Ellis, G. B. Moore, and A. M. Saunier, "Forced Ranking: Not So Fast," Perspectives, June 30, 2003,

7. D. Rooke and W. R. Torbert, "Transformations of Leadership," Harvard Business Review, April 2005, pp. 67–76.

8. J. R. Katzenbach and D. K. Smith, The Wisdom of Teams: Creating the High-Performance Organization (Boston: Harvard Business School Press, 1993), p. 45.

viii J. R. Katzenbach and D. K. Smith, The Wisdom of Teams: Creating the High-Performance Organization (Boston: Harvard Business School Press, 1993), p. 45.

5. https://www.pymnts.com/earnings/2018/starbucks-rewards-mobile-app-stocks-loyalty/

13. W. Taylor, "Control in an Age of Chaos," Harvard Business Review, November–December 1994, pp. 64–70.

5. K. Spors, "Do Start-Ups Really Need Formal Business Plans?" The Wall Street Journal, January 9, 2007.

4. Adapted from Kinicki and Williams, Management, 2009, pp. 146–147.

ix D. Katz and R. L. Kahn, The Social Psychology of Organizations (New York: Wiley, 1966); A. Kinicki and B. K. Williams, Management: A Practical Introduction, 4th ed. (New York: McGraw-Hill/Irwin, 2009), p. 371; and T. S. Bateman and S. A. Snell, Management: Leading & Collaborating in a Competitive World, 9th ed. (New York: McGraw-Hill/Irwin, 2011), p. 454.

16. http://money.cnn.com/2016/12/15/news/economy/us-trade-canada-china-mexico/index.html.

i Adapted from Robbins and Coulter, Management, 2007, pp. 64–66; and Kinicki and Williams, Management, 2009, pp. 243. Based on T. E. Deal and A. A. Kennedy, Corporate Cultures: The Rites and Rituals of Corporate Life (Reading, MA: Addison-Wesley, 1982).

2. https://www.als.org/ice-bucket-challenge-spending#:~:text=The%20%24115%20million%20in%20donations,services%20for%20people%20with%20ALS

1. From Cabaret, John Kander, Fred Ebb, line from song Money, Money.

3. https://www.forbes.com/sites/mikecollins/2015/05/06/the-pros-and-cons-of-globalization/#3fc87121ccce.

6. J. Pfeffer, in A. M. Webber, "Danger: Toxic Company," Fast Company, November 1998, pp. 152–161. https://ethisphere.com/2018-worlds-most-ethical-companies/

10. B. A. Blonigen and J. Piger, " Determinants of Foreign Direct Investment," Canadian Journal of Economics/Revue canadienne d'économique 47(3) 2014, pp. 775–812.

6. Definition adapted from InvestorWords, www.investorwords.com/629/business_model.html.

10. https://tradingeconomics.com/country-list/personal-income-tax-rate

18. "The Home Depot Foundation Increases Disaster Relief Commitment to $3 Million," HomeDepot.com, News Release, September 29, 2017, http://ir.homedepot.com/news-releases/2017/9-29-17-hurricane-maria.

1. "Starting a Furniture Making Company," startupbizhub.com, http://www.startupbizhub.com/starting-a-furniture-making-company.htm.

1. S. F. Brown, "Wresting New Wealth from the Supply Chain," Fortune, November 9, 1998, pp. 204[C]–204[Z]; N. Shirouzu, "Gadget Inspector: Why Toyota Wins Such High Marks on Quality Surveys," Wall Street Journal, March 15, 2001, pp. A1, A11; and M. Maynard, "Toyota Shows Big Three How It's Done," New York Times, January 13, 2006, pp. C1, C4.

https://careertrend.com/benefits-importance-ethics-workplace-7414.html

1. A. B. Carroll, "Managing Ethically with Global Stakeholders: A Present and Future Challenge," Academy of Management Executive, May 2004, p. 118. Also see B. W. Husted and D. B. Allen, "Corporate Social Responsibility in the Multinational Enterprise: Strategic and Institutional Approaches," Journal of International Business Studies, November 2006, pp. 838–849.

9. J. Antonakis and R. J. House, "The Full-Range Leadership Theory: The Way Forward," in B. J. Avolio and F. J. Yammarino, eds., Transformational and Charismatic Leadership: The Road Ahead (New York: JAI Press, 2002), pp. 3–34.

8. https://www.entrepreneur.com/article/270556 (Feb 9, 2016).

The website or other source

2. A. Martin and R. Lieber, "Alternative to Banks, Now Playing Offense," New York Times, June 12, 2010, pp. B1, B5.

6. J. R. Katzenbach and D. K. Smith, "The Discipline of Teams," Harvard Business Review, March–April 1995, p. 112.

11. F. Herzberg, B. Mausner, and B. B. Snyderman, The Motivation to Work (New York: John Wiley & Sons, 1959); and F. Herzberg, "One More Time: How Do You Motivate Employees?" Harvard Business Review, January–February 1968, pp. 53–62.

9. https://www.sba.gov/managing-business/running-business/energy-efficiency/sustainable-business-practices/small-business-trends

10. R Uhl, "Investor Perceptions Are Your Reality," Westwick Partners, July 24, 2013, http://westwickepartners.com/2013/07/investor-perceptions-are-your-reality/.

1. https://taxfoundation.org/corporate-income-tax-rates-around-world-2016/

12. http://www.acc.com/legalresources/quickcounsel/cnela.cfm.

3. A. Martin and R. Lieber, "Alternative to Banks, Now Playing Offense," New York Times, June 12, 2010, pp. B1, B5.

1. D. R. Baker, "Hyping 'Free Gas' to Fuel Sales," San Francisco Chronicle, June 22, 2008, pp. C1, C4.

16. http://money.cnn.com/2016/12/15/news/economy/us-trade-canada-china-mexico/index.html.

15. https://taxfoundation.org/overview-pass-through-businesses-united-states.

5. A. Kinicki and B. Williams, Management: A Practical Introduction (McGraw-Hill Companies, Incorporated, 2009).

C. Song, "Stock Market Reaction to Corporate Crime: Evidence from South Korea." Journal of Business Ethics, Vol, 143, No. 2., pp. 323–51; https://www.sixsigmaonline.org/six-sigma-training-certification-information/the-consequence-of-unethical-business-behavior/

xi A. Maslow, "A Theory of Human Motivation," Psychological Review, July 1943, pp. 370–396.

16. 16. S. Parrish, "The Profit Potential In Running An Ethical Business,"Forbes.com, February 4, 2016, https://www.forbes.com/sites/steveparrish/2016/02/04/the-profit-potential-in-running-an-ethical-business/#5f5a24076876.

2. https://www.als.org/ice-bucket-challenge-spending#:~:text=The%20%24115%20million%20in%20donations,services%20for%20people%20with%20ALS

7. J. P. Kotter, "What Leaders Really Do," Harvard Business Review, December 2001, pp. 85–96.

3. Susan Adams, "11 Companies Considered Best For The Environment," Forbes.com, April 22, 2014, https://www.forbes.com/sites/susanadams/2014/04/22/11-companies-considered-best-for-the-environment/#4a51343612ae.

http://westwickepartners.com/2013/07/investor-perceptions-are-your-reality/

2. https://www.medicare.gov/pharmaceutical-assistance-program/

3. Global Entrepreneurship Monitor, 2002 study by London Business School and Babson College, reported in J. Bailey, "Desire—More Than Need—Builds a Business," Wall Street Journal, May 21, 2002, p. B4.

   https://www.acfe.com/rttn2016/docs/2016-report-to-the-nations.pdf

7. https://www.marketingbinder.com/glossary/countertrade-definition-examples/.

13. https://fred.stlouisfed.org/series/GDP

3. Adapted from S. P. Robbins and M. Coulter, Management, 9th ed. (Upper Saddle River, NJ: Pearson Education, 2007), pp. 361–366; A. Kinicki and B. K. Williams, Management: A Practical Introduction, 4th ed. (New York: McGraw-Hill/Irwin, 2009), pp. 317–318; and R. W. Griffin, Management, 10th ed. (Mason, OH: South-Western Cengage Learning, 2011), pp. 408–411.

5. https://www.ams.usda.gov/grades-standards/organic-standards

7. https://www.entrepreneur.com/article/270556 (Feb 9, 2016).

8. Tweriod website, http://www.tweriod.com/.

6. N. Koenig-Lewis, A. Palmer, J. Dermody, and A. Urbye, "Consumers' Evaluations of Ecological Packaging—Rational and Emotional Approaches," Journal of Environmental Psychology 37 (2014), pp. 94–105.

1. Adapted from Robbins and Coulter, Management, 2007, p. 185; and Kinicki and Williams, Management, 2009, pp. 141–42.

13. V. H. Vroom, Work and Motivation (New York: Wiley, 1964).

2. Investor Dictionary, www.investordictionary.com/definition/mircopreneur; and A. Robertson, "Are You a Micropreneur?" WebProNews, August 17, 2006, www.webpronews.com/expertarticles/2006/08/17/are-you-a-micropreneur (both accessed May 31, 2011.

1. J. Pfeffer, in A. M. Webber, "Danger: Toxic Company," Fast Company, November 1998, pp. 152–161.

14. https://www.entrepreneur.com/franchises/lowcost/2016/2.

9. http://www.newsweek.com/north-koreas-kim-jong-un-starving-his-people-pay-nuclear-weapons-573015

   https://www.hrw.org/world-report/2017/country-chapters/north-korea

9. http://money.cnn.com/gallery/news/economy/2013/07/10/worlds-shortest-work-weeks/index.html.

4. Adapted from eight steps in K. M. Bartol and D. C. Martin, Management, 3rd ed. (Burr Ridge, IL: Irwin/McGraw-Hill, 1998), pp. 360–363.

15. E. A. Locke and G. P. Latham, Goal Setting: A Motivational Technique that Works! (Englewood Cliffs, NJ: Prentice-Hall, 1984); and E. A. Locke, K. N. Shaw, L. A. Saari, and G. P. Latham, "Goal Setting and Task Performance," Psychological Bulletin, August 1981, pp. 125–152.

   xiv B. F. Skinner, Walden Two (New York: Macmillan, 1948); Science and Human Behavior (New York: Macmillan, 1953); and Contingencies of Reinforcement (New York: Appleton-Century-Crofts, 1969).

7. https://www.als.org/stories-news/ice-bucket-challenge-dramatically-accelerated-fight-against-als